INCONSEQUENT NONSENSE

A LIFE WITH DOGS AND HUMANS

BRAD LANCASTER

Library of Congress Cataloguing in Publication Data:
Lancaster, Brad.
Inconsequent Nonsense: A Life with Dogs and Humans

ISBN 978-0-9986435-4-0

Published by:
  Saint George's Hill Press
  17503 10th Avenue N.E.
  Shoreline, Washington 98155

First Printing: 2020

This book is printed in Times New Roman font.

Printed in the United States of America.

For every dog and person, named and unnamed, in this tome,
Who contributed value or dross to my fractured existence,
Issuing in this meaningful (to me) jumble of events,
Joyous, immiserate, excruciating, blissed,
Hilarious, tortured, testy, ecstatic,
All intertwining, then melding
To become tensile alloy
Which I imagine
Might be
me.

"Life is a series of dogs."

George Carlin

SUZY

TABLE OF CONTENTS

Dedication 3
Opening Thought 4
Introduction: Listening to Dogs and Humans 9

1. Sweetness 13
2. Alice's Restaurant 15
3. Blunt 17
4. Woody 19
5. Frank 21
6. Death 23
7. Certainly Uncertain...25
8. Departing Jesus Ecclesiasticus.......................................27
9. Selassie 33
10. Symphonies 35
11. Civility 37
12. A Tale of One City 39
13. Peace in Our House 41
14. Moms 45
15. *Cull: Choosing Well* (Section I excerpt)......................47
16. Ox Mountain 59
17. Arrogance 61
18. Regret 63
19. Guns 65
20. A Suessical Wedding..67
21. Knitting from the Tangled Skein 69
22. Mental Illness...71
23. Jerry and Hercules 73
24. Friends 75
25. Jazz Walk...77
26. Ruckus 79
27. YMCA 81
28. Work 83
29. Truly Selfish 85
30. Yachakas 87
31. Suicide 95
32. Dispute with an Absent Friend 97
33. Arthur the Rotarian 99
34. Adipose Oscillations 101
35. Intimacy 103
36. Kidist 105
37. John Henry: Elegy 107
38. Teacher 109

39. Mentors 111
40. Teams 113
41. Childless..115
42. Bear Children Only If You Must...117
43. Perseverance..131
44. Ship-shaped...133
45. President with a Mirror 135
46. Truth-speaking 137
47. Trash 139
48. News 141
49. God Talk: Truths..143
50. God Talk: Encyclopedia..145
51. God Talk: *Via Negativa*..147
52. Mack for Judge..149
53. Drug Diversion Court..151
54. Pacifist Assassin..153
55. Tone Poem for the Deaf 155
56. Rabuor 159
57. Forbearance...161
58. Thicket 163
59. Trubble Talk..165
60. Fear 181
61. Good 183
62. In My Back Yard..185
63. Yammer at Shoreline City Council 187
64. The Other America...207
65. Decaffeination 211
66. Squirrel Buddha 213
67. Loss 215
68. Three Miles 217
69. Howard and Bev...221
70. Woodhaven 225
71. Requiem Lucy 227

Appreciations and Apologies 229

LUCY

INTRODUCTION
LISTENING TO DOGS AND HUMANS

A core privilege in life is listening. We do with ears and an attentive mind what can be accomplished in no other way.[1] One enters the life of another. Perhaps only briefly. Perhaps only a bit, say, to the mudroom or, of sacred spaces, the vestibule. But one opens a door and approaches (with welcome, if one is fortunate) the innerness of another. One hears stories, tales of woe and wonder. One audits distant places and odd states of consciousness. One dabbles, from a respectful distance, in intimacies and execrations. Listeners tiptoe into foreign precincts, limned in tales of luminous triumphs or shrouded allusions to cabined blushing.

We are our stories. When our accounts fall on ears deafened by distraction or judgment or alienation, we deflate. We murmur inwardly, "I do not matter. I am negligible." When heard by an eager ear, we blossom. We matter. We joy in being known. Often quietly, even privately. We murmur, and occasionally even say, "I am here. I am glad." One subsists in the attention one gleans from the other. In South Africa, the Bantu term "Ubuntu" teaches that I am because we are. A common greeting among the tribes translates to "I see you." To be seen matters. To be heard matters. Our stories, if cherished by friends, fill our emptiness with recognition, as spring wine nestles in a well-loved goatskin.

> **ONE HEARS A STORY EVEN IN THE SILENCE OF OTHERS.**

When working, I am a lawyer. Contrary to what you see on television, I mostly listen. Tales, woven from tendrils of fancy and conflict, press into my ears. These narratives are often welcome, like surprise rain on parched land. A chance to care, a moment to beckon healing. A happiness. Some stories, however, wear, grinding compassion, as torrents chew plowed fields. A chance to persevere, a moment to hope amidst despair. A challenge. One client comes with a history of sibling bitterness, now raging as the last parent has passed. Can the probate avoid Armageddon? Another arrives spewing fears of fiduciary thefts, born more of suspicion than evidence. Can the family warp be re-woofed? A mother sits with her tale of spousal betrayal and needy children and sparse wages. Is amicable resolution beyond the pale? Much is said. Much is left unsaid, but even what remains inaudible lingers in the conversation. My job, on good days, is to imagine an outcome that appeals to antagonists, a vessel carved from hard wood by the keen blade of attentive listening.

---

[1] A friend objected, on reading this sentence, that she reads, and that's not an ear-thing. I counter that reading is just fancified listening. Audition predates orthography, both historically and logically. Besides, one "hears" with eyes when one listens actively. To listen engages an entire human.

Some clients require more. I had a lovely client for whom I managed finances and health care decisions. She suffered aphasia, both receptive and expressive, due to a brain lesion decades ago. She could not understand my words, nor I hers. Gibble garble, garble gibble. A grim beginning for a listening project. And yet, we connected. Warmly. I read her records. I attended her details. I closed up her house, noting the fabric of her life lived there. I pieced together a person from the scraps, a simulacrum which I hope is faithful to her complexities. She also fabricated a story, apparently favorable, from her observations of me. We listened to each other, though our ears were handicapped. Affection ensued, bridging a chasm dug by wordlessness.

Dogs present a grave challenge. They not only do not speak, they have no linguistic capacity at all. A spring of intelligence burbles in their verbal desert. But the species divide, our respective modes of living, dog and human, yawns. Dogs have reached humans, despite the interspecies gap, forging a vibrant symbiosis in affection and protein-sharing. This fortunate conjunction modified us both, down to our plasm, the canine and the human.

With canine friends, listening is not useless. Dogs lack words. But they are vocal. Ruby, our third miniature pinscher whom you will meet later in this ramble, a pup of one year, went out for a pee last night and returned at breakneck pace, terrified. I never learned why. Raccoons? Coyotes? Imagination run amok? Her piercing miniature pinscher bark roiled the deep of night, vibrating our ceiling fan for twenty minutes, pouring salt on my sluggish sleep. Consolation mattered not a bit. Ruby could not abandon her doggish shrieks, her unnamed horror, until secure in her dark cubby, where, so far as she knows, nothing menacing may intrude. Listening, one distinguishes Ruby's moods and needs in this groan or that look. Postures are part of Ruby's vocabulary. She has a "let's go" gambol, a "let's walk" bob, the ubiquitous play bow seeking a ball toss or a sock pull, a "dinnertime" stare, a "shouldn't I have a treat" stretch, and an "I want attention" ear-licking. And, as I have mentioned, there is the "I am scared to death" barking torrent. A canine lexicon expresses much, though humans struggle to recognize its terms. Fortunately, dogs are patient with their humans. Though we appear retarded as to things doggish, these children of wolves nurture us along toward pack-itude. Mongrels teach us to sleep akimbo on one another. Mutts instruct us in eating protocol, to gobble and beg like any self-respecting hound. Whelps know when to walk, and when to snooze. Dogs have domesticated me. Thank God. I needed it. I have studied in Canine Academy. I learned much, though I, regrettably, guttered near the bottom of my class.

So, one listens, if she wants to tread the precincts of others. Human or companion animal—the task is the same. Ears and inquiry. Attention and curiosity. Imagination and observation. The listening trifecta.

I call this thin volume *Inconsequent Nonsense*, because, if, while reading, one fails to listen ably, the text is nothing more than that. Where, however, practiced audition intervenes, one may discover in the collection's vagaries, a fraction of a life—my life, not all that dissimilar from your own (or so I suppose). You might construct a doppelgänger of me, from my opinions and events and feelings. You might even suffer a wan existential encounter. Perhaps that is too much to hope from a pastiche of snippets.

Nevertheless, I invite you to listen.

LUCY

1
SWEETNESS

Life brings unexpected sweetness. Dawn's illumination of hanging mists in Hamlin Park. Eclipse of a harvest moon over Lake Washington. Rose petals after rainstorms in North City yards. A thoughtful speaker over lunch at Rotary. Wenatchee tree-ripened peaches. Odd conjunctions of disparate ideas, spilling laughter over beer. A friend's ear when needed. Great old books. Kim's snuggle in darkness.

Immense sweetness erupted when Lucy, our first miniature pinscher, arrived. I intended to get my wife a dog. I got a child, friend, student, and teacher. We instructed Lucy in humanity. Her knack for personhood made me laugh out loud *every* day. I flunked as alpha pack leader. Patiently, Lucy schooled me. I came to feed, greet, forage, and sleep properly. I grew canine; Lucy grew human.

One night, a thief invaded. Kim had taken dying friends for a final visit with Manitoba relatives. Lucy dashed out her doggie door for a midnight pee. Raccoon jaws waited. Canine screams ejected me from bed. A blur of snarling fur, dog and raccoon, rolled across our patio. I seized and flung the masked raider. Righting himself, that intruder glared defiantly. I raised my hands. I roared, a flaccid urban gorilla. The raccoon, unimpressed, nevertheless conceded and withdrew. Lucy stained the family bedroom crimson while

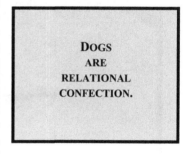

DOGS
ARE
RELATIONAL
CONFECTION.

coagulating. As dawn glimmered, we finished cleaning and cuddling. Antibiotic goop oozed. The vet said Lucy would live to err another day.

I negotiated a new balance of power with the indigenous raccoon population by introducing them to my BB gun. I coined new language with Lucy. "Big Dog," inflected with urgency, warned of predators, raccoon or otherwise. Lucy still considered most of my commands mere advisory opinions. Obedience is a term erased from the min-pin lexicon. But when I grated "Big Dog," Lucy found my leg and hovered, that violent night dancing again in her tiny skull.

Dogs are relational confection, one of life's startling sweetnesses. Charles DeGaulle (French WWII leader, 20th century A.D.) said, "The better I get to know men, the more I find myself loving dogs." Most days, I concur. Dogs are the best humans I know.

SOFIE

2
ALICE'S RESTAURANT

Driving out State Route Six from Portland to Oregon's beaches, afternoon hunger drove my car past elk warning signs to Alice's Country House. Alice's diner hugs the highway in the low foothills of Oregon's coastal range, just miles from Tillamook's dairy pastures, where live the udders from which squirt their famous cheddar. The front of Alice's menu proclaims, "If you are in a hurry, this is the place to forget." Every meal is home cooked. The ladies at Alice's are serious about that promise. I tasted sincerity in my Big Spruce club sandwich and fries.

Alice's welcomes city folk streaking through to beach getaways. I got a big "Hello! Grab any seat you want" when I shuffled inside. There were even a couple Subarus and Audis in the parking lot. But the parking stalls were wide, sized to Ford F-250s and Dodge Rams. Alice's serves migratory urbanites, but survives on locals. The décor told me so. Eleven buck racks, shorn of their skulls, decorated walls. A black bear skin with marbles for eyes and a red felt fringe draped a showcase. A stuffed grouse with a patina of dust stared from its wall mount. Farm implements proliferated. Pitchfork tines supported bow-saw blades, nailed to a tractor steering wheel. Basketballs in an acrylic case commemorated Portland Trailblazer and local high school glories. A framed Philadelphia front page declared World War II over. Vague hints of felled spruce and lubricant wafted from a worn chainsaw.

Two regulars sauntered in, fresh from frustrated fishing. Hugging them, my waitress demanded, "I want to know where my steelhead is?" Her victim smiled, "Still swimmin' in the river, hon." Cook came out; she introduced the duo to a third at the counter. "Jus spent a thousand bucks on new tires. Right front sidewall blew. Thought we wuz gonna die, haulin that boat an all." Locals exchanged knowing nods.

NOT YIT.

The Greeks say that cities are great solitudes. Thoreau (American, 19th century A.D.) described the city as "millions of people being lonesome together." There is less social isolation in the cattle, dairy, lumber lands of coastal Oregon, at least at Alice's. The locals' yammer reminded me of a city slicker's exchange with a farmer in Carl Sandburg (American, 20th century A.D.): "'How do you do, my farmer friend?' 'Howdy.' 'Nice looking country you have here.' 'Fer them that likes it.' 'Live here all your life?' 'Not yit.'" (*The People, Yes*).

A freezer display by the cash register suggested Tillamook ice cream. The cows down the hill compelled me to taste their product, with a bit of chocolate added, in a waffle cone. Within the boundaries of the law and culinary joy, you can get anything you want at Alice's restaurant. Maybe Bob Dylan had a Route 6 chicken fried steak sandwich there. Who knows?

SUZY

3
BLUNT

In the summer of 1960, my parents finished their new rambler in Dalton Gardens, just north of Coeur d'Alene, Idaho. The home sat on three pastoral acres, its east picture windows filled with Canfield Mountain. All things were new. My folks hoped and worked. The year before, I almost flunked out of first grade at Bryan Elementary, which was hard to do. Mom and dad prayed I might improve at Dalton Elementary. Second grade teacher, Mrs. Smith, stumbled, coping with me. She called me "precocious," which was polite for "unruly." But by November, Mrs. Smith had wrangled me. In class, I progressed beside rural ruffians, of which I was one. During recess I showed less restraint.

November delivered a frigid week, every cheek bitten by Arctic jaws. The gutterless two-story Dalton Elementary building, poorly insulated, produced abundant roof melt. That dripping froze at eaves, icicles jutting down three, four, five feet. I found those stalactites irresistible. I was not alone.

Being new to Dalton, I followed. Ron, the tallest of Dalton's crop of second-graders, organized our recess raid. Seven boys crunched snowballs, then marched around the corner to the thickest crop of icicles. We launched our missles. Cracking, spears of ice tumbled, exploding on frozen ground. Cheering, we reloaded. Distantly, a door creaked. Ron pushed me forward alone, "Go for it, Lancaster." One boy giggled, a signal I missed. Honored, I split off a big one, just as Principal Chariton rounded the corner. Ice chips skittered. "Mr. Lancaster, come with me," he growled. We crunched toward his office, when he spun, an eyebrow raised. "Ron, you come with us too." Ron slunk up behind.

We got a lecture, which was lost on me. The principal painted sordid tales of icicle impalements, pointed at rules plainly explained only yesterday, and decried thoughtlessness. I was distracted by plans to knock the rest of the ice down after school. The diatribe ended. "Grab your ankles," Principal Chariton said. Ron and I folded ourselves. Then we met Mr. Woody. The plank slapped hindquarters, first Ron's, then mine. Once. Twice. Thrice. Alternation left sufficient time to savor each previous impact. The pain was startling. I cried, which salved none of the sting. It was my first blunt conversation, that talk between Mr. Woody and me. My father had administered amateur spankings; Mr. Woody was professionally licensed to afflict. The board's elemental logic convinced me. I never again liberated Dalton icicles.

Culturally, we have decided against corporal punishment of children. Abuses warrant that prohibition. But some of us may need measured pain to focus attention. I did. Talmudic rabbis (1st to 6th centuries A.D.) advise: "If you are visited by pain, examine your conduct." Mr. Woody visited. I suppose I might still be standing under falling icicles were it not for his blunt talk with my buttocks.

WOODY AND SOFIE

4
WOODY

Woody the alpaca has moved in next door to our home. We northernmost Shoreline Lancasters live next to a storm water retention pond. This time of year, the pond grounds are fervent with dandelions, new growth brambles, and hip-high grasses. Once or twice a year, a city employee comes to tamp back the exuberance so that the fenced pond does not become a jungle in our midst. Occasionally, we scale the fence to pick up garbage or do some whacking ourselves. In 2012, Woody the alpaca has shown us weed control done by a professional. Woody has pared back all the grasses and weeds. The camelid does not prefer woody materials, but pulls the leaves from the brambles, leading to their retreat and demise. I hear Woody has companions, goats and sheep, at other ponds who eat the tougher stems. These friends will soon arrive to finish Woody's job. Woody's patient munching has left the pond grounds clad in a short green carpet, one that brings to mind lush groomed expanses of pastoral Swiss meadows. I do not know what the City of Shoreline is paying for this Andean pack animal experiment, but it is a bargain. We Lancasters much prefer Woody's humming and little piles of highly-digested llama poo to the cantankerous hornet's nest of mixed gas-oil engines and sometimes-neglected overgrowth.

Do not think that Woody is just a happy replacement for weed-eaters. Woody is a phenom. Parents bring their children by the scores. Teens stop their incessant social jockeying to say hello to the rented alpaca. I even saw one adolescent put down his smart phone (for only a moment). Walkers eat their granola bars in Woody's company. All the dogs want a sniff of him. Woody gives us something to talk about with strangers. He boosts us Shoreliners over the "who-are-you-and-why-are-you-talking-to-me" hurdle. Woody is no dull cud-chewer. When people come to visit, Woody often stops browsing and comes to greet them. He has made himself a neighbor, a welcome one.

Woody may be a bit lonely. The alpaca and our little dog, Sofie, have built a bond. I read that alpacas are herd animals. I am told that Woody has a bit of an attitude with other animals, due to testosterone overload. Perhaps Woody should run for Congress. Woody beds down just outside our television room's window, where he rolls in the dust and

WOODY
FOR
CONGRESS

watches the sound and fury of Shoreline hurtle past. When bored, Woody watches television with us through the window, as the sun goes down and it grows difficult to see the grass. We think Woody prefers Downton Abbey, from among our NetFlix selections. We could be wrong.

To the persons who conceived and authorized this experiment in drubbing Shoreline's weeds, congratulations. Genius. Pure genius. Thanks for making life a little bit better in Shoreline.

RUBY

5
FRANK

As University of Idaho undergraduates in 1974, Fred and I built youth programs together at Moscow Presbyterian Church. We became friends. Fred was a brilliant biologist. He studied cougar foraging and duck injuries in his doctoral work. Acne plagued Fred. When our friendship reached a point where I could speak frankly, we sorted out how to tame his complexion. I was gaining weight (as usual); Fred made helpful nutrition suggestions. Fred fought Oregon fires one summer. I visited and found his sleeping bag rotted. After some direct talk, we discovered a local thrift held cheap replacements. I tended to burn the candle at both ends. I would study well past midnight, then set meetings before morning classes. Fred told me "one or the other, not both." He was right. Finally, Fred found Linda, a gem among women. Linda grew discouraged in their relationship. After candid talk, I learned Fred had not told Linda his feelings for her. Fred did so. When Fred and Linda married, the couple chose nuptials in a field in the woods. The morning of the ceremony, I learned Fred had tasked no one to police the cattle pasture. I shoveled dung in my tuxedo, then stood as best man. Imagine that chat.

A core privilege of friendship is frank conversation. Ralph Waldo Emerson (American, 19th century A.D.) saw: "Better be a nettle in the side of your friend than his echo" (*Friendship*). True friends must show one another grace and forgiveness. Joseph Joubert (French, 19th century A.D.) said: "When my friends are one-eyed, I look at them in profile" (*Pensees*). Still, deep humans show grace even to strangers. Frankness they hoard for friends. An honest word spoken by a beloved companion is spiritual elixir. Wounds heal. Barriers fall. Fears flag. William Penn (American, 17th century A.D.) said: "They have a right to censure that have a heart to help" (*Some Fruits of Solitude*, §1.46). Friendship boils down to frank love. A friend's plain-speaking stimulates reflection and mediates ill-conceived excesses. Heart-to-heart companionship warms the cold nut of existence. Sophocles (Greek, 5th century B.C.) asserted: "To throw away an honest friend is, as it were, to throw your life away" (*Oedipus the King*).

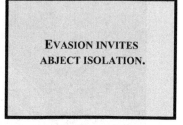

EVASION INVITES ABJECT ISOLATION.

Where friendship sickens, the disease is dishonesty. Some believe friends do not argue; I doubt they have friends. Friendship thrives in passionate disagreement. Friendship rots where deceit is suspected. Solitude craves politeness. Strings of sincerity weave human bonds. Moliere (French, 17th century A.D.) agreed, "The greater one's love for a person the less room for flattery. The proof of true love is to be unsparing in criticism" (*The Misanthrope*, 1666, §2). A friend's core responsibility lies in compassionate candor. Djuna Barnes (America, 20th century A.D.) said, "To love without criticism is to be betrayed" (*Nightwood*, 1937).

Sit down with a friend. Give a hug. Be frank.

KITTY

6
DEATH

My father the veterinarian brought the kitten home from work. We three kids, too young to be clever, named the creature Kitty. Kitty became a ten-pound white yard tom; a mottle of black and brown spilled over one eye. We kids loved Kitty and Kitty adopted us, in the manner of cats, as well. The Lancaster urchins were Kitty's odd pride, in both the human and feline senses.

When I got boyish enough to be so stupid, I caught a ricochet from my BB gun in the right cornea. Interior bleeding clouded my eye's light canal. Dr. Barclay prescribed two weeks strict bed rest, flat on the back with both eyes covered—a calamitous sentence for eleven year old boys from Dalton Gardens.

Kitty, who sensed my distress, kept vigil over me, as though I might be dying. The protective old nightmare-of-mice draped himself across my neck, rear claws anchored in one shoulder and head plopped on the other. And we waited. Kitty departed occasionally to scratch in the yard or to pick at his bowl, but never for long. Kitty laid his soul alongside my own, and waited for developments. When I was released, Kitty returned to patrolling the barnyard and I to fort building and cow pasture baseball with the Cuddy boys across the street.

WAIT FOR DEVELOPMENTS.

On a gray winter's morning years later, my vigilant mother found Kitty's bed cold, his dinner untouched. Mom whispered with my father. Then came the report: Kitty is missing. After searching the usual places, I reached the grim conclusion. I squeezed behind bales, poked under the tack barn, checked the neighbors' pigeon roost and tool sheds. My own vigil began. I walked the country roads of Dalton, inspecting the ditches for a week before and after school. In the end, fresh snowfalls ended my sad plodding and any hope of finding Kitty's remains before spring's thaw.

Socrates of Athens said that philosophers prepare for life by practicing death every day. Kitty knew. When death, or even the fear of it, looms, one lays his soul alongside a friend, and waits for developments.

NEIGHBORHOOD BASEBALL

7
CERTAINLY UNCERTAIN

Plagued by my incessant seven year old questions, Mrs. Smith blurted: "Brad, everything that can be known is known. So, be quiet." Not the sentiment of a second grade teacher having her best moment. Mrs. Smith repented. She thrust Jules Verne's *20,000 Leagues Under the Sea* into my hands. Verne's tale drove me to Coeur d'Alene Public Library's science fiction collection. As one starving, I gorged on Asimov and Heinlein and Bradbury, banquets of ripe speculative universes. Truths, certainties quavered in master hands. The demi-gods of science fiction drove me, for the first of many times, to ask: what do I *know*?

At three, I worked out shoe-tying for myself (to this day, I tie my laces backwards). I knew then that I knew everything important. From that triumphant day, education increased, but certitude shrank. At four, I crushed off the tip of my right index finger in my bicycle sprocket. At eight, the principal thwacked my tusch for tossing snowballs at icicles on school eaves. At ten, I discovered just how much my classmates liked fat, smart people. At twelve, I learned that Jean Hall did not pine for me as I did for her. At thirteen, I scored in an elementary school basketball game--for the other team--twice. At eighteen, I adopted religious certainty with Protestant odors. At nineteen, I saw that religious certainty is not all that certain. By twenty-two, I understood my mind was second-tier. By twenty-four, I fathomed that churches don't want smart-alecks leading them. By twenty-six, I gleaned that I did not know what truth is. At forty-three, I found that crooks may prosper and facts may not matter. At forty-five, I grasped that I could not coherently explain evil. At forty-eight, I learned that bad men of ignoble purpose may be more eloquent than me. At fifty-three, I started writing these little bits, publishing my ignorance.

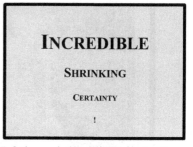

Certitudes wane for me. Hordes of messy facts, heaps of worthy perspectives gnaw at my knowing. Socrates (Athenian, 5th century B.C.) assaulted confident knowing. He withered opponents: "[N]either of us really knows anything fine and good, but this man thinks he knows something when he does not, whereas I, as I do not know anything, do not think I do either. I seem, then, in just this little thing to be wiser than this man at any rate, that what I do not know I do not think I know either" (*Apologia*). The Enlightenment's scion, Voltaire (French, 18th century A.D.), put it simply: "I am far from being certain" (*Philosophical Dictionary*, "Certitude"). That captures it. I am certainly uncertain.

PUDDLES WITH GRAMMA ADA

8
DEPARTING JESUS ECCLESIASTICUS[2]

Many encounter Jesus, or his semblance.[3] I did.

Our meeting came during an initial dive into the New Testament as a high school sophomore in northern Idaho. Jesus won me: his sassiness, blunt wisdom, and that persistent preference for anti-Roman underdogs and unschooled laborers. I savored the Galilean's bemused solitudes, juxtaposed, often uncomfortably, with unbridled chatter and clueless incomprehension from his students. Jesus' metaphors and parables grabbed me, each rooted in his rural conviction that wan urban religiosity had played itself out. Yahweh[4] trembles, in Jesus' rendition, poised to irrupt[5] into human ordinariness. Jesus announced himself as Yahweh's scion,[6] the divine sword of incursion, honed for final judgment. Jesus believed he was the Son of man.[7]

Parochial eschatology[8] aside, I found Jesus disarmingly heartfelt and alarmingly direct. He captured me. I laid aside my nets. I followed.[9]

---

[2] This text is an excerpt from the introduction to my little book, *Gethsemane Soliloquy: An Epitome of the Reliable Sayings of Jesus*.

[3] In 2016, seventy-eight percent of Americans self-identified as Christians.

[4] "Yahweh" is a transliterated approximation of the Hebrew tetragrammaton (יהוה, rendered in English as "YHVH" or "YHWH"), which is the personal name of the god of Israel (see Genesis 21:33 or Exodus 3:13-15).

[5] To "irrupt" is to suddenly break into something, as in an implosion. See Mark 14:61-62. Note how the gospel writer conflated messianic identity with Son of man language.

[6] A "scion" is a descendant of an aristocratic family, or a shoot grafted onto a mature plant. The concept of branch resides in the eschatological rescue passages of Jeremiah 23:5-6 and Isaiah 11:1-10.

[7] See Daniel 7:9-18, and Mark 2:27-28. In the prophet Daniel's vision, the Son of man stands before the Ancient of Days, who is arrayed in all his divine glory, poised for final judgment upon the four kingdoms of earth. The Ancient of Days gives the Son of man dominion over all peoples of earth, perpetually. He will be served by mankind, as shall all the saints of the Most High. The denomination "son of man" is used in other ways as well in the book of Daniel. At Daniel 8:17, the term is used of Daniel himself, and appears to mean "human." Elsewhere, the term is used to distinguish lowly humankind from the unutterable magnificence of divinity, e.g., Numbers 23:19. The term "son of man" (בן אדם, rendered in English as "ben 'adam") appears 107 times in the Hebrew canon, mostly in the apocalyptic visions of Ezekiel and Daniel. Some interpreters have construed Jesus' use of the term "son of man" as an emphatic form of the personal pronoun. I dispute this construction, since it is inconsistent with the eschatological vision of John the Baptist, to whom Jesus went for baptism and with whose ministry Jesus associated his own (see Mark 1:4-9, Mark 1:14, Mark 9:11-13, Mark 11:30) and with Jesus' own eschatological view of his ministry as the fulfillment of time and the leading edge of the oncoming kingdom. See Mark 1:15. As a sophomore in high school, I understood nothing of these eschatological sentiments. I cannot claim greatly improved comprehension now decades later. Perhaps, these logia are intentionally elusive.

[8] "Eschatology" refers to ruminations upon the end of the world, and the ultimate destiny of mankind.

[9] Mark 1:17-18. Much to the dismay of my parents, I might add. But that is another tale entirely.

A numinous[10] Presbyterian sequel arrived. In the social adhesion of young adults transported by the thrum of guitars and song, I recognized that life exceeds my comprehension of it. I glimpsed *noumena*.[11] We are more—much more—together than alone. I have, in my dotage, clumped together words to describe my youthful song-borne intuition of abyssal existential depth. I presume in that work, probably unsuccessfully, to describe the bramble that is human social interpenetration.[12] At the time, however (it was 1972), the church taught me to call this odd experience a supernal incursion of "the holy spirit." I was, for some months, content enough with my good-hearted pastor's interpretations. I, at that time in my early life, ill-appreciated the mental mutations and mutilations worked by theological jargon. Along with Jesus, who moved me, I imbibed the church, its theology and liturgical habits, and its problematical attitudes. I kept the ecclesiastical bathwater along with its scrubbed and divinized baby Jesus. And I called the burbling batch "faith." I was styled "born again," in the manner evangelicals use those words. At this characterization, I, for reasons I then little understood, chafed. But I shrugged off my misgivings. I chewed at length upon that sinewy muscle that is the church. It proved a tough jerky.

Years of study and life among permutations of Christianity ensued.[13] I undertook studies of biblical materials and various theologies at Fuller Theological Seminary in Pasadena, California. I earned a master's degree, and commenced doctoral studies in

---

[10] "Numen" denotes implicit influences that can be perceived, but not by the senses. In the Roman usage, numen trended toward suspicions of divine nudging, though some authors use the term to mean "impressive potency." In sycophantic moments, emperors were applauded for the numen that attended them.

[11] "*Noumena*" is a term for things-as-they-are, set over against "*phenomena*," things-as-they-appear to a human. So, the distinction registers recognition that humans see only part of what ultimately exists, bounded as we are by the constraints of our sense organs. Yet, humans imagine (or, possibly, even experience) glimpses of hidden matters. Immanuel Kant denied that humans know anything of *noumena*. See Kant, *Critique of Pure Reason*. I now suspect (but did not always do so) that Kant is right. We unconsciously fabricate much of what we perceive, and (wrongly) call that construction "insight." Reality, as humans experience it, consists in observations pasted together with supposition and superstition. A person spreads that jumble onto a psychic canvas conformed to the survival demands of the African veldt. Gods leak imperceptibly through the canvas, if the divine, in fact, leaks into the cosmos at all.

[12] See Lancaster, *Cull: Choosing Well*, Sections I and II, and Lancaster, *Cull: Epitomes* on Berger's *Sacred Canopy*, Buber's *I and Thou*, Cicero, *On Friendship*, and Aristotle, *Nichomachean Ethics*, Books 8 and 9.

[13] By background, I was Presbyterian. I participated in youth ministry programs with four different congregations of that Scottish ilk. A college friend directed Lutheran youth ministries in the small college town where I spent my sophomore year of college; I worshiped with his congregation occasionally. In my freshman year of college, I helped in youth ministries at a Methodist congregation, one mired in a town awash in immoderate Mormons. I coached an Episcopalian boys' basketball team (which is a measure of just how hard up they were for a coach), and worshiped with the priest's group on campus occasionally. I tasted Pentecostal, Catholic, and non-denominational community churches as opportunities presented themselves. In each community, I found people of good faith attempting to ascertain the will of God for themselves. I also discovered others in their midst devoted to alternative, and to my taste less worthy, purposes.

systematics.[14] Experience and insight grew, as did disillusion. I left seminary, part way through my Ph.D. work under mentor, Paul Jewett. And I forsook the church. My exits were graceless pratfalls, freighted by unresolved anger and trenchant disappointment. Paul Jewett, a quiet and decent man of the church, never plumbed my ecclesiastical dysphoria. The church, for its part, jammed spasmodic fingers in its metaphorical ears, so to remain ignorant of my numerous theological broadsides. Justifiably so. I was obnoxious.

I have, since those dual departures from seminary and churches, nevertheless harbored a grave affection for Yeshua the Galilean.[15] My continuing attachment to Yeshua is grave for two reasons. Interest in Yeshua has been a demanding enterprise. It has taxed me. And many exquisitely painful events in my life emerge from heeding Yeshua. He has asked much. Thoughts often run to the Jewish peasant. Shall I subvert this authority? Shall I comfort that person? What matters? Shall I give time or money? How will I make my living? Who may become my friend? What do I owe governments, and my family? How fares my heart? What of enemies? When I make decisions, Yeshua weighs in. He lingers, enigmatically, near the back of every room, close by the exit. He murmurs advice and the occasional snide aside. Yeshua's tongue, and wit, remain whetted edges. They cut. Who, or what, is this Yeshua of Galilee? What did he say? Critically, how is Yeshua the Galilean related to the church's Jesus of Nazareth?

My experience within the Protestant orb falls in two regimes. For five years, I absorbed the church's theology, read the Bible devotionally (but with some intensity), and directed youth programs within the various organizations I attended. The second five years saw formal theological inquiry, critique (sometimes virulent) of churches,

---

[14] Systematic theology indulges the presumptuous inquiry of the biblical canon, What is the whole counsel of God? Systematics tends to fold philosophy and alternative religions into the conversation about the meaning of the Jewish and Christian canons. New Testament or Old Testament theology asks of the relevant books, What do these collections, as a whole, teach? Biblical theology focuses on individual books of the canon, asking, What does this book teach? New Testament or Old Testament studies attempt to place a book or collection in its historical circumstance, in an effort to invest obscure language with a then-current human context.

[15] "Yeshua" is the Aramaic name of Jesus, before that name was transliterated into Greek and a Latin masculine suffix added. Matthew 2:23 calls Yeshua a "Nazorean," often dubiously translated in KJV and NRSV as Nazarene. No historical evidence for Nazareth, as a village, exists before the third century A.D. Nazareth probably did not exist in the lifetime of Yeshua. It seems likely that early Christian writers confused the terms Nazirite (Numbers 6:1-23), the third century Galilean village of Nazareth, and a first-century designation for a murky ascetic sect known for fastidious religiosity, the Nazoreans. Toranic Nazirite vows require the worshipper to set himself apart for Yahweh, avoiding alcohol and grapes. The Nazirite did not cut his hair or go near dead bodies (even close family members). If a person died suddenly beside a Nazirite, the Nazirite must shave his head, and make appropriate sacrifices, which are specified. Upon completion of the term of a Nazirite's vow, he made sacrifices and shaved his head at the door of the tent of meeting and burned the hair in the fire of the sacrifices. Then the Nazirite was allowed to drink wine (Numbers 6:1-23). Matthew 2:23 proof-texts to associate Yeshua with the Branch of Yahweh described in Isaiah 11:1. It does appear that Yeshua's early home was Galilee. Matthew 4:23. Thus, I prefer to call this man "Yeshua the Galilean."

and textual criticism of the church's canon. I quested for means to remake the church catholic. Nasty tracts, alternative theologies, and house churches issued. I bluntly castigated ecclesiastical institutions and their unfortunate ciphers, my senior pastors. I offended by arrogant excess and paucity of peacemaking. Maturing, I recognized the church as a matrix of sociologically ossified organizations. After years of painful exchanges, I left my church and the church. We are happier parted.

Passing decades have bequeathed me rubrics[16] more apt, quarried from minds more penetrating than my own, in which to frame theological angst.[17] I found in personalism, both theological and secular, frameworks of utility.[18] Albert Schweitzer's *Quest for the Historical Jesus* exposed the penchant of churches and their opponents to cut-and-paste Jesuses to preference. The final alfalfa leaf that tipped my theological haystack came on a crisp October dawn in 1980. I strolled to seminary beneath a cerulean blue dome, before obscuring smog mashed against Pasadena's hills from the tailpipes of Los Angeles's belching horde of ill-tuned cars, trucks, and buses. A seditious thought dawned, as had the sun. I undoubtedly knew more—no, much more—of Jesus than did Saul of Tarsus, the writer of portions of the New Testament.[19] From that moment, the canon eroded for me. I came to regard the apostles and their successors, as well as subsequent church fathers, not as mentors or icons or heroes. I held them as struggling, relatively narrow, people. The apostles and fathers sought to deflect an existential threat to their affection for Jesus—the revisionist mongrels of the Roman-Hellenic empire. To defeat the syncretist hordes, the church adopted their methods. The church faithful wrote Jesus Ecclesiasticus. Back in Pasadena, church dogma became, for me, equivocal. I recognized in my Christian co-religionists a nasty streak, which rooted also in my heart in a peculiarly putrid manner.[20]

I commenced a search. How might one disentangle Yeshua the Galilean from the church's mash-up, Jesus of Nazareth? This latter is the ecclesiastical god-man,

---

[16] A "rubric" can mean an explanatory framework or a gloss, or even an organized way of speaking of something.

[17] "Angst" is persistent dread about something that may prove to be essentially trivial.

[18] Consider Martin Buber's *I and Thou*, or Levinas's *Otherwise Than Being*, or the personalist Neo-orthodoxy of Emil Brunner. Brunner's three-volume *Dogmatics* merits a careful reading, if you savor Christianity.

[19] Saul of Tarsus renamed himself the Apostle Paul, after his conversion from Pharisaical Judaism (see Philippians 3:5) to nascent Christianity. Paul never met Jesus, unless one counts the odd event Paul recounts from a trip to Damascus. See Acts 9:1-22. Paul wrote several letters to churches which became part of the canon of the New Testament. Their exact number is indeterminate, because the practice of pseudonymity (attaching a false, and usually more famous or authoritative, author's name to a work) leaves the writer of several New Testament books equivocal.

[20] A character flaw common to religious ideologues of diverse persuasions, and one from which I, for some years, suffered acutely. I was narrow, and valued narrowness.

the churches' Messiah, their metaphysical Son of God, and an occasional apocalyptic Son of man. The former, Yeshua, hunkered beneath churchly Jesus. This essay recounts some intellectual components of sorting Yeshua from Jesus.

If you find yourself satisfied with the Jesus whom your church has taught you, do not read [*Gethsemane Soliloquy*].[21] Yeshua the Galilean is not Jesus of Nazareth. You will learn next-to-nothing about how to co-exist with Christian people of faith, especially bumptious bible-bangers, by reading this book, except to the extent those brethren are human.

Yeshua belongs to mankind, as do Homer and Plato and Aristotle and Cicero and Augustine and Kant and Wollstonecraft and de Beauvoir. Yeshua shared our struggles and confusions, and ultimately, our death. Jesus, the Jesus invented in those first few centuries of ecclesiastical struggle, belongs to the church, in the way protagonists belong to their novelists. I do not so speak to injure or disparage the church. I use this language because the metaphor is apt.

Jesus Ecclesiasticus hovers, at least a little bit, above our merely mortal fray. What other has been resurrected? Clerical persons claim authorial rights to Jesus. In this, many are more than a bit uppity. Still, their claim has merit. Jesus belongs to the church. For, at least in part, the church made Jesus up. The Fathers painted and prettified their Jesus. They perched their Nazarene, scrubbed and freshly garmented, on a lonely shelf far above pedestrian criticism.

Those clerical dominators have long quashed critics who explore heretical irreverence. They have hoped to silence those who extricate Yeshua from beneath their fractured Jesus—people like me, and possibly, if you are still reading, people like you.[22] Despite the church's fervent obscuring, Yeshua leaked through. I, and many, have whiffed him. We dog Yeshua's trail.

---

[21] Consider yourself warned.

[22] Jan Oppermann styles *Gethsemane Soliloquy* a "personal anti-Christology." Oppermann wonders where the author hides amidst the analysis. I certainly have important personal feelings about the topics touched in this little work. But my purpose is not self-revelation (though I do a fair bit of that anyway), but analysis and sorting of the sayings of Yeshua, which I have not found to my satisfaction in other works, followed by a sympathetic summary of Yeshua's residual tuition. Oppermann doubts that I can (or anyone can) follow Yeshua's thoughts from the far side of the two thousand year chasm that separates us. I am sure my friend, Jan, is correct. Yet, Yeshua matters to me. I want to hear him. Ecclesiastical editing excised, I listen. Personal correspondence with the author, spring 2017.

PUDDLES

9
SELASSIE

I shook the hand of a king or a god.

August 1974, Addis Ababa, Ethiopia. Our bus filled with college students rattled down a long, straight road of spotty asphalt. Scores walked narrow shoulders as we jostled toward the Imperial Summer Palace. Ethiopians are a warm, generous people with an ancient culture. But they are poor, desperately poor. Lacking facilities, pedestrian roadside urination was the rule. I pointed out a line crew tending utilities. Our guide corrected me, "Thieves pilfering telephone wire for the copper." Despite their difficulties, smiles adorn Ethiopian faces like bees on flowers.

Palatial gates opened. Ratty militiamen lounged on two parked jeeps. The guide warned: "Those guns have real bullets; these communist rebels lack humor." Ornate doors swung to reveal Emperor Haile Selassie. The short, frail man in excellent uniform patiently gripped our hands one by one. Scruffy guards with submachine guns surveyed us from either side. Ostensibly protecting Selassie, their weaponry insured rather his compliance and incarceration. The Emperor's captors and their bloody Mengistu successors, with Soviet backing, inflicted communist Red Terror upon Ethiopia, murdering thousands. In 2006, Mengistu was convicted *in absentia* of genocide.

Haile Selassie rose to power without violence in 1930. Upon Selassie's coronation, Jamaican Pan-African enthusiasts declared Selassie the living God incarnate and promised Messiah for Africans. A community of 200 Rastafarian families ("Ras" means prince; "Tafari" was Selassie's birth name) persists at Shashamene in southern Ethiopia.

Emperor Selassie was much loved, but an ineffective administrator. The 1972 Wollo Famine killed more than 40,000 people. Selassie's popularity plummeted. Edmund Burke (British, 18th century A.D.) said well: "Nothing turns out to be so oppressive and unjust as a feeble government" (*Reflections on the Revolution in France*).

Military elements seized power. Selassie endured house arrest (at which time I shook his hand), then died or was murdered in 1975. He was buried under a concrete slab on the palace grounds. After Mengistus and their Soviet bankroll collapsed (1991), Selassie's body was exhumed, given Imperial honors, and entombed on holy Ethiopian Orthodox ground. Rastafarians attended, but denied the body laid to rest was that of their Messiah, who they believe lives on in hiding.

I have pondered Haile Selassie. In most accounts, the Emperor was a good man overwhelmed by his country's many challenges. Robert Louis Stevenson (Scottish, 19th century A.D.) said: "Our business in this world is not to succeed, but to continue to fail, in good spirits" (*Reflections and Remarks on Human Life, §4*). I met Selassie as his life's work collapsed. He bore defeat with equanimity.

JESSIE AND SOFIE

10
SYMPHONIES

Singers massed at Spartan Gymnasium. Youthful voices rattled retracted backboards. The gym, usually salted with hoopla and sweat, purred with harmony and syncopation. The Sixth Grade Honor Choir Concert showcased an army of elementary school vocalists, as well as ensembles from both local high schools. Instructors stood proud and nervous. Educators received well-deserved, praise-stuffed bouquets. And music erupted. Five of eleven selections were ecclesiastical: John's Christology or sassing the devil or Negro spirituals or jubilation to the Bible's god. Boys swaggered in celebration of the *Drunken Sailor*. Girls charmed the socks off hundreds with sweet antics, rendering *When You're Smiling* with excessive joy (if there is such a thing). Even the full moon applauded, fresh from eclipse, bestowing a blue winter's wink from behind backlit clouds. Humans approximate paradise in song. This festival chorus dipped toes in eternal seas. Songs ended; all welcomed respite from hard bleachers. Chairs were restacked. Full lots emptied. Cars of tired choristers and glowing parents rolled to their abodes.

A grander, quieter symphony rung simultaneously at Spartan Gymnasium, crooning behind choirs' offerings. Performers included parents, schools, children, citizens, taxpayers, educators, administrators. Their selection was *Nurture the Future*, a goodwill opera sung to an orchestra of young heartstrings. Each family, each life added its melody. Each kinfolk beat its peculiar percussion of progress. The communal "symphony" soared lyrical, though dissonance (we know) erupts occasionally. Success was palpable. Sixth graders, fresh to song, plugged along bravely. High

> **OUTPACING**
> **DOGGED**
> **CATASTROPHE**

schoolers, only three to six years their elders, waxed poetic. One imagined wonders ahead: chorales or madrigals, musics from Islam or Borneo, atonal poems and structured classics, rhythms of timeless or timely tempo. Perhaps Shoreline fledges voices destined to one day spellbind mankind.

H. G. Wells (British, 20th century A.D.) said: "Human history becomes more and more a race between education and catastrophe." At Shoreline's Honor Choir Concert, education was a full lap ahead.

JESSIE

11
CIVILITY

Shoreline is a peach of a town, with a spot of blight. Shoreline elects her officials to address civic issues directly and efficiently. For the most part, we get that. I thank city government. But the last election was a squeaker; the outcome polarized Shoreline. Sore-losers carried the election to court, filing suit against three current (and one former) Council members, alleging Open Meetings Act violations. The sum at issue is a few hundred dollars. Attorney's fees substantially exceed $100,000. Plaintiffs paint themselves defenders of open public process. I doubt that. At best, their bag is mixed. Plaintiffs seek political blood. Taxpayers' wallets are pillaged. Rancor grows as the fall election approaches. Some have indulged gender bashing, *ad hominem* dismissal of concerns, intentional impoliteness, bitter invective. Plaintiffs and their supporters care little how much their pound of flesh costs Shoreline taxpayers. And civility in Shoreline has taken a beating. The Open Meetings lawsuit reeks of revenge.

Marcus Tullius Cicero (Roman, 1st century B.C.) wrote: "A most wretched custom, assuredly, is our electioneering and scrambling for office. . . . [W]e should regard only those as adversaries who take up arms against the state, not those who strive to have the government administered according to their convictions. . . . Neither must we listen to those who think that one should indulge in violent anger against one's political enemies and imagine that such is the attitude of a great-spirited, brave man. For nothing is more commendable, nothing more becoming in a pre-eminently great man than courtesy and forbearance. . . . [We must avoid developing] a sour, churlish temper, prejudicial to ourselves and offensive to others" (*On Duties*, Book I, §87-88).

Political lawsuits abuse our constitutional system. We must address political questions with ballots, not pleadings. Political lawsuits are social gangrene. They choke dialogue; they sicken the body politic. Witness Shoreline's recall elections, those ill-conceived boils. Council members (and now the school district) are distracted from public business. Political lawsuits squander dollars that might otherwise buy books or pave sidewalks. Political lawsuits poison our candidate pool. Who seeks office when debilitating litigation follows? Shoreline hires its City Council to dispute with one another, in the conviction that good policy flows from open, occasionally spirited, dialogue. But most of us prefer political "fighting" that exudes the spirit of Gandhi: resolute, principled, forbearing, possibly kind.

> **POLITICS NEED NOT BE THE "SYSTEMATIC ORGANIZATION OF HATREDS."**

If you do not like the last election's outcome, then win the next election--fairly. **Dismiss that revenge lawsuit.** Do not support those who support revenge lawsuits.

Some City Council members, current and former, are my acquaintances. I count among them friends, even clients. To those who support revenge lawsuits I say:

When you disparage other council members, you damage all of us. When you attack opponents, instead of their positions, you diminish the dignity of your office. Henry Adams (American historian, 20th century A.D.) called politics the "systematic organization of hatreds" (*The Education of Henry Adams*). Prove him wrong. Win arguments by facts, reason, and persuasive talk. Compromise with opponents. Every City Council member is intelligent and cares deeply about Shoreline. Try to discover that in the others. Biting your tongue is permitted. You must not build our physical infrastructure to the neglect of our interpersonal and communal well-being. Relationships matter. We are all part of one another. Every community has a spirit and identity. I ask you to lavish the same care you have shown in creating our streets and parks upon building our communal identity and civic spirit. Be led by your *best* lights. We are counting on you.

JESSIE

12
A TALE OF ONE CITY

With apologies to Charles Dickens (English, 19th century A.D.), I tell a tale of one city (my own), which, unfortunately, mirrors the tale of many cities. Shoreline, Washington, has stumbled through the best and worst of times, a season of deeds, a spell of despond. Shoreline has traded cherubic youth for awkward, adolescent pimples. As is customary in matters civic, Shoreline's tale pivots on purses, mostly developers' purses. Lately, Shoreline, like Dickens's Mr. Lorry, passes life "turning an immense pecuniary Mangle" (*Tale of Two Cities*, Book I, Chapter 4).

Shoreline is not alone. Recently, *USA Today* reported bellicose city council ire in Ashland, Oregon. Their noise sounds familiar. The paper also cited council rancor in Atlanta, Dallas, Cincinnati, Reno, Wilmington, Cedar Rapids, and twelve other cities. Charles Mahtesian, editor of *Almanac of American Politics*, asserted: "The public arena is a much louder and nastier place, and civility has really disappeared." The trend "reflects a general decline in civility in society" (*USA Today*, "City Council pays for lessons in civility," October 4, 2007).

Shoreline began as hinterland in imperial King County. Citizens were frustrated by dawdling police response, permit delays, and unkempt (occasionally squalid) parks. Maggie Fimia boosted Shoreline's incorporation with civic-minded locals. In 1995, Shoreline pulled up a chair at the table of cities. Shoreline's first city council took on the obvious. It hired police and staff. It refurbished parks. It began gateways, the Interurban Trail, the Fifteenth Avenue resurrection, and approached our core eyesore, Aurora Avenue. Real estate developers and big contractors salivated. Shoreline's council hired assertive city manager, Steve Burkett. Burkett, no dummy, knew who buttered his bread. He served the council majority better than its minority. Burkett rammed projects through public process. He got things done, pleasing developers and builders, but angered unheard citizens and businesses squashed by heavy-handed process.

Those angry dissenters helped Maggie Fimia take Kevin Grossman's Shoreline council seat in 2003. Fimia asked hard financial questions. She butted heads with the old guard, especially city manager Burkett. Fimia demanded open, participatory process in Shoreline. Burkett stonewalled her. Power on Shoreline City Council flipped in 2005. Minority became majority. Burkett resigned, got on his horse and rode out of town, negotiating a substantial severance package as he galloped past city hall. I know Burkett. He is a good man; I wish him well. He left when Shoreline needed different leadership.

Not everyone got that message. Members, present and past, of the council's former majority chose the moral low road: character assassination, political litigation, disinformation, and attack ads. They formed Pro Shoreline, a developers' and builders' political action committee, and enlisted the like-minded. Pro Shoreline members brought a recall petition against new majority members. Then dismissed it. Pro Shoreline plaintiffs brought politically-motivated Open Public Meetings Act ("OPMA") allegations against the new council majority. After two years of litigation and hundreds of thousands of dollars of public costs, plaintiffs unearthed no evidence from mountains of documents and emails. They lost their motion for summary judgment. The writing was on the wall. Pro Shoreline's supporters dismissed their limping case, but not before extorting a portion of their attorney's fees from the City of Shoreline.

As has become the rule for defeated armies, Pro Shoreline formed up its tattered troops and declared victory--before scuttling for the bushes. From the brambles, Pro Shoreline misled newspapers (including the *Seattle Times* and *Shoreline Enterprise*). Those presses proved incompetent (or unmotivated) to analyze OPMA facts and law. Both papers regurgitated Pro Shoreline's prevarications. Robert Armstrong (British, 20th century A.D.) satirized a public falsehood: "It contains a misleading impression, not a lie. It was being economical with the truth" (*Daily Telegraph*, November 19, 1986). So too, the *Times* and *Enterprise*: very economical.

Now Shoreline's tale finds its cliff-hanger. Elections are upon us. Urban futures are debated, but deliberated in the shadow of misguided press coverage. What will Shoreline choose to become—a developer's haven, or a chorus of lively civic voices? We shall decide on Tuesday, November 6, 2007. In the meantime, Pro Shoreline's incivility rages unabated. Pro Shoreline mailed another attack ad. In that hit piece, Pro Shoreline intentionally misrepresented State Auditor Brian Sonntag's support of Maggie Fimia. The piece was a cheap shot. Pro Shoreline's boorish rancor seduced opponents to follow suit. Opponents issued two attack ads, also boorish, against Paul Grace and Pro Shoreline. They were wrong to do so. Our low road grows well-trodden.

Numerous American cities suffer the incivility plague, not just Shoreline. Dickens's tale concerned two cities: London and Paris. London labored under outrageous classist inequities. Paris suffered the French Revolution's Reign of Terror, with regicide and guillotine purges. Shoreline, and other cities as well, should learn from Dickens. Conflict degenerates, if we let it fester.

Without civility, public life is just brawling. Do we really want our civic dialogue reduced to fistfights? I, for one, do not.

13
PEACE IN OUR HOUSE

The Open Public Meetings lawsuit ("OPMA suit") settled. Finally. City council defendants make no admissions. That is appropriate. Defendants did nothing wrong. The plaintiffs abandon their meritless allegations. That is appropriate. Plaintiffs lacked evidence of OPMA violations. The City of Shoreline pays plaintiffs (Connie King, Kevin Grossman, and John Hollinrake, supported by Pro Shoreline and real estate developers) $159,000 (a fraction of their attorney's fees) to drop their OPMA suit. That, however painful for us taxpayers stuck with the bill, is necessary. OPMA suit costs spin skyward. After jury trial, city costs might have reached one million dollars. So, the City covered some of plaintiffs' losses, and plaintiffs dropped their OPMA suit. At last. Good enough. Shoreline might have peace.

"Might" is the operative word. Now Pro Shoreline begins its spin, compounding their meritless, dismissed lawsuit with a campaign of disinformation. Pro Shoreline befuddled newspaper editors. The Shoreline Enterprise opined that plaintiffs possessed "damning" evidence of defendants' OPMA violations. The Seattle Times ignored plaintiffs' lack of proof, leaping to condemn defendants' purported stubbornness. Both papers are wrong. Utterly wrong. In twenty months of litigation, plaintiffs gathered no evidence proving their case. We know this certainly. In lawsuits, when one party has both indisputable facts and the law on their side, courts declare them the winner. It's called summary judgment. Plaintiffs *lost* their motion for summary judgment. Lawyers do not dismiss lawsuits when they possess "damning" or "compelling" evidence. They move for summary judgment. They move to win.

Evan Smith of the Enterprise, with troubling temerity, writes that accused council members should have perjured themselves to quash the OPMA suit. Really, Mr. Smith? Shoreline Enterprise staff, and the Times as well, lack the skills to competently evaluate the thousands of pages of evidence in the OPMA lawsuit or analyze the OPMA statute and interpretive cases. Both seem ignorant of perjury law and civil procedure. Nevertheless, the papers blurt, as is their right. In America, one can spout groundless political conjecture with impunity, as have the Enterprise and Times. A. J. Liebling (American journalist, 20th century A.D.) identified a problem: "Freedom of the press is guaranteed only to those who own one." (*New Yorker*, May 14, 1960). I would add, "or to those who buy ad space." Like myself. The Enterprise and Times editorial staffs erred.

The OPMA suit has been Shoreline's "tempest in a teapot," a pricey foray into hostile divided-government, Pro Shoreline's moral backsliding toward politics-by-litigation. Remember our past. Events may rupture teapots. Our United States has suffered boiling bloodbaths. Abraham Lincoln (American, 19th century A.D.) predicted three years before the Civil War: "'A house divided against itself cannot stand.' I believe this government cannot endure, permanently half *slave* and half *free*. I do not expect the Union to be *dissolved*—I do not expect the house to *fall*—but I *do* expect it will cease to be divided. It will become *all* one thing, or *all* the other." (June 16, 1858). In this prophecy, Lincoln was right. A month earlier, on May 18, 1858,

Lincoln said: "To give the victory to the right, not *bloody bullets*, but *peaceful ballots* only, are necessary." In this prescription, Lincoln was wrong. Six hundred thousand Union and Confederate soldiers died. No one will perish in our city's tempests. Still, we might debilitate Shoreline.

Pro Shoreline and its supporters brought us the OPMA lawsuit. Can Pro Shoreline forsake yesterday's battles? Can they silence their spin sweatshop, finish their fib frenzy? Can Pro Shoreline be "pro Shoreline?" Fall elections may strengthen one block or the other. In November, Kim and I will support Maggie Fimia and those who support her. We ask you to vote with us. Decisive victory at November's polls will consolidate hard-won gains—South Woods, the final phase of our Aurora project, Fircrest, parks, sidewalks, and a generally more inclusive and fair and courteous public process. That's what Shoreline gets from Maggie.

From Pro Shoreline, we get political lawsuits and attack ads. Pro Shoreline deserves no thanks from Shoreliners. Pro Shoreline spent gobs of **our** money on **their** political revenge lawsuits. Pro Shoreline disparages our best public servants. Pro Shoreline backs Maggie Fimia's election opponent, whose primary qualification appears to be that she is "not Maggie." Be pro Shoreline. Vote **against** candidates supported by Pro Shoreline. Enough said.

Regardless how the election turns, victory will plant no peace. Peace is a commitment of the heart. Peace is an action; it must be chosen. Peace never just "happens." If we want peace in our house, factions must forsake arms. Pro Shoreline might replace their OPMA suit with worse debacles. Consider Belfast. Consider Gaza. Consider Darfur. Conflict in Shoreline can get worse, if we let it fester. Calgacus (Scot, 1st century A.D.) complained of the Roman war machine: "They make a desert and call it peace" (Tacitus, *Agricola*, Chapter 30).

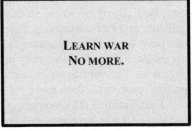

LEARN WAR NO MORE.

To find meaningful peace, opponents must forsake battle and make prosperity. Together. We can resolve a shared horizon. All agree about so much. To find peace, we must stop teaching war to others—and to ourselves. Isaiah (Hebrew, 8th century B.C.) said of choosing peace: "They shall beat their swords into plowshares, and their spears into pruning hooks: nation shall not lift up sword against nation, neither shall they learn war any more" (*Isaiah* 2:4). Remove war from your list of options. Peace surpasses winning. Peace with health makes joy. War precludes all three, even for winners.

Choose, Shoreline. Swallow, do not chew, bitterness. Bite your tongue occasionally. Set a banquet of sidewalks and neighbors and arts and parks and schools and safety and weal. Invite all. Savor the feast together.

Choose peace in our house.

CHEWY, WITH DEAR FRIENDS

BUTCH, KITTY, AND THREE LANCASTER URCHINS

14
MOMS

Everything comes from something: mountains from subterranean pressures, a child's smile from words of encouragement, avalanches from one flake too many, and the universe itself from We Know Not What.

I came from Beverly, with Howard's enthusiastic collaboration. The two became high school sweethearts in sleepy Selah, dancing to Glen Miller 78s scratching from a Victrola "talking machine" in a mahogany cabinet. Howard and Beverly tackled the brunt of adulthood in Coeur d'Alene, Idaho, with their brood of three and a hand-to-mouth veterinary practice. My task, it appears in hindsight, was to torment my mother. Case in point.

At age four, my first bicycle (training wheels, no coasting gears) gleamed. Boyhood demanded that I demonstrate to a fellow ruffian how (extremely) fast I could spin its rear wheel. Upended on handlebars and seat, pedals spun. My right hand flipped into the rear sprocket, grinding off the tip of my right index finger.

A crimson trail scored my path to home's front door. Blood-slick, my right hand could not work the latch. I pounded and wailed. Mother never described that mess. Dad worked in our only car. Stranded with her distressed child, Mom drafted ancient Ralph from down the street to careen to the hospital. Surgical repairs ensued.

> **THANK YOUR MOTHER.**
> **YOU WERE A PAIN.**

I woke the following morning; Mom was momentarily absent. Four year old wisdom demanded that I extract myself from bed and hide in a nearby broom closet. Mother and wide-eyed nurses eventually discovered me cowering. Back in bed, I cried. Mom snuggled me. I began healing.

The next week, a beat-up blue Dodge sat in our drive. We urchins littered it with beach sand, popsicle sticks, and, eventually, discarded surgical gauze.

Mothers repair what children tear. Mothers (and most fathers) labor at earth's most crucial and thankless job. Ann Taylor (English, 19th century A.D.) wrote: "Who ran to help me when I fell, And would some pretty story tell, Or kiss the place to make it well? My mother" (*My Mother*, stanza 6).

Mom, thanks. Fifty years late.

KATE

15
CULL: CHOOSING WELL (SECTION I EXCERPT)

I. CULL[23]

Think, **Kate**, *about decision-making, yours and humanity's.   Examine its flow and eddies. We choose well or poorly, alone and together. Have we erred? Almost all would answer that we have chosen poorly, though for diverse reasons.*[24] *Let us converse about character, that is, our aloneness with ourselves and our togetherness with friends, acquaintances, and strangers. Let us deliberate what augments or erodes meaningful community. Let us contemplate human flourishing. Taste ethics I adopt or reject; weigh objections and replies. Pull together fragments that fix in mind what humans are: evolved moral and social animal brains-in-bodies, riven by jostling subconscious drives and emotions, frequently conscious but fitfully rational.*[25] *You have complained that I, as a teacher, suffer comic incapacity in expressing myself. You are undoubtedly correct. Bear with me. A little slack in my tether, please. Scoff, Kate, when appropriate. Like chili pepper in one's sleepy oatmeal, friends jolt. Let us mull strenuous topics. Let us cull. Together.*

1. **Choosing.**   To act, one culls.[26]   One sorts for and adopts good; one identifies and ejects evil.[27]   One hopes, by culling, to undertake actions that portend worthy

---

[23] "Cull" means: a) to select the best from among others (as in gathering), or b) to remove the defective from among others (as in winnowing). See *Webster's Third New International Dictionary*, s.v. "cull." For example, one culls excellent essays in creating an anthology, and one culls sick animals from a healthy herd.

[24] Gregory Bateson styles the way we think as a "maze of hallucinations." Bateson, *Steps to An Ecology of Mind*, 483. The Dalai Lama advises: "Analyze. Think, think, think. When you do you will recognize that our ordinary way of life is almost meaningless." Dalai Lama, *How To Practice*, 37.

[25] Some readers lament my resistance to including the "soul" as a fundamental component of any description of humanity. I resist because not all share that view of mankind, but all acknowledge humans are animals with brains. I offer several thoughts on the mind-body problem in the course of this text, not all of which evidence reserve about expressions of human spirituality.

[26] William Godwin, in 1793, argued (in a fit of eighteenth century irrepressible optimism) that human nature is perfectible, and one approaches such perfection by means of comparison of one idea or course of action with others, which leads one to a preference. Preference among competing options leads to action. [♪] Godwin, *Political Justice*, Vol. I, 43, 169-170 (Book I, Chapter VI). Michael Tomasello argues that instrumental rationality is nothing other than imagining likely outcomes of possible actions and choosing among them for maximum benefit. Tomasello, *A Natural History of Human Thinking*, 14.

[27] Plato argues that wickedness is more to be feared than death, because moral evil is harder to avoid. [♪] Plato, *Apologia, §39A*, 137. I do not employ the words "good" and "evil" in their solely moral sense. Impulses of attraction and repulsion drive the behavior of all living things, and establish the ancient and biological basis of our conscious dichotomy "good and evil." The Chinese philosopher, Mo (5th century

outcomes.   One aspires, by culling, to avoid actions that threaten ill results.[28]
Moral action begins when one recognizes good acts and evil acts amid life's hurtle,
and adopts a stance concerning these events.[29]   Conduct-culling fashions, to the
extent they are plastic, the member and her community.   What sort of person are
you?   What sort of person do you want to become?   What sort of social world
issues from people possessing the character you hope takes root in you?[30]

Good acts build meaningful human community.[31]   Evil acts injure meaningful
community.   Humans nourish themselves and nurture one another in meaningful

---

A.D.) advocated an ethical system of propagating what benefits and eschewing what harms. [♪] *Mozi*, 41
(Part III, §16). In the Buddhist tradition, King Milinda asked sage Nagasena the nature of virtue. Nagasena
replied that one pursues dharmas, some of which are wholesome and others unwholesome. The virtue of
mindfulness draws attention to helpful dharmas, to the detriment and neglect of injurious dharmas. [♪]
Conze, *Buddhist Scriptures*, 152 (citing *Milindapañha*). But within the Buddhist tradition, Seng-ts'an dis-
agrees. He asserts that preferring one state of affairs over another diseases the mind. Peace pervades those
who find perfect emptiness of mind, an absence of preferences. Seeking right and wrong confuses, and
jeopardizes emptiness. [♪] Conze, *Buddhist Scriptures*, 171-172 (citing Seng-ts'an, "On Believing in
Mind.") Again, in the Pali Buddhist tradition, wise men transcend assessments of good and evil. [♪]
Dhammapada, 39, 267. But, elsewhere, a Buddhist seeker abstains from what hurts and seeks what helps,
in the process, purifying the mind. [♪] *Dhammapada*, 183, 268-269. The *Qur'an* teaches that good acts
positively repel evil. [♪] Muhammad, *Qur'an* 28:54. Ethical culling, that is, sorting good from evil, proves
to be the foundational meta-scheme of most systems of ethics. Plato takes this question, whether one trends
toward goodness or badness, to be the great test of men. One must not let money or acclaim or influencing
others tempt one from becoming a person of justice and virtue. [♪] Plato, *Republic*, 330 (§608b).

[28] And yet, Master Zhuang warns that the Great Man "knows no line can be drawn between right and
wrong, no border can be fixed between great and small. *Zhuangzi*, 101 (Autumn Floods, Section 17).

[29] This task may not prove so simple as it may sound. Richard Weaver asserts that getting real people
to make real decisions about their own lives by sorting what is better from what is worse proves widely
problematical. He suspects that modern man has grown morally moronic. Weaver, *Ideas Have Consequences*, 1. William Godwin believes men always choose what they deem preferable, and never knowingly
adopt what they deem evil, nor return to evils previously abandoned. [♪] Godwin, *Political Justice*, Vol.
I, 70-71 (Book I, Chapter VI). I wish Godwin were right. Godwin wildly underestimates cultural momen-
tum, which induces men to persevere in patently dysfunctional behaviors despite their misgivings. Our
age butts bluntly against the brick wall of failed imagination. Aristotle asserts that where such deliberative
culling is well-done, it constitutes practical wisdom, which seeks the best among possible alternative
goods. [♪] Aristotle, *Nichomachean Ethics*, 110 (§1141b). Michael Shermer, surveying the arc of human
history, concludes that *homo sapiens* grows more and more moral. Shermer, *The Moral Arc*, 3.

[30] John Dewey identifies the core issue, in deliberations of any sort, the kind of person that issues
from such a decision, and the sort of world the decision will fashion. [♪] Dewey, *Human Nature and
Conduct*, 217. Dewey argued that progress means that one increases the present meaning of choices of
conduct. [♪] Dewey, *Human Nature and Conduct*, 280, 282. David Hume finds that human instincts do
not govern, but rather the core concept is public utility of this or that rule. We ask, What world emerges
from this rule? What features of common life will be hobbled by that rule? Hume, *Enquiry Concerning
the Principles of Morals*, 97 (Chapter 3, Section 47).

[31] Aristotle opines that the best lives emerge from living in a community that well-governs life in a
manner that is as good as it can be under the circumstance. Members are happy to the extent their acts
accord with wisdom and excellence, provided they have enough external goods to undertake good acts.
[♪] Aristotle, *Politics*, 166-168 (1323a.18 and 1323b.22, 39). Robert Owen concurs. A member's happiness emerges from conduct that promotes her community's happiness. Owen, *A New View of Society*, 14.
Pregnantly, Jaak Panksepp argues that humans are heirs to a mammalian motherload of meaning encoded
in our emotional lives. He calls humans "inheritors of ancient biological values that constitute the very

community. Meaningful community distributes human necessities, such as food, drink, shelter, clothing, rest, membership, security, money, political office, political power, professional office, professional power, kinds of work, leisure, education, kinship, friendship, love, divine approbation, honor and recognition, and sex.[32] Of greater importance, human community provides a framework for investing these necessities with import within the cooperation of a human group.[33] For humans, meaning outweighs happiness.[34] Humans, with great regularity, sacrifice happiness to purchase meaning. We suffer, even die, to promote group action, real

---

ground of meaning within our minds." Panksepp and Biven, *The Archaeology of Mind*, 494. Meaning is a pervasive affective state that tinges all of consciousness, provided we do not live and think in a manner that precludes its psychological tinting. Hannah Arendt argues: "Action, as distinguished from fabrication, is never possible in isolation; to be isolated is to be deprived of the capacity to act. Action and speech need the surrounding presence of others no less than fabrication needs the surrounding presence of nature for its material, and of a world in which to place the finished product." Arendt, *The Human Condition*, 188. When we act, for good or ill, we act within a human community. We act to affect that community.

[32] Michael Walzer argues that human society, as a whole, distributes social goods to its members. Doing so well, without the domination of one sort of social good over others, constitutes complex equality. Each good has its own sphere, and ought not be translated into another, or dominated by another. Walzer takes complex equality to be the essence of a good society. Walzer, *Spheres of Justice*, 3-20.

[33] Muhammad urges Islamic communities to avoid dissension. Successful communities urge what is good and forbid what is wrong, acting as brothers, because God brought them together. [♪] Muhammad, *Qur'an*, Sura 3:103-104.

[34] "Happiness" denotes a human emotional state characterized by various degrees of pleasant affect; one seeks to perpetuate such states. See *Webster's Third New International Dictionary*, s.v. "happiness." "Meaningful existence" connotes welcomed integration into the purposive activity of an intentional human community. Thinkers disagree about the role of happiness in human motivation. Aristotle argues that the goal of human activity is *eudaemonia*, which may be translated a "flourishing life in the company of friends" or, less adequately, "happiness." [♪] Aristotle, *Nichomachean Ethics*, 193-199 (1176b-1179a). Sigmund Freud argues that humans are never happy, but cannot stop seeking happiness. Freud, *Civilization and Its Discontents*, 27-28 (Section 2). Bentham changes the focus to outcomes. Bentham advocates a cost-benefit scheme for evaluating human actions. An act is measured by its social consequences. Bentham's scheme is sometimes called "consequentialism" or, his own preferred term, "the principle of utility." Bentham argues that act is best which promotes the greatest happiness of the largest number of individuals. [♪] Bentham, *The Principles of Morals and Legislation*. Peter Berger changes the focus from happiness to meaning. Berger argues that human communities fabricate a psychological universe in which members of the community find their meaning and place. [♪] Berger, *Sacred Canopy*. Panksepp augments Berger (and contradicts him) by asserting that much of human meaning is inherited from mammalian evolution, and lies implicit in our mostly-subconscious affective lives. Panksepp and Biven, *The Archaeology of Mind*, 494. Victor Frankl argues that mankind searches not for happiness, but for meaningful existence, the acquisition of which is the primary goal of human life. Frankl, *Man's Search for Meaning*, 99. In Sessan Amakuki, *On Hakuin's Zazen Wasan*, a Zen Buddhist argues that by meditating, one discovers that everyday life gleams with personal meaning. [♪] Conze, *Buddhist Scriptures*, 137. Epictetus, the Stoic slave, asserted that the good for humans is moral purpose. Epictetus, *Discourses*, 63 (Book I, Section 8.16). Schopenhauer styles our desire for happiness an "inborn error." We cannot but long for happiness, but soon learn that the world trends against us. Hence, suffering is inherent in experience. Schopenhauer's thought tails into Brahmanist and Buddhist concepts, recapitulating themes of those metaphysical systems. Schopenhauer, *The World As Will and Representation*, Volume II, 638.

or imagined, when we believe our acts nurture those whom we love and with whom we identify.[35] Absent meaningful community, humans sicken and perish.[36]

The good in human existence is meaningful participation in a meaning-laden community.[37] What conduct[38] might one undertake to create such a community?

As used in this book, a "**community**" aggregates a number (say, ten) of constituent social groups, which are called "**circles**," themselves each numbering around 150 members.[39] Families and their supportive mentors and alloparents, small groups

---

[35] Such meaning-aimed action is most evident in soldiers on missions, but also in parents rearing well-attended children. We see sacrifice of happiness for common weal when politicians adopt unpopular, but necessary, stances; when firemen rush into smoking houses; when obese people prune food choices or fast-food lovers munch broccoli; when one reads difficult books; when congregations welcome smelly or surly people; when food banks are flush; when electorates vote to tax themselves for meritorious purposes unlikely to personally benefit them. That for which we sacrifice a good is a superior good. Meaning exceeds happiness.

[36] Watzlawick calls the mental structure within which people find their sense of meaning a "third order" perception. First order perceptions are raw sense data. Second order perceptions are those data constructed into useful concepts. Watzlawick calls this second order perception "knowledge about knowledge" or "meta-knowledge." The aggregate pattern of one's experiences, which melds into one's worldview in which one is socially embedded, is the third order perception (meta-perception of one's meta-knowledge). Man perishes in despair where his third order perceptions prove less-than-compelling to him. Watzlawick, Bavelas, and Jackson, *Pragmatics of Human Communication*, 248-249. Tolstoy laments his dearth of meaning, despite a well-heeled, relationally-rich, aristocratic, and morally-exemplary life. He recounts the intellectual and spiritual tale of how he found some meaning. [♪] Tolstoy, *A Confession*. Sebastian Junger argues: "Humans don't mind hardship, in fact they thrive on it; what they mind is not feeling necessary. Modern society has perfected the art of making people not feel necessary." Junger, *Tribe*, xvii.

[37] Martin Buber calls genuine community among persons the preeminent aspiration of history. Anything less than a sociality rooted in the actual relation of one man with another is counterfeit. Buber, *Paths in Utopia*, 133. Sarah Blaffer Hrdy notes that human babies gauge how older others around them evaluate objects of shared attention, looking to those elders for keys to meaning. Hrdy, *Mothers and Others*, 115. Stirner acknowledges that a human's natural state is togetherness, but urges all to seek self above all, and to subjugate any person or thing which one might fancy. Stirner, *The Ego and Its Own*, 271, 275. I suspect we all know a Stirnerite or two, and wish we did not.

[38] "Conduct" denotes deliberated activity, especially insofar as the choice of activity reflects moral conviction. The term may be distinguished from mere "behavior," which is human activity that may emerge without conscious choice. See *Webster's Third New International Dictionary*, s.v. "conduct" at §3c. Aristotle argues that choice concerns matters potentially within one's control, and not matters such as fate, nature's laws, and randomness. One deliberates a choice by selecting among alternatives by some process of rationalization. One deliberates when outcomes are uncertain. With human choice comes responsibility for means and outcomes, though deliberation primarily addresses means, in Aristotle's view. One bears responsibility where acts are voluntary, meaning that the agent originates the act under a known set of circumstances. Where acts derive from forces outside oneself and one makes no contribution to the act, the outcome is involuntary, and one bears no responsibility. [♪] Aristotle, *Nichomachean Ethics*, 117-141 (Book III, §§i.1-iii.19).

[39] The particular community size recommended in this work emerges from Zhou, "Social Group Size Organization," 440. The research underlying Zhou's estimate of the maximum number of active social connections the human cortex can manage derives from the work of Robin Dunbar. Dunbar, *How Many Friends Does One Person Need?*, 21-34. The estimate of 150 as the maximum number of human social connections is sometimes called the "Dunbar Number." Zhou estimates the usual tribal population at

of collaborating colleagues, or small associations of intimates (friends), called "**ca-dres**," identify themselves with a circle, or among various circles in a community.[40] A community's ten or so allied and overlapping circles share an economic organization and social ethos, which its members select and manage. Communities are, for the purposes of this book, the basic building block of the human world,[41] each having a voice, both directly by technological means, and representatively, through chosen speakers, in the "**Commons**," the global community of communities.[42] This

---

1,000-2,000. Henri Bergson notes: "Man was designed for very small societies. . . . The original state of mind survives, hidden away beneath the habits without which indeed there would be no civilization. Driven inwards, powerless, it yet lives on in the depths of consciousness." And a bit farther along, Bergson says, "Humanity must set about simplifying its existence with as much frenzy as it devoted to complicating it." Bergson, *The Two Sources of Morality and Religion*, 275, 307.

[40] Maoist ideology employs the term "cadre" to identify a party official. [♪] Mao, *Little Red Book*, 109 (Chapter 10). I use the term in its English sense of a core group of persons or trainers. See *Webster's Third New International Dictionary*, s.v. "cadre," definition 2a. Aristotle argues that friendship and genuine community are coextensive. Friendship requires community. Communities without friendship are hollow shells. [♪] Aristotle, *Nichomachean Ethics*, 154, Book VIII, Chapter 9 (1159b-1160a). Robin Dunbar notes the hierarchy of threes in friendship. One has three to five intimates, people with whom one shares everything. The next level comprises about fifteen members, sometimes called the "sympathy group." The subsequent level involves thirty to fifty or so members. An intermediate grouping includes about 500 members. The tribal grouping includes 1,500 people. So, there exists a rough increase by factors of three: 5, 15, 50, 150, 500, 1500. Dunbar says no one knows what these numbers correspond to in real life. We tend to have contact with the smallest circle at least once weekly, at least once a month with the circle of fifteen, and at least once yearly with the circle of 150. Dunbar, *How Many Friends Does One Person Need?*, 32-33.

[41] Leidloff, speculating on revising our shared Western culture, contemplates just such a diminution in social scope from millions to tens. We need groups of tribal size and comprehensible expanse. Leidloff, *The Continuum Concept*, 141. Aristotle finds that ten people do not constitute a polis, but that a hundred thousand cannot constitute a polis, since the polis is the seedbed of friendship. [♪] Aristotle, *Nichomachean Ethics*, 180 (1170b). Aristotle goes so far as to say that friendship is community, and that our social relations mirror our relationship to ourselves. [♪] Aristotle, *Nichomachean Ethics*, 182 (1171b). Thomas Jefferson, reflecting on what he had learned from observing how the American Constitution functioned, advised that we form "wards" in which every man is engaged in making choices about his most local and pressing concerns. "[T]he whole is cemented by giving to every citizen, personally, a part in the administration of public affairs." Jefferson, *Writings*, 1400 (*Letter to Samuel Kercheval*, July 12, 1816).

[42] The word "community" serves several uses in this text. First, it denotes approximately ten circles of around 150 members each, thereby organizing mankind in tribe-sized communities of 1,500-2,000. Second, the term identifies the global Commons, the worldwide community of communities, which this author anticipates might, at some point in the distant future, supplant the national governments that plague humanity presently. Finally, the word "community" enshrines not only a social structure, but also a qualitative aspiration and goal, that every person should matter deeply to some particular group of people more broadly construed than those from whom he is genetically derived. In this latter sense, persons who share my concerns might "build community" or "advocate community." Buber argues that every viable commonwealth is a "community of communities." Buber, *Paths in Utopia*, 136-137. The details of what I define as "human community" will be expanded at length in what follows.

concentric "cadre-circle-community-commons" structure constitutes a "Quad social-ity."[43]   This form of consensual, friendship-laden society is called "kithdom."[44]

This book offers no vision of ideal human existence. Quad sociality is no uto-pia.[45] It, rather, suggests a process for choosing meaningful forms of living, and for ridding oneself and one's community of forms from which vitality has leaked or forms that were misguided from inception.[46] By this process, communities may move

---

[43]The term "quad" derives from the Latin word *quattuor*, meaning "four." Quad tallies the first letter of each of the four components of *Cull*'s sociality: cadre, circle, community, and commons. Each level of human relating (the four Cs) catalyzes companion levels robustly. I advocate Quad sociality to attempt to redress depersonalization of member existence that plagues most Western cultures. First-world persons have traded being known for the pseudo-efficiency of semi-personal existence: citizenship, identification numbers, or unitization. Quad sociality is equivocal. When better evidence indicates a more appropriate size or shape for human social organization, that better theory should be adopted. My point is this: mean-ingful human existence is never impersonal; regimes that treat human relations impersonally should be abandoned, minimized, or allowed to crumble under the weight of their own misdirected fragility. I employ a diagnostic criterion: when a community must coerce its members to participate in their own well-being, that community should discorporate itself and seek a fresh approach to meaningful life.

[44] Aristotle asserted that such a structure to social life is a natural phenomenon. He hypothesized that the relations of men, women, and slaves gave rise to families, which aggregated into villages, which aggregate into towns (the *polis*). Towns exist, according to Aristotle, to create for members a good life. Man participates naturally in town-sized social groups. Such towns are voluntary associations of intermar-rying families, a community of friends whose association aims to create for all in a town the good life. [♪] Aristotle, *Politics*, 12-13 (1251.25-1253.1), 74-75 (1280.30-1231.1).

[45] Jan Oppermann calls kithdom a "pragmatic utopia," meaning that kithdom presents a social struc-tural opportunity that does not, but could, actually exist, either in discourse about political choices, or possibly even in praxis. The problem with all pragmatic utopias, Oppermann argues, is history. How does any people step past its bitternesses, prejudices, and stubbornness in sufficient measure to step into kith-dom? Oppermann urges that answers lie in the potency of education. Jan Oppermann, personal corre-spondence with the author, dated October 14, 2015. Robert Nozick, in contemplating the application of utopian theories to actual living, presents a framework for utopian endeavors that closely tracks that pro-posed in *Cull*. (In my view, when Nozick abandons utopian theories and speaks of actual application to human society, he has left utopian thought behind in favor of a process of living and improving communi-ties.) Given the diversity of people, no one sort of community might suffice for all. Rather, utopia, as actually lived, is meta-utopia, the framework within which utopian experiments are welcomed, and mem-bers pursue their highest visions of the good life. All those who aspire to better societies will welcome the framework, except those of totalitarian sentiments. [♪] Nozick, *Anarchy, State, and Utopia*, 307-320. Nozick calls his framework of diverse community experiments a "utopian process" rather than a utopian state. [♪] Nozick, *Anarchy, State, and Utopia*, 332. Some bloggers (such as Heather Schlegel and Kevin Kelly) have coined the term "protopia" for views of the future that are neither pessimistic (dystopian) or perfectionist (utopia). Rather, protopian views present a positive take on the human future, without claim-ing to solve every problem or achieve all humans might desire or imagine. The process, which *Cull* de-scribes, of culling conduct in Quad communities in a global kithdom may well be styled "protopian." The process is incremental. Michael Shermer offers a similar emphasis on improved decision-making and step-by-step modifications of the human cultural norm. Shermer, *The Moral Arc*, 398.

[46] Jonathan Haidt suggests that, apart from theodiction, no answer exists for the question: What is the purpose *of* life? Such a question presupposes the existence of a designer, who dwells, for the agnostic, in an epistemological black hole. Haidt answers, instead, the question: What is human purpose *within* life? Haidt answers that happiness exceeds grabbing what we want. We bring portions of happiness with us. We receive portions of it from others. And we participate in happiness by embracing purposes larger than ourselves. Haidt, *The Happiness Hypothesis*, 238-239.

together toward troves of meaning that are now, in our benighted stumbling, hardly recognized and seldom seized. This process of sorting is a core concept: "finely-elaborated culling of conduct."[47]

In culling conduct, one assesses purposeful actions or inactions for their moral outcome. One puts squarely in mind competing courses of action, and rehearses the likely sequels of each.[48] On a turbulent moral sea, one seeks purpose(s) by which to rudder action. The human twilit morass does not readily resolve itself into dichotomies of day and night, that is, of good and evil. We wallow in half-light, never certainly knowing, when we make choices, if the light we see waxes toward dawn or wanes toward nightfall.[49] The human actor, as she chooses, must act or abstain. Moral dichotomy, you see, ultimately impresses us into its service.[50] Life is choice; to cower in hand-wringing indecision is itself a moral choice. None evades moral

---

[47] Bateson argues that we need not determine what is best to do under existing rules, but rather determine what other rules might better serve us. Bateson, *Steps To An Ecology of Mind*, 484-485. *Cull* asks readers to change the rules by which we govern ourselves. Sextus Empiricus disposes of all of ethics simply with his skeptical razor: "There can be no expertise in living either. If there is such an expertise, it has to do with the study of good, bad and indifferent things. So since these are unreal, expertise in living is unreal." Sextus Empiricus, *Outlines of Scepticism*, 205 (Book III, Section xxv).

[48] [♪] Dewey, *Human Nature and Conduct*, 190. Aristotle calls such thinking "practical wisdom," by which one chooses what creates the good life as a whole. [♪] Aristotle, *Nichomachean Ethics*, 107 (§1140A). Herbert Spencer argues that conduct includes "all adjustments of acts to ends." A good act is one well-adjusted to its end; a bad act is ill-adapted. A good act is a "highly evolved" act. Spencer considers moral phenomena to be evolutionary phenomena. Spencer, *The Principles of Ethics*, Vol. I, p. 39, 58, 78, 96. Hence, Spencer is often criticized for a doctrine of social Darwinism, which theory plainly distorts Darwin's Darwinism.

[49]Normal people are certain; the sage explores tentatively. [♪] Lao Tzu, *Tao Te Ching*, 64 (20). Life is little more than a long struggle in the dark, so feeble is reason. Lucretius, *De Rerum Natura*, 59 (Book Two, Line 54).

[50] Jaak Panksepp warns that dichotomous schemes (such as good-evil) are tempting, but are not supported by neurobiological research. Panksepp, *Prosocial Brain*, 151. He opts instead for seven foundational emotional neurological subsystems: FEAR, RAGE, SEEKING, LUST, CARE, PANIC, and PLAY. Panksepp, *Prosocial Brain*, 146. Panksepp capitalizes the systems to indicate his technical use of the words. These systems interact in complex, non-dualistic fashion. I argue, *contra* Panksepp, that culling is the most basic of biological impulses, those of approach and withdrawal. Panksepp's neurological subsystems issue drives and motivations that play in moral choice. I argue, *contra* Panksepp, that culling underlies all the impulse and affect systems of the human organism. Culling expresses the urge to homeostasis, to preserve one's life, to maintain equilibrium. Our propensity to cull unconsciously impels us toward life's sweet spot, silently sidesteps life's poisons. I argue that rudimentary ethical culling characterizes all non-pathological human neuroanatomy.

culling.[51] One chooses well or poorly.[52] The point of making decisions well is to fashion for oneself and for one's fellows a flourishing life.[53] One who embraces careful culling improves her chances of establishing a robust, flourishing life for herself and her companions. Perhaps one even renders planetary weal[54] more likely.

One expects some outcomes if the changes proposed by this book come to pass. The human focus migrates from financial capital to social capital.[55] And the means of enforcing rules jags from formality (laws, crimes, judges, police) to informality (mores, intervening friends, raised eyebrows, smiles, consensus). One envisions plummeting coercion. The human social interface grows less fearsome and intricately amicable.[56] David Brooks would call this transition a change in "moral ecology." Moral ecologies are communal patterns of behavior, beliefs, and habits. These

---

[51] The Buddha taught that one should make his conduct competent and friendly. [♪] *Dhammapada*, 376. Hrdy reports human one year olds find joy or shame in the attitudes of others toward them. Hrdy links this essential moral propensity in human children to our long evolutionary journey during which sensing the intentions of others aided survival. She calls these perceptions "intersubjective involvement." Hrdy, *Mothers and Others*, 117. Henri Bergson says, "Mankind lies groaning, half crushed beneath the weight of its own progress. Men do not sufficiently realize that their future is in their own hands." Bergson, *The Two Sources of Morality and Religion*, 317.

[52] James cites Fitz James Stephen to the following effect: Human decisions are stabs in the dark. We choose, never knowing with certainty the outcome. It is as though we were blind, freezing, lost, standing at a crossroads. To choose a path may lead to death. To choose no path guarantees death by hypothermia. So we choose, knowing our uncertainty. We elect courage and hope. If we choose the wrong path, we die, but we die well. [♪] James, *Will to Believe*, 62.

[53] Kwame Appiah so styles Aristotle's concept of *eudaemonia*. See Appiah, *Experiments in Ethics*, 202ff. Rousseau, in contrarian acerbity, finds self-improvement the root of all evils. Rousseau, "A Discourse on the Origin of Inequality," 60. Oppermann argues that Rousseau intends here, not a rip at self-improvement so much as historical pessimism about human consciousness itself. The more human we become, the unhappier we get. Oppermann believes that Rousseau countered this grim assessment in later works such as [♪] *The Social Contract* and *Emile* and *Reveries of the Solitary Walker*. Jan Oppermann, in correspondence with the author, dated October 14, 2015.

[54] "Weal" designates a state of sound, healthy prosperity. See *Webster's Third New International Dictionary*, s.v. "weal."

[55] Robert Putnam identifies indicators of high social capital. People in high social capital areas are more likely to serve on committees or as officers of a club, and join civic organizations and attend them. Citizens form more clubs. They vote and attend government or school meetings. People visit friends and invite them to their homes. They trust people, are honest with them, and anticipate that others will treat them in like manner. Putnam, *Bowling Alone*, 291.

[56] According to Christopher Boehm, conflict-suppressed egalitarianism is the human norm for (illiterate) small groups. Members actively tamp down individual spectacles of egoism and emotion (which Boehm styles "upstartism"), securing for all (male) tribal members rough political equality. Leaders are hidden, and lead mostly by generosity, and direct groups by indirection. The preemptive suppression of upstarts seeks to utilize them by cooling their hearts and making them gentle. Boehm, *Hierarchy in the Forest*, 45, 55, 65.

ultimately issue revised institutions, which encourage members to adopt characters that nestle well in those institutions.[57]

Human feelings are, according to Jaak Panksepp, evolutionary memories. Emotions about the prospective weal or woe of choices are genetic ciphers for encouraging adaptive choices or discouraging catastrophic ones.[58] Good choices are emotionally compelling; our thoughts about emotions rein in those affects that exceed what circumstances warrant. A well-deliberated choice expresses a basal urge, diverted by an affective preference, and supported by reasonable review and practiced examination. Colloquially, we aim to desire, feel, think, and only then, in light of experience, act. Our moral impulses consist in ancient priorities bred into the human line, emotive predilections all. In culling, we carefully edit and choose among their diverse thoughtless directives. To cull is to edit mammalian priorities thoughtfully.[59] Where culling is done well, that culling is "finely-elaborated."[60]

One seeks self-knowledge. Just who is the culler in your skin, Kate? Life, absent moral deliberation, is hardly worth the bother.[61] Prudent decision-makers cast

---

[57] Brooks, *The Road to Character*, 261. I am less hopeful about the utility of societal institutions than Brooks. But I believe every human group's persistent actions issues some form of institution after a time. Brooks argues for a return to the crooked-timber school of thought, a view of man plagued in his inmost recesses by sin and called to acts of self-denial and thoughtful reshaping. Brooks finds that people, recovering a now-lost moral realism, should seek holiness (which sounds in his usage very much like "meaningful existence"), recognize character flaws side by side with one's amazing capacities. He finds humility needful, and pride blinding. Moral struggle defines the good life, which aims at generation-spanning goals and commitments. The good person requires help from her community, tolerates setbacks resiliently, shepherds an inner quiet, knows when she does not know or cannot know, works at needful occupations, seeks incremental change in herself and her community, avoids debacles, and perseveres in seeking what is better. Brooks, *The Road to Character*, 262-267. Much recommends Brooks's effort, in *The Road To Character*, to cultivate a strong character and wise heart, and to save his own soul, as he puts it (at page xiii).

[58] According to Jaak Panksepp, emotions are odd memories, because one need not be able to recall them and comprehend their purposes. Good-or-bad is an evolutionary shorthand for the survival import of choices. Panksepp, *Prosocial Brain*, 150-51.

[59] De Waal calls this a bottom-up morality, since it is not given to mankind by gods or reason. Rather, he argues, human moral priorities are primordial. De Waal, *The Bonobo and the Atheist*, 228.

[60] Epictetus argued that the right use of a human mind is to ferret the true from the false, and to forestall decision when a matter is doubtful. Epictetus, *Discourses*, 51 (Book I, Section 7.5).

[61] [♪] Plato, *Apologia*, 38A. "[T]he unexamined life is not worth living." I depart somewhat from the Socratic formulation. Rebecca Goldstein summarizes the Greek view: "One must *exert* oneself in order to achieve a life that matters. If you don't exert yourself, or if your exertions don't amount to much of anything, then you might as well not have bothered to have shown up for your existence at all." Goldstein, *Plato at the Googleplex*, 8. Dewey notes that the culling enterprise befuddles most men, who desire to be good buddies rather than good human beings. [♪] Dewey, *Human Nature and Conduct*, 5. The Buddha sees moral deliberation as a temporary expedient. When one rises above *samsara*, the perpetual rebirth to suffering, his mind awake and blossoming, ethical distinctions seem childish and are abandoned. [♪] *Dhammapada*, 39. I question Buddha's metaphysics. Rousseau, consistent with his penchant for being entertaining but wrong, opines that when men commenced studying virtue they lost theirs. Rousseau, "A Discourse on the Arts and Sciences," 12. Max Stirner dissents utterly. Morality is to States what faith is

conceptual nets broadly in their struggle to recognize and elect goodness. The culler sweeps away intellectual detritus, making room for fresh comprehension. The careful decision-maker's far-flung haul includes our evolutionary origins, human eusocial animality, the social genesis of culture in niche construction, the tangled trajectory of fitness guiding the jumbled evolution of human consciousness, our essential sociality and the role of members in it, humanity's predilection for certain conceptual errors, the wisdom of history's finest moralists, withering scrutiny of coercions and violence and governments, exploration of irenism and quasi-anarchist kithdoms, and humanity's efforts in culling a course toward a deliberated human future, to spy the farsight horizon.[62] . . .

Culling appears, at first blush, a narrow-minded, self-centered mistress. The culler asks, What may help *me*? What might harm *me*? Subsequent sections of this work relieve the cull's harsh, unhewn lines by convening the far-flung considerations mentioned above. These blur boundaries between individuals and elevate communal life to its due pre-eminence. These considerations also make of friendship, rather than anonymity, the template for all human relating.[63] Such diverse considerations elaborate and inform our culling, refining its rude simplicity. *Good decision-making consists in finely-elaborated culling of conduct.*[64]

---

to churches. Moral thought keeps all a State's sheep safely within its fences. There is nothing, according to Stirner, sacred enough to rule over man the individual. Stirner, *The Ego and Its Own*, 200. Isocrates argues that the best thing in a man is his good judgment. Isocrates, *To Demonicus*, 25. Hobbes argues that men deliberate when they allow desires and aversions, hopes and fears to attach to the same object or purpose, so that in one moment one desires the outcome, in another flees the outcome, and in choosing we terminate our liberty to vacillate. [♪] Hobbes, *Leviathan*, 44 (Chapter 6).

[62] Albert Schweitzer, in his autobiography, call such thinking "elemental." Elemental thinking examines fundamental human relations, meaning in human lives, and the nature of goodness in human behavior. Schweitzer, *Out of My Life and Thought*, 224.

[63] I intend nothing obscure by the term "friendship." A. C. Grayling describes friendship nicely: "[W]e meet someone and take a liking to him or her which is reciprocated, and thereafter we enjoy each other's company, laugh together, share interest and views, and over time come to feel that we are part of the fabric of each other's worlds, a valuable part, so that we develop a mutual sense of obligations owed and trust given, and meet each other's needs for boon companionship, comfort, confidences and sharing." Grayling, *Friendship*, 1-2.

[64] Aristotle asserts that good deliberation calculates and inquires, leading to correctness of thought. [♪] Aristotle, *Nichomachean Ethics*, 112 (§1142b). B. F. Skinner denies the possibility of moral thought and the importance of entertaining any. All that matters, in Skinner's view, is moving on from morality to a viable technology of behavior. [♪] Skinner, *Beyond Freedom and Dignity*, 1-25. Jean Jacques Rousseau argues that people's opinions shape their morality. To improve morality, renovate human decision-making. [♪] Rousseau, *The Social Contract*, 174 (Book IV, Chapter 7). Anthony Shaftesbury argues that the human moral sense is inborn, and our opinions and beliefs can under no circumstances dislodge it. Shaftesbury, *Characteristicks*, 25 (Volume II, Part III, Section I).

Guidance is the best for which one can hope. Every particular circumstance beggars our decision-making capabilities.[65] In every case, it remains for you, dear Kate, to worry together the particular pieces of your personal and communal moral puzzles. Most of virtue consists in the commitment to cull well.[66]

---

[65] That a task exceeds us does not recommend forsaking it. Lao Tzu called the Way and the sage-devoted-to-the-Way an "uncarved block" (or "unhewn log"). [♪] Lao Tzu, *Tao Te Ching*, §72 of the Ma-wang-tui manuscript, or §28 of the now-superseded standard text. These Chinese masters acknowledge that the unhewn log, which is the Way, may be sawn or cut, and doing so serves human purposes. But they admonish that the skillful master receives the Way just as it comes to him, without cutting. Nevertheless, analysis and comprehension plague some, especially the philosophical few.

Systematic treatment of all factors involved in finely-elaborated conduct culling may exceed human grasp. Upon careful deliberation, ethical thought frequently devolves into quandaries. Recent philosophical ethics, in which trolley problems and various competition games command an inordinate share of philosophical attention, slides into this conceptual eddy. One must avoid the "quandary quandary," as Appiah terms the conundrum in his *Experiments in Ethics* (page 193ff). Meaningful life exists not to untangle moral birds' nests, but to be lived. Game quandaries and meta-ethical conversation call to mind garage chatter among mechanics debating fuel injectors. It is shop talk, scarcely benefitting those put to the task of driving. Of the Prisoner's Dilemma (criminal partners are offered deals to implicate the other; if neither informs, both go free; if one informs, the informer goes free, but his hapless partner serves eight years; if both inform, each serves five years. Shall one inform?), one can say only that acting in self interest, according to the dilemma, is less desirable than cooperating. See discussion in Singer, *The Expanding Circle*, 47.

Moral puzzles often reflect the competing impulses of neural programs that derive from the human evolutionary past. Quandaries illuminate too little of life to provide useful guidance. To expand Appiah's simile, reliance upon ethical quandary deliberation can be likened to finding one's way through benighted woods with a laser pointer (Appiah, *Experiments in Ethics*, 194). If it proves true that the modularity of our moral cognitive capabilities creates our ethical conundra, then any adequate ethics will prove neurologically eclectic, picking and choosing among available behavioral impulses as deliberated circumstances recommend. Our several moral voices generate cognitive cross-talk. One's inner moral sanctum rings with a din akin to that of a classroom of expectant second-graders.

[66] The biggest obstacle in any task is finding the will to commence it. So too, is one waylaid in becoming a good man. Seneca, *Epistles 1-65*, XXXIV, 3. John Stuart Mill asserts that people have a duty to assist one another in sorting good from evil choices, and having distinguished, to muster motivation to elect the good. [♪] Mill, *On Liberty*, 73.

SARGE

16

OX MOUNTAIN

Omar, aged eighty-three, loved the Mariners and ship traffic passing on the Sound. Time eroded Omar's memory. He forgot cooking. The washer stumped him. Unfortunately, Omar's attorney (call him Smutch) "helped" Omar. Smutch made Omar's son-in-law (call him Dolt) Omar's legal agent. Dolt, with Smutch's assistance, pilfered Omar's ready cash. Then Smutch helped Dolt refinance Omar's residence, so Dolt could "manage" what remained of Omar's funds. Omar found out. He came to me. I confronted Smutch, who lied. I brought the problem before the court. So, Smutch lied to the court. Smutch, it appears, lies better than I tell the truth. The court waffled. Our judge appointed a guardian to wrest Omar's money from Dolt. The guardian did not. Omar grew depressed, suffered strokes, and died. Even in the grave, Smutch "helped" Omar one last time. Smutch encouraged Dolt and his sister to contest Omar's Will, which left them nothing. The dim duo snatched most of Omar's estate from those Omar loved.

> **AVOID BECOMING EVIL CRUD.**

How did Smutch get to be Smutch? He was not born evil crud. Boy Smutch, undoubtedly, was the apple of his mother's eye: smart, cute, promising, studious, earnest. What happened? What cataclysms left Smutch a moral cripple? I was baffled. Years later, I read the parable of Ox Mountain. (Mencius, Chinese, 5th century B.C.) battled Hsun Tzu, who believed men evil. Mencius disagreed: men are innately good. By Ox Mountain, Mencius explains human corruption.

Ox Mountain lay beneath a verdant umbrella of trees near a city. Exuberant foliage burst from its slopes. But humans encroached. Men axed trees. Sheep and cattle grazed. Resilient, Ox Mountain sprouted new shoots and grasses. Scythes and herds returned. Then yet more people and flocks. Soon, Ox Mountain grew barren. Still, hordes came. Livestock stomped roots. Men trampled earth. Soil trickled off precipices. Dust blew from corpses of meadows. Only a bare, rocky knuckle remained. Nothing could ever grow. Mencius said: "Can what is in man be completely lacking in moral inclinations? A man's letting go of his true heart is like the case of the trees and the axes. . . . Given the right nourishment there is nothing that will not grow, and deprived of it there is nothing that will not wither away. . . . It is perhaps to the heart this refers."

Smutch made himself Ox Mountain--overgrazed and eroded. To Mencius, Smutch seethes no elemental evil. Smutch grew incapable of goodness. For us who must cope with life's Smutches, this seems a distinction without much difference. Smutch let life corrode his true heart; a scorched knob remains. Mencius would argue even Smutch's perversity portends good. Smutch makes his life an object lesson for Ox Mountain. Smutch's existence, like red-emblazoned freeway signs, warns people headed onto life's off-ramp: WRONG WAY.

To preserve a functioning conscience is one of life's subtle and elusive tasks. Smutches help. If you find yourself behaving like your Smutch, change course.

KARMANN GHIA

17

ARROGANCE

In Selah, Washington, my grandparents' fruit ranch topped a hill. I ran amok with local pre-adolescent boys through parched, snake-infested hills, doing things against which mothers warn. The Yakima River meandered the valley below; the sky shone cerulean blue. Sun-baked dirt shimmered. The neighborhood sons were tough, progeny of seasonal Hispanic fruit workers and hard-drinking African ranch hands.

In the dusty heat one afternoon, we ruffians (perhaps I was only a wannabe) set our minds to a rock war. Discarded fruit pallets became forts, twenty paces apart. After much jostling and giggling, our opponents hollered, "Done." I stood to set them straight. We were erecting defensible walls, and they should promptly reconsider their ramshackle affair. A ping-pong ball of river rounded granite arced toward me as I opened my mouth to correct their failure of prudence. I remember the thwack.

When I regained consciousness, blood was pouring down my forehead into my eyes. Mixed with tears, red goop spread down my face and neck to bloody my white tee. I hobbled back to Grandma Ada's kitchen. My mother gasped. Rapid descent to the hospital in Grandmother's cherry red Karmann Ghia ensued. A doctor swabbed and injected. Antiseptic bit my forehead, then stitches. Maternal recriminations, a bit of well-deserved cursing, warm caresses. My father just frowned and sighed. He shook his head slowly. I was abashed.

KEEP YOUR HEAD DOWN, STUPID.

Muhammud reports that Luqman, an Arabic sage, advised his son: "Turn not thy cheek in scorn toward folk, nor walk with pertness in the land. Lo! Allah loveth not each braggart boaster. Be modest in thy bearing and subdue thy voice. Lo! The harshest of all voices is the voice of the ass" (*Koran*, Surah XXXI: 18-19).

I lost the rock war in an instant. I gained a permanent scar, and (maybe) a lesson. Hee-haw. Hee-haw.

BUTCH

18
REGRET

Butch spent his first nine years of life in the lap of a spinster. When her infirmity deepened, she left Butch the Boston terrier with my father, the veterinarian. Dad brought the dog home to his three young kids.

Butch's life changed. No more sedate walks and long afternoons gazing out a quiet window. Butch engaged, fetching homered baseballs and shredding sweaty socks in pull contests. Butch chased deer and stole cat food. He snorted his congenitally smashed nose. We kids squealed in mirth. Butch scented our world with digestive aromas for which Boston bulls are infamous. We giggled and pinched our noses. Butch bathed us at every opportunity with a long, slathered tongue, and ran with us until he dropped—quite literally keeled over. So young, I never pondered Butch's repeated swoons, his frequent faints. In retrospect, Butch was happy, but getting old.

Drifting sub-zero snows drove us kids underground. We transformed the unfinished basement into our playground, skate park, trouble zone. Butch careened, typically. A brainstorm: I suspended Butch's favorite pull sock with the big knot in its end, on an elastic rope from a basement rafter. Butch seized his prize, swung up in the air, a bulldog pendulum on a muscular neck and vice-like jaws. He loved the game. Our excitement and laughter spurred him. Butch fainted, then rose to attack his sock afresh. Then collapsed.

When Butch stood again, tongue lolling, he wanted out. Fatefully, I opened the back door for him. Butch dove into drifts and rooted in the arctic snowscape. Father hollered, "Don't let Butch out. He's overheated." Too late.

THINK, BEFORE OPENING DOORS.

The end came slowly. Butch lost interest in food, began vomiting. Dad took Butch to his veterinary clinic and nursed him with intravenous ministrations. Still, our friend weakened. Some days later, Father shook his head. We shuffled to Butch's cubicle. Butch lay glazed. Dad said, "It's time." We kids consented silently. A fatal injection; Butch breathed his last. We rode silently home in our green Oldsmobile. Mom turned to her brood in the back seat. "It's okay to cry." We erupted. Butch was gone.

I cry now, as I write, these decades later. *I killed Butch* imprinted on my juvenile soul. The adult in me knows better—declining immune system, opportunistic infection, congenital cardiac insufficiency, nine years in a lap, love of life to excess. These killed Butch. But the adult yields. A tar of regret has congealed. *What if I . . .* is forever glued to my memory of Butch. T. S. Eliot (American, 20th century A.D.) wrote: "Footfalls echo in the memory Down the passage which we did not take Towards the door we never opened Into the rose-garden" (*Burnt Norton*).

Butch bequeathed me joy, and the wisdom that a thoughtlessly flung door may open to unwelcome loss. Dog mentors boy.

ANNIE AND CAESAR

19
GUNS

I own guns. An 1870s Argentine rifle graces my bedroom wall, an immigrant from father's Idaho mantle where it hung during my childhood. No one has produced ammunition for that weapon in 100 years. This gun is art and reminiscence. Rifles and shotguns huddle in cupboards, asleep in their form-fitting covers. Boyish enthusiasms made me terror of squirrels and wanna-be deerslayer. In my teens, I woke one morning no longer a hunter. Killing grew pointless. I quit. These guns are retired tools of past fascinations. Most ominously, a shotgun and revolver hide in my home. An ill-intentioned intruder might find himself profoundly unwelcome. These guns are deterrents. I hope violent deviants worry, at least a bit. But I stew as well. The pacifist in me groans. The Turks say "A weapon is an enemy even to its owner."

Recently, the United States Supreme Court decided no government agent can prohibit non-exotic guns in the home. District of Columbia et. al. v. Heller, 554 U. S. 570 (2008). Justice Scalia said: "The Second Amendment protects an individual right to possess a firearm unconnected with service in a militia, and to use that arm for traditionally lawful purposes, such as self-defense within the home" (Slip opinion, page one summary). The District of Columbia's handgun ban has fallen. The Justices' vote was five to four. Four conservatives lined up against four liberals, with the ever wishy-washy Justice Stevens tottering between those ranks of titans. A French proverb warns "Between two stools, one sits on the ground."

> **ARE GUNS OUR GODS?**

In the Heller case, the high Court was Everyman. The conservative in each of us demands home and hearth secure from criminal assault. The liberal in each of us recoils at a culture awash in weaponry, streets bathed in crimson gun carnage. And the Justice Stevens in each of us dithers, ready to inflict rough hewn justice but longing for a world in which none is needed or even possible.

I keep my guns, with deep reservations. I fret about the poetic foresight of Rabindranath Tagore (Indian, 20th century A.D.): "He has made his weapons his gods. When his weapons win he is defeated himself" (*Stray Birds*, 45).

SOFIE, A-SNUGGLE

20

A SUESSICAL WEDDING ON AN OCTOBER SUNDAY

Dear Audrey and Cory are wedding today,
We gather with laughter the Suessical way.
We tell little tales that rhyme just a bit
To capture a moral with goodness in it.

Audrey stands long like a tall sarsaparilla.
Cory comes bald like a hairless gorilla.
The straw takes a cue ball to husband today
To learn from our Suess like puppies at play.

The Suessical Cat with the big red-striped hat,
Pokes at our schools in their waste and their fat.
The Cat warns us all with cute subtle patter,
To avoid being stuck in old subject matter.

Big old gray Horton hears his strange Who
Warns us to love those different too.
Those not from our country may seem very strange.
Rejecting them, though, does our own minds derange.

The Grinch who stole Christmas made wailing so shrill
By poaching the stuff of the Yuletide's good will.
Suess teaches us all to question our ways
In thinking that junk will bring better days.

The Sneetches all quibble over stuff of no weight.
They make of starred bellies some quibbling freight.
Stars always snubbing as they get fatter,
Ignoring the truth that Plain Sneetches Matter,

So, marry today, you tall and you slick.
Cling to each other, through happy and sick.
Make life and some babes, if chance should befall,
They'll be long drinks of water with no hair at all.

For Audrey and Cory we gather today
In Bellingham beauty so close to the bay.
I ask you to question each Suessical day
How best to live in your love and your play.

ANNIE

21
KNITTING FROM THE TANGLED SKEIN

A BIRTHDAY REVERIE

Maggie knits. You may imagine I mean that Maggie plops in an armchair, watches professional wrestling, and produces scarves and gloves and sweaters from a thread of yarn bent to the rhythmic clicking of fingers and needles. She may. I do not know. Nevertheless, I say, Maggie knits. Not every knitting produces garments. When bones break, the fractures knit. When relationships fray, tattered feelings require knitting. Even history, a chaos of threads, begs a careful hand to untangle the skein and weave a useable fabric. Maggie knits in this latter sense.

Like all American families (except perhaps a few Amerind tribes from ancient migrations), events exploded Maggie's historical family. Shards fell everywhere: Italy, Cuba, Ireland, across the United States. The human dynamite was probably pedestrian enough, the typical corrosives of modern life. Cheap land over the hill sends a brother packing. A war kills a young wife, and grief drives her bereaved across mountains. A corrupt landowner connives to seize a poor family's homestead; they move on. A job beckons in another land. Plague decimates. A lover begs to return to her family of origin—elsewhere. Oceans intervene. Mail gets lost. Elders die. Exigencies preclude travel. Connections moulder. Records perish in fire and rot. Relationships languish. Finally, memory fails. What had once been ancient, spreading, oaken "family" becomes scattered seedlings with shallow roots. Histories grow blank.

Maggie lost her parents young. Her siblings were problematic. Don and the girls and Don's family were Maggie's all, which, though much, was not enough. So, Maggie took up knitting. She plies her family's photos, guessing connections. When she discovers one, Maggie calls, then visits. She sniffs Irish church records. She knocks on doors of Sicilian "Fimias." Maggie thwarts political impediments to build ties to Cuban cousins. She drafts Mormons to her tasks, ferreting connections in their vast archive of the unbaptized dead. She intervenes with nieces in the Ozarks, and summers with distant relatives' children. Maggie has even tortured a bishop or two, in a kind, mostly civil manner. All in the name of knitting together the fragments of that explosion we call post-Enlightenment modernity. All in the name of knitting a family.

To knit is to create. All creativity takes something that exists and bends it in a fresh direction, creates associations that would otherwise go unnoticed. So, family is to Maggie an art form. Her medium is pastiche. She glues history's detritus back into a meaningful shape. She introduces members to other members. She writes letters, makes calls. She weaves in a global web of associations, her living work of art. Few understand her obsession. That is typical of creative work. Most do not get it.

So, when Maggie's grandchildren ask what Grandma Maggie did, tell them she knit.

KIM

22
MENTAL ILLNESS

The worst day of my life ransacked me on a drizzling winter's evening in 1986. My lovely bride Kim lay crushed by depression and intractable parenting litigation. She fled our home, bent on suicide. Just before dawn, I stopped searching. I sobbed and waited for the inevitable phone call. It came from Idaho. "Kim survived," said a stranger. In relief, I sobbed again.

Thus, our saga of return began. Ralph Waldo Emerson (American, 19th century A.D.) said, "Nothing is at last sacred but the integrity of your own mind" (*Self-Reliance*). Kim was shattered. Psychiatrists, tests, drugs, side-effects, counseling ensued. For years, we catalogued her demons (and mine). The first decade was hardest. Kim feared she might relapse, that I might leave. Truthfully, I was uncertain I could persevere. But slowly prayers for cure became determination to cope. Seneca (Roman, 1st century A.D.) said that with, "diseases of the soul, the worse one is, the less one perceives it" (*Epistle LIII*). Kim's path required painful admissions and self-encounter. In the end, Kim stabilized.

Jesus (Roman, Province of Judea, 1st century A.D.) cast demons from a mentally ill man into swine (Mark 5:11). Kim exorcised her torment into rags and Windex. Our world sparkled. Fastidious compulsion, however, proved insufficient. Kim sought wider outlets. She listens to and stands beside the bipolar afflicted who cross our path. She devotes herself to empathic conversation. Frequently, some player in our legal cases is psychologically unwell. Kim understands, and helps. She counsels. She cares.

> **FIND DETERMINATION TO COPE.**

Kim endures the cultural stigma of being nuts. She hides nothing. Her frankness shames those moral Munchkins who castigate people for the diseases they suffer. Kim takes each day as it comes. She must. Her brain changes frequently. Kim focuses on now, striving for equanimity. "There are more things likely to frighten us than there are to crush us; we suffer more often in imagination than in reality" (Seneca, *Epistle XIII*). Unlike most wars, Kim's has no end. She does not contemplate a day when her battle ceases. She faces that interminable challenge with quiet courage.

If you sense admiration in my words, you got that right.

SAM

23
JERRY AND HERCULES

Jerry stopped at my office to talk last summer. He did not know me; he did not need legal services. Jerry had seen Kim and me working on our office grounds. Introducing himself seemed like a good idea. So, Jerry turned his sassy electric cart into our driveway and made acquaintance. Hercules, Jerry's seven year old 155 pound black Newfoundland-Labrador mix gave me a sniff, then consented to ear and tail scratching. In 1965, Jerry lost his left leg at the knee to bone cancer after he served in the Navy. His craft, before retirement, was plumbing. We talked about prostheses and sidewalks (that Jerry has the one and Shoreline lacks the other). Hercules wondered why Jerry interrupted their daily stroll, but thought sniffing our back yard an exceptionally good idea. Jerry and I chatted on a bench in the back yard. We spoke of South Dakota, where Jerry might move. We spoke of Shoreline, its wonders and bedevilments. Jerry has returned repeatedly, for no particularly pressing reason other than getting to know one another. Our visits cheer us.

Jerry's stops at Lancaster Law Office matter. Jerry and Hercules mortared a brick in Shoreline's communal house. They made connections where none had previously existed. They brightened our day, and possibly we theirs. Jerry helped me wish well for Shoreline, and know another's view of our togetherness—

CREDIBLE
CORN

the helpful and the horrid. Jerry broadened me. Hercules the giant dog informed Lucy the miniature pinscher that she is not the Big Canine she imagines. I wished for sidewalks everywhere to keep Jerry and Hercules safe. I thought I may stroll more, and introduce myself to complete strangers for no reason at all. Gratuitous kindness seems warranted. I may pick up others' trash. In grim moments, I may hope; gray faces spawn only gray faces. Jerry and Hercules stirred me up.

Gestures cumulate. Kindnesses knit strangers into communities. Ella Wheeler Wilcox (American, 20th century A.D.) captured the truth: "So many gods, so many creeds, so many paths that wind and wind, while just the art of being kind is all the sad world needs." That may be corny, but it is credible corn.

Thanks, Jerry and Hercules. Good to know you.

LUCY, ON HER FRIGHTFUL OUTING.

24
FRIENDS

I am my friends. Their lives are mine; mine theirs.

I once believed otherwise. I was an individual in the American, the Emersonian, sense. Ralph Waldo Emerson (American, 19th century A.D.) said, "Society everywhere is in conspiracy against the manhood of every one of its members. . . . Insist on yourself; never imitate" (*Self-Reliance*, 1841). I imagined, unconsciously following Ralph, *I am a lone ship amidst storms, grateful when another vessel appears on the horizon, signaling, even sharing plight for a moment. But eventually, inevitably, I am alone. And storms abound.* I was proud. I felt grim.

Life happened. Connections blossomed, and confidence in my capacities flagged. There was Mike with his lovely bride and two kids, she who got thyroid cancer, he with the contracting business and back troubles. Their challenges became mine. There came Kim with her mental illness and son and endless line of medications and courageous struggle to be useful despite it all. We became one person together. There came (and departed) Kirk's psychological distress at work and spouse Lisa's need to fit in. They wandered off in a boat, to my distress and displeasure. Kathy's obesity, along with my own, occupied years. Maggie's political battles and Don's exuberant biking, Ken's spiritual growth and Janet's devoted parenting: all penetrated. Law clients arrived, with lives blossoming and disintegrating and spinning toward war and rising from ashes. And YMCA basketball guys, and ethics reading group

THE MYSTICAL LINKAGE OF FRIENDSHIP.

friends, and Rotary colleagues, and good-hearted opposing counsels. Each intruded, implicated me. Deep connections emerged. I learned I control little. Pride waned (slightly). I struggle; they struggle; finally, we struggle. Insight blossomed: I am my friends, conjoined in deeps of existence. We are unconsciously linked. Their web and my own form one skein of living. Aggregately, in all our various conjunctions, we are humanity. Individually, I am a lone shifting thread in time, soon snipped. Together, we are history, the interwoven tapestry of consciousness. Aristotle (Athenian, 4th century B.C.) concluded, "Friendship is a single soul dwelling in two bodies" (reported by Diogenes Laertius in *Lives and Opinions of Eminent Philosophers*, V.20, 3rd century B.C.). Or, I speculate, one soul in many bodies, maybe hundreds, maybe thousands. It is a mystical thought, an insight that occupies me, frequently preoccupies me.

Horace (Roman, 1st century B.C.) captured the implication: "Your own safety is at stake when your neighbor's wall is ablaze." (*Epistles*, 1.18) All human fires are my fires. It is overwhelming. The little I can do, however, is not nothing. Besides, I no longer feel grim. For I am my friends.

FIFI, WITH GRAMPA PAUL AND GRAMMA ADA

25
JAZZ WALK

Good citizens of Shoreline gathered in gobs. Trills and riffs tickled August evening breezes. Dixieland reigned. North City strutted proud sidewalks, flower baskets, and sassy small businesses. Five venues, five flavors of jazz, a new street, a fresh event. Neighbors cruised the bands, strolled at leisure, knitted by shared joys. Airy sax, nimble keyboard, brooding bass, pungent cabernet, summery chardonnay, witty desserts. A setting sun raked pink through cloud wisps. Despite themselves, city council foes tapped their feet in unison, obeying imperative cadences of New Orleans. Duke Ellington (American, 20th century A.D.) once snickered: "By and large, jazz has always been like the kind of man you wouldn't want your daughter to associate with." Not so in North City. Yes, the music piped hot from Bourbon Street. But the sidewalks and venues were pure Americana: wholesome, strapping, bursting with vivacity.

People, possessed of Ragtime, seized Fifteenth Avenue. Judge Michael Trickey (what a name for an attorney...) warmed the street, handsome and smart as ever. Charlotte Haines and Sally Granger shouldered backstage labors, as is their habit, greasing event gears. (We must thank them more.) Gary Batch rustled more tickets; Jazz Walk ran out in the welter of popularity. Keith McClelland teased his keyboard to utter mirth and joy and rhapsodic blues. Keith is a gifted man. Pierced, tattooed teens shuffled amid business wonks and snow-capped seniors. Councilman McGlashan beamed, savoring respite from poker-faced politics. Harry Weidenaar, a local pastor fresh from summer South African service projects, introduced his lovely wife, Grace. Cell phones, perhaps, receded. No televisions blared. Robin McClelland charmed the avenue with North Carolina inflection. Jazz and a belle's smile— forces of nature for which to thank the South. Fifteenth Avenue teemed with jazzophiles.

Shoreline's election cycle dysphoria swooned in a boogie-woogie spell. North City's blood-driving timbre and rhythm convinced us walkers, if only for a time, that our disputes lie in that great shadow cast by what we share: affection for children and commitment to their nurture, exuberant green of summer grass, lilting laughter, tickle of a good joke, salty wet of tough workouts, gustatory glee of summer fare, evening breezes, sunsets at Richmond Beach, jazz. We knew, if fleetingly, that we must abandon Mark Twain's (American, 20th century A.D.) epithet about political practice: "In all matters of opinion our adversaries are insane" (1907). With Dwight Eisenhower (American, 20th century A.D.), we should decline to "confuse honest dissent with disloyal subversion" (1954). Make good faith dissent safe. Such civility ennobles American governance. Besides, life exceeds our disputes.

Louis Armstrong (20th century A.D.), America's most famous trumpeter and jazzer, said: "You blows who you is." North City's Jazz Walk, a piece of "who we is." Well done, Shoreline.

RUCKUS AND LUCY

26
RUCKUS

Ruckus huddled in a blanket beneath the passenger seat of my friend Judy's old car. The young puppy peered at me with intense black eyes. Those orbs talked. They flashed the insecurity of dogs fresh from the pound, and the silent interrogatory of every dog, *Are we friends?* I reassured puppy Ruckus.

Ruckus soon journeyed to my home, where he met then-puppy Lucy, our miniature pinscher. Ruckus caromed into the fenced back yard, where he tore fifty foot circles until he collapsed in delighted exhaustion. He taunted Lucy for refusing to join his sloppy, silly sprints.

Ruckus sprang from alley breeding, a terrier's ebullient heart in a body of ungainly dachshund stretch. His long low body and powerful legs carried his sweet face at tremendous accelerations, bounding off walls, tearing around corners. When Judy traveled, Ruckus visited Lancasters, to sniff out Hamlin Park, to splash at Richmond Beach and Edmonds dog park, and most to torture Lucy. Ruckus was Life itself gushing through a dog-shaped orifice.

One leap too many, one vault down stairs beyond the pale. Ruckus injured his improbable spine. His hindquarters no longer obeyed terrier imperatives. Hydro-therapy helped, but offered no cure. Time passed. After consultations, Judy bore Ruckus to Washington State

> **LIFE ITSELF GUSHING THROUGH A DOG-SHAPED ORIFICE.**

University. Spinal surgery improved function, but not greatly. Ruckus's bladder still needed manual expression. Bowels moved naturally, but unpredictably. Ruckus got diapers and a cart for his back half. Muscle memory gave him occasional jumbled walking motions, like a drunken sailor in a bobbing skiff. Slowly, the dog improved; Ruckus's gait peeked out. But recovery was not to be. Ruckus reinjured his spine. The cart and diapers would be permanent.

Though Ruckus's pain must be substantial, he never betrays it. Sores on limp feet must be bothersome, the chafing of his cart an annoyance. One would never know. Ruckus runs with the same abandon as his first trip around our yard. He tires sooner, dragging half a dog on a cart behind him. But Ruckus's ecstatic thirst for life perseveres. Troubles do not deter Ruckus.

If Ruckus were a talking creature, he would implore us that all is well. Ruckus does what a Ruckus is born to do: careen with abandon and spill laughter. William James (American, 19th century A.D.) said: "For to miss the joy is to miss all" (*On a Certain Blindness in Human Beings*). Ruckus knows.

GRAMPA PAUL LOVING ONE OF HIS MANY AIREDALES.

27
YMCA

Around 1959, Grandfather Lancaster shuffled me through the door of my first YMCA in Yakima, Washington. I floundered in their swimming pool for Grampa Paul, demonstrating half-learned strokes from Red Cross swimming class. After I had mostly drowned myself, Paul towed me to the locker room. We stripped off our trunks. He handed me a white towel scented with bleach. A foggy door swung open. I sat on the steam room tile bench, my rag draped to obscure what needed hiding. I listened to the naked sun-wizened fruit men of Yakima valley: Selah cherry farmers, Wapato barons of red delicious, Moxee lords of peach and plum. My grandfather regaled the fortunes of Yakima Fruit and Cold Storage, of which he owned a part. The orchard burghers spoke of dogs (grandfather loved his Airedales) and liquor (of which Grandpa Paul was fond to a fault) and Yakima. Protruding paunches jiggled in mirth. Sagging jowls frowned at hated taxes and scurrilous scandals. In this senate of sweat, a bond was built, a promise offered. Bits of Yakima emerged from rivulets of perspiration rolling down hairy backs, as steam boiled off stainless pipes. Those conversations proved prophetic. Alan Kay (American, 20th century A.D.) noted, "The best way to predict the future is to invent it."

More than two thousand years ago, Roman patricians spent afternoons at swimming pools, which they called baths. There, the Roman elite conversed, read, gossiped, exercised, massaged, philosophized, and (oh, yes) washed. The Imperium maintained communal baths for purposes far beyond diversion and a brisk scrub. Romans struck deals, vetted candidates, built muscles, debated wars, and nurtured friendships. Rome was invented in baths. Baths housed libraries and lecture halls. Time ravaged Rome, but baths, a great community-building idea, endured. Britain restated Rome's baths (and the Greek *gymnasium*), baptizing them to different values. In 1844, Britons formed the Young Men's Christian Association. The YMCA built its reputation on swimming pools, steam rooms, and civic purposes. The Y inculcated values Christian in origin, though the organization came to emphasize service over evangelism. Character development became the Y's watchword: caring, honesty, respect, and responsibility. Ys build healthy spirits, minds, and bodies for all, so their saying goes.

> **PREDICT THE FUTURE BY INVENTING IT.**

In the late 1970s, I played basketball as often as studies permitted at Pasadena's YMCA. My parochialism got buffeted. Men of every color, culture, and character pulled on sneakers to jump, shoot, foul. Diversity annoyed me—unfamiliar lingos, impenetrable accents, reprehensible values. But years passed; differences found context. Mutual respect frayed xenophobia, as we learned one another's game, as we made ourselves teams.

In the mid-1980s, I joined Shoreline's YMCA. Old guys played gentleman's basketball on the short court: play stopped when roundballers fell; cursing was tolerated, but discouraged. I heard that familiar YMCA song. The grunting of hard exercise. Chatter of common concerns. Back-slapping, laughter, and warm hand-shakes. Networking and decision making, dreams floated and plans hatched. Shoreline's YMCA flaunts a jewel, its front desk traffic cop, Cheryl Medin. She juggles phones and front door like a Ringling Brothers act. Cheryl greets governors and homeless people with equal courtesy and aplomb. Through decades, Shoreline YMCA's excellent string of directors has tended a mission that issued from Jesus of Nazareth, though none preaches a gospel of words. Shoreline YMCA serves. It takes two incomes to rent in Shoreline, so the Y provides subsidized daycare. Some teens appear lost; the Y offers places and guidance. The Y's doors open to all. And, of course, the Y proffers baths, sweating, education, and a deluge of good faith.

Shoreline has outgrown its YMCA building. The Y erects a new, more appropriately-sized, facility at Echo Lake. The new Y has a pool (a bath, if you will). Join the Y; contribute to its capital campaign. Come splash in the bath. Converse. Predict Shoreline's future by inventing it. Imagine Shoreline.

FIRDALE OFFICE AND LUCY WITH KIM

28
WORK

I got my second real job the summer of 1969. I was fifteen, my high school freshman year completed. The National Boy Scout Jamboree convened at Farragut State Park near Lake Pend O'Reille in north Idaho. Pepsi won the soft drink contract to quench the assembled thousands. The local distributor needed a tangle of teens to distribute product. Scores of pop machines sprouted from parched fields, amidst Scouts' tents. I made $1.85 per hour (then, a fortune). Work began at dawn, loading trucks at the factory. Since Big Boss watched, all kids worked hard. We caravanned to the Jamboree, then filled and cleaned soda machines until noon.

After lunch, four trucks awaited afternoon reloading. Storage tents baked. Dust roiled. Six hours of lifting wearied backs. That first day, our supervisor left for a beer in Bayview, the nearest tavern. Boys worked and complained. By the third day, our Jamboree super vanished before lunch and emerged when afternoon circuit neared completion. One by one, teens stopped lunch loading. I complained at the dinner table. My father advised, "Do what you were hired to do, son." I labored alone restocking trucks in the midday swelter, the butt of teen jokes. On about day ten of that two week Jamboree, a truck rolled up during afternoon reload. Big

> **WORK HARD**
> **AT WORK WORTH DOING.**

Boss plopped a cowboy boot into Jamboree dust. Boys lazed in shadowy brown grass. I steamed past, lugging two canisters. Big Boss cast a weary glance.

The Boy Scouts departed. Pepsi had two summer factory jobs. I got one, and a big raise to $2.15. That first day, the factory men, with wry smiles, put me on "table," a rotating steel disk where filled bottles marched. They instructed me: grab four bottles, two in each hand. Put them into a case of twenty-four, six grabs per case, eight cases per pallet level, six levels per pallet, and an unending stream of empty pallets. I offloaded 176,000 full bottles of pop that day. The crew guffawed at my blistered hands. Each had once suffered initiation himself. When the line whined to a stop, they offered beer. I declined, to avoid mother's scowl, but enjoyed a good laugh with the men at my expense.

I have had many jobs: lawn mower, youth minister, doorman at Frederick & Nelson, prosecutor, daycare buffoon, theologian, used car lot boy, painter, preacher, 7-11 clerk, lawyer, mansion finisher, janitor, and pop factory worker. I enjoyed each duty, but not equally. Theodore Roosevelt (American, 20th century A.D.) noted, "Far and away the best prize that life offers is the chance to work hard at work worth doing" (Labor Day address, Syracuse, New York, 1903). Teddy was right.

BAILEY, WITH TANYA AND KATE

29

TRULY SELFISH

In 1845, Henry David Thoreau (American transcendentalist, 19th century A.D.) cobbled together a cabin in woods near Walden Pond, outside Concord, Massachusetts. Thoreau rhapsodized nature and solitude. He ruminated, "The mass of men lead lives of quiet desperation" and "have become the tools of their tools" (*Walden*). Thoreau sought escape. "I went to the woods because I wished to live deliberately, to front only the essential facts of life, and see if I could not learn what it had to teach, and not, when I came to die, discover that I had not lived" (*Walden*). Thoreau asserted taxes fund war and slavery; a local constable famously jailed Thoreau for refusing to pay poll tax (*On the Duty of Civil Disobedience,* 1849). America heralded Thoreau an archetypal bootstrapping loner. Henry David (mostly after his death) grew famous.

Thoreau downplays critical facts of his Walden years. Friends visited and provisioned the cabin. When unrelenting solitude chilled Thoreau's heart, dinner at Ralph Waldo Emerson's house thawed him. Friends paid Thoreau's poll tax, bailing him after only one night's incarceration. Thoreau sent out his laundry and mending. Henry David tired of isolation in Walden's woods after twenty-six months; he returned to Concord, working at odd jobs. Thoreau was never so independent as acclaim (or he himself) painted him.

Shoreline little resembles Thoreau's Walden. His century was nineteenth; ours twenty-first. His earth housed one billion persons; ours seven. We queue at freeways and latte stands. Cards identify us as often as names. Misbehavior of Saudi princes boosts or dings our paychecks. We long outlive Thoreau's New Englanders. And our taxes beggar Thoreau's annual pittance. Daily, half our fruits transfer from individual to communal weal. So, Ronald Bog is not Walden Pond. America's romance with self-sufficiency succumbed to webbed interconnectivity. Some call us poorer for the change. I demur.

> **SELF IS A MORAL DISEASE**
> **CURED BY**
> **BUILDING COMMUNITY.**

Seneca (Roman, 1st century A.D.) answers individualists: "There is no such thing as good or bad fortune for the individual; we live in common. And no one can live happily who has regard to himself alone and transforms everything into a question of his own utility; **you must live for your neighbor, if you would live for yourself**" (Epistle XLVIII, emphasis added).

Seneca understood better than Thoreau. Taking care of oneself entails serving neighbors, not avoiding them. Excellent individuality spices our communal stew, but alone provides little nourishment. To be truly selfish, build neighbors. Elevate the poor. Embrace retarded and insane persons. Educate the ignorant. Find people jobs. Heal the sick. Tolerate dissenters. Stifle the reckless. Punish wickedness. Praise noble acts. Address injustice. Hope for the best, especially when desirable outcomes are in doubt.

To seize goodness, give goodness. It is a rule. The ship founders; all drown. The ship harbors; all prosper. Be truly selfish.

YOKWAT SPIT ON NOOTKA SOUND

30

YACHAKAS (EXCERPT FROM CHAPTER 2 OF *RAVENRY*)

NOOTKA SOUND
WHAT WOULD BE LATER NAMED VANCOUVER ISLAND
1565 A.D.

Tootoosch poked his head through the smoky entrance to the longhouse. Broad cedar roof planks were shoved aside to let smoke out and sunshine in. The days shortened as morning frosts of Burning waned toward blustery Rough Sea and snowy Elder. The bronzed, heavily-muscled Tootoosch scanned the longhouse interior with intense black eyes. Children played. Women cooked and sewed. A few, the oaf Shewish among them, slept. Finally, Tootoosch's eyes landed on his brother's son helping his mother hang dried salmon in the longhouse rafters.

"Yachakas, you little fleck of sandpaper. Today we chase flat rocks."

Little Yachakas, whose name meant Dogfish, looked up with surprise.

"What?" he asked, wondering what his beloved uncle meant. Tootoosch stuck his arm further into the beam and plank building. Ornate halibut hooks dangled from his fingers. Dogfish squinted. A great smile lit his face. Yachakas would accompany his uncle in a great cedar canoe, and they would tempt halibut.

"Hali—," Dogfish clapped his hand over his mouth before he could finish. Tootoosch shot him a severe look, one which reproved the boy wordlessly. The youngster sprinted across the sunlight mottled interior, littered with debris and fish bones. Older women scolded and shook their heads gently in disapproval.

Tootoosch scuffed his nephew's head. "Boy, do not speak old green slate's name. You will alert him to our stroll today," Tootoosch warned. The hunter never spoke of his quarry. Dogfish nodded aggressively, now reminded that the Spirit of Halibut might be eavesdropping. Dogfish's careless mention of their outing could alert the halibut of Nootka Sound to danger.

"Uncle, how do you know when flat rock spirit might be listening?"

Tootoosch sighed. "More questions, young one?"

"I have many. About our life. About the old stories."

"That is certainly true," Tootoosch laughed, and walked on.

None in all the thirteen houses of the Mowachaht tribe fared so well with the Spirit of Halibut as did Tootoosch. Once he had brought to Yokwat, the Mowachaht's summer village, exposed to the open ocean, a chief of the halibut. Four men groaned lifting the fish from the water, and a great feast was held that very day to appease the spirits of the halibut peoples beneath the sea. The bones and guts of that fish were carefully returned to the water that they might take flesh anew and live once more.

"Follow me," Tootoosch commanded, and pointed to the spit of basalt which sheltered their little cove from the Pacific inclemency of Nootka Sound.

Tootoosch strode gracefully. Dogfish clambered clumsily. Blockish, black rocks tripped him. Thickets grabbed his feet. Nettles pricked him. Dogfish clamped his jaws. Nothing would convince him to shame himself before Tootoosch with whining or complaint.

The two wrenched loose cedar boughs. In the cold Pacific inlet, they scrubbed themselves. When red with irritation, and blue with cold, their lice drowned. Yachakas followed his uncle's incantations, appeasing the many spirits that crowded their watery world. Dogfish could have sung along. He had learned. Though clumsy, the young man's mind skipped, nimble and supple. His many questions annoyed some of the Mowachaht. Insistent probing had earned him his childhood name, Yachakas, which means dogfish. Dogfish are nuisance sharks. Their skins, once dried, are used as sandpaper to smooth carvings and polish mollusk-shell blades and points. Little Yachakas abraded some, counterpoint to a generally compliant crop of youngsters at Yokwat. He asked where the pole attached, the one that held up the disk of the world. If lightning was Thunderbird's pet snake, why did He keep so many pets? Women hissed at Yachakas. Such knowledge lay with shamans, not boys. Yachakas frowned, and yearned for the day he would receive his adult name. Then he would be a man of the village. He might get answers.

Tootoosch asked, "My son, have you touched Arima, who is heavy with child?"

"No, uncle. I have avoided her."

"That is good. Flying turtles hate the stink of pregnant women." The hunter winked.

"My son, have you walked past a bleeding woman?" Tootoosch raised his eyebrows, to indicate the sort of blood he meant.

"That too I have avoided, uncle."

Tootoosch handed Yachakas a tiny woven cedar ball, with a long string attached. "Bind this on. It will help us find flat rocks in the trees." Yachakas laughed with his eyes. He wound the strap around his upper arm. Inside the ball hid a fragment of a blind snake Tootoosch had killed, which scent masked human odors, so offensive to spirits.

Tootoosch thanked Ichtope, the humpback whale spirit, and Sky spirit for the good hunt they hoped to have. Dogfish matched his uncle's obeisances. As they paddled toward open water, elder in the stern, youth at the bow, the beach bustled. Canoes smoldered, blankets wove, and planks split. Children danced the Wolf whirl, awash in the Tlokwana's cultic imagination, preparing for the big party. Over all hung an unspoken pall, the crisis chief Qwistok suffered with whales. Because of that, Yachakas avoided chewing pitch. Gum bothered whales and salmon. No villager chewed when the winter's supply of food grew uncertain.

Tootoosch paddled briskly. Yachakas's eyes widened. The open Pacific, outside the shelter of the spit of Yokwat, might gulp a two-man canoe. If they hooked a large halibut, it might drag them miles before death frosted its eyes. This outing might sorely test Yachakas's endurance. His paddle bore Raven's image. The two sliced through swells. Tootoosch noted the fiery, nettled welts on his nephew's forearm. The boy met today's challenge with quiet confidence, and a bit of trepidation.

"You stroke well, little Dogfish," Tootoosch encouraged. Yachakas smiled.

The expanse of the sea stretched before them. These waters fed the people. The ocean was their highway. Snow, the mange scales of Sky Dog, whitened peaks and leaked down valleys. Fog burped from the kneecaps of Crane, lying in low smudges against shadowed shores. A profusion of steep, green islands dotted the thalassic seascape. Glacier-carved verticality made Yokwat spit a prize. Twice in Dogfish's short life the tribe had defended their summer village from insurgents paddling north. Prime village sites were few and prized.

The broken necks of bullwhip kelp flopped past in currents. Small crests atop swells splattered the paddlers. Seabirds played in the stiff onshore wind. This turbulence scared Yachakas. Tootoosch saw his nephew's back tense.

"You know Raven and Bear sought flat rocks, as do we today," Tootoosch probed. Of course Yachakas knew. Every Mowachaht heard these stories from infancy. Yachakas nodded, struggling to hide his growing alarm. Of all the Mowachaht legends, Yachakas best loved those of Raven.

Tootoosch settled into a cultic voice, the smooth talk of an oft-repeated liturgy.

Raven the Trickster was a chief of the Mowachaht. He asked Black Bear to go halibut fishing one day. Bear dug his toe into the dirt, staring fixedly. He fidgeted.

Bear said, "I will go, but promise you will do me no harm. You are clever and a trickster. I am just a stupid bear." Bear slobbered a bit from the corner of his mouth, like nervous brutes do.

Raven replied, "Why, Bear! What harm could I do to you? You are fifty times my size, and a thousand times as strong. Can I lift you with my wings? Can I pierce your hide with my beak?"

Bear found muddled truth in Raven's words. He fetched his paddle. Bear checked his hooks and lines. He grabbed octopus for bait. But Raven brought no bait. Bear wondered, but shrugged it off.

Bear took the bow, Raven the stern. They paddled far up Muchalat Inlet.

"We have gone far enough," Raven decided. "Throw out the anchor."

Bear tossed the stone from their canoe, and played out cedar bark rope until it bottomed. Bear rigged for halibut. Raven turned his back to Bear, fussed with his gear. Bear lodged the octopus tentacle on his hook. Both wetted their lines. Immediately, Raven caught a halibut. Then a second. Soon, the bottom of the canoe brimmed with Raven's catch. But Bear caught none.

Bear was embarrassed. How would he explain the outcome to the villagers? They would laugh at him. And Bear hated being the object of scorn.

Bear asked, "What are you using for bait, Raven, that you have caught so many of halibut's family?"

Raven smirked, "If I told you, you would not bait your hook as I have baited mine."

Bear, the dim hibernator, disagreed, "I would do anything to avoid being the butt of jokes, Raven." Bear tried to look cute, as coy as a slobbering bear can look.

"Alright, Bear," Raven sighed. "I have used my dick for bait. I cut it off and put it on the hook. Halibut love it, as you can see."

Bear's slack jaw dropped open. He wanted to avoid humiliation. But he also wanted to keep his privates. Bear protested, after thinking it over for a time, "If I cut off my ladysnake, how will I put it back on when we are done with halibut fishing?"

Raven's eyes danced their jig of amusement. He laughed, Cawk, Cawk. He pulled a lump of gum from his beak. "We paste it back on with this gum when we are done. That is how I do it."

Bear hesitated, then said, "Alright. Let's do it."

Bear lay back and parted his legs. Bear raised his shell knife to slice off his genitals. Bear entreated Raven, "Is this going to hurt?"

Raven responded, "Removing your holepoker will hurt, Bear, but not so much as returning to Yokwat fishless."

Bear sawed off his dingus. Bear groaned. Raven said, "Lay back your head, brother. Take a nap."

The bottom of the canoe filled with blood. Soon, Bear kicked twice, and died.

Raven paddled to shore. He put Bear's stiffening corpse beside a great fire he built. Raven covered the corpse with mosses. He poured water over Bear's bulk. When cooked, Raven ate Bear—fur, muscles, ears, claws, and all. Bear's winter fat burned, creating an oily cream that wafted deliciously. This, Raven drank, then belched. Raven gathered Bear's bones and hid them beneath a salalberry bush.

Raven paddled home to Yokwat spit. He turned the six largest fish so their heads pointed toward Bear's seat. Mowachaht situate their halibut in this manner to indicate who caught them. Raven began to wail. He crunched onto the pea gravel beach.

The Mowachaht gathered around Raven. Raven said, "Bear caught these six fish. The seventh was gigantic. Bear tangled his feet in the line, and was hauled overboard. He never surfaced."

The villagers puzzled. Did Raven speak truly? Or was this one of his many tricks?

Raven belched again. It smelled of bear grease.

Regardless, most believed Raven's tale. Some grumbled, certain Raven can craft a lie like no other. Raven deceives to amuse himself. All knew that.

Raven gave some halibut to Bear's widow, but kept the rest for himself.

And that is why, to this day, ravens laugh around Yokwat, but no black bears.

When Yachakas emerged from the story of Bear and Raven, he and Tootoosch had paddled far. They could no longer see Yokwat. They dropped anchor against the incessant shoving tides.

Their fortune was good. Several small halibut lay in the canoe. They would make a meal for the families of Yokwat. Two large bottomfish were tethered through their gills to the side of the canoe with cedar bark rope. Tootoosch bashed their tiny brain boxes.

As they paddled, Yachakas jabbered. "Why would Bear agree to cut off his dick? Did he not know that Raven plays practical jokes?"

Tootoosch shrugged. "Of the Spirits one can never know."

"And how could a raven eat a whole bear? How could he move the corpse to the fire? He is so little. The bear is so big."

"Size may not matter to Spirits," Tootoosch ventured.

Yachakas opened his mouth to voice more pestilential questions. Tootoosch raised a hand for silence.

Yachakas and his uncle turned the canoe homeward. An image of Raven splashed into the water on the boy's paddle. In and out, in and out. As the two neared the mouth of the Sound, a tiny island slid up aport. A knuckle of granite poking from the water, only five war canoes long. On the ocean side, it was precipitous. Landward, it sloped gently from the water. Scraggly firs clung to its rocks, rooting in quartz and feldspar dust, organic detritus, and a fertilizer of bird droppings. It was an unexceptional island, except for the ravens. Several score hopped and clacked and strutted, a winging for avians. Usually, ravens gathered to quarrel over carrion. But no carcass was evident. The ravens were agitated.

Tootoosch paddled faster. Yachakas asked, "Why hurry, uncle?"

"Because that island is a Ravenry. The Spirits are strong, so it is dangerous. Those ravens potlatch with the Trickster himself," murmured Tootoosch. Dogfish knew he too should fear. But he did not.

Yachakas asked, "Uncle, has any man of Mowachaht claimed that little hill for his ritual place?"

Tootoosch shook his head. "I do not believe so, boy. It is far from Yokwat across open water. I would not return to that place. Raven will capture your dreams, make you crazy. I saw one raven shaking a rattle over a rotten log. The log writhed at the jester's croaking. I heard groaning, like cedars bending in gales."

Yachakas had not seen or heard these things. He held his tongue. At that instant, there germinated within Yachakas a seed, the sprout that would become a towering cedar of obsession in his clan. Monomania amidst polyanimism. Fixation dissenting from generalism. From among the hidden world's many divinities, Raven seized Yachakas. The Trickster disturbed dreams, drove desire, dug direction.

In the open sound, Tootoosch poked Yachakas, pointing behind them. A dark wall of cloud loomed. "The old man has farted." Legend had it that southeast winds, the violent sort, are flatulence of an ancient mythic spirit. Mink, it was said, could calm the old man's bowels. Tootoosch began the song of Mink. Chanting paced their paddling. Growing waves slid beneath them as the waters turned gray and turbulent.

The smudge of Yokwat fires beckoned. But the storm rose. Yachakas's paddling stuttered.

Tootoosch turned again to story. "I will tell you again of your namesake, Yachakas." Dogfish nodded stiffly.

Three Mowachaht boys ventured into the woods, much farther than their mothers permitted. The boys were Yachakas, Spirit of Elk, and Small Clam Boy. This last was eldest son of the Mowachaht chief, and so, a person of great importance in the village. The boys spied a river, the Mowinis. They paddled up its meander.

Far from Yokwat, these bad boys met an ugly woman sitting on the river bank. Beside her sat a huge basket. She chewed gum furiously. The boys paddled up to her, over Yachakas's objections. She looked, to him, evil.

Near the bank, Small Clam Boy spoke to the hag. She whirled, blowing shaman dust over the boys. All sank to the bottom of their canoe. She leaned over them. Yachakas recognized her. She was Malahas, the Woman of the Woods.

Malahas took gum from her mouth, dripping with her spit. She smeared it on Yachakas's eyes, sealing them shut. She plucked him up and dropped him in her great basket. Then she gummed Spirit of Elk and Small Clam Boy. She dropped them on top of Yachakas. As she traveled, little Yachakas squeezed through the weave of her basket. He fell to the ground behind Malahas and felt his way to a big rock. Malahas did not notice.

The Woman of the Woods, when she arrived home, took a long pole and tied the feet of Spirit of Elk and Small Clam Boy to it. She hung them over her hearthfire and smoked them to death.

Dogfish pried the pitch from his eyes, and made his way back to Yokwat. He told the tribe his story. The mother of Small Clam Boy, the chief's son, was overwrought. Tears gushed like spring streams. She bawled for four days. At the end of those days, she blew her nose and threw the snot on the ground. The muck lay there.

The next day, her mucus moved. It grew a little head, then some arms. On the third day, it was long as his mother's hand. On the fourth day, the snot child began to cry. His mother swaddled him in a corner of her cedar bark blanket, and tucked it away beneath a giant spruce, behind a clump of licorice fern. She told her husband, the chief, of the strange incident. The very next day, Snot Boy walked into the Mowachaht village. He had become a young man overnight. The chief adopted him, since his wife begged.

Snot Boy heard his mother crying. He asked, "Why do you cry, Mother?"

She said, "You were born from my tearful snot. Before I blew you from my nose, the Woman of the Woods stole my baby, Small Clam Boy, and killed him. She murdered also Spirit of Elk. Only Dogfish escaped. Woman of the Woods kept those poor boys up the Mowinis River."

Snot Boy made himself a bow of yew and two straight arrows, which he tipped with mussel shell. The next morning, Snot Boy's mother painted his face, and adorned his ears and nose with abalone jewelry. He was most beautiful. Snot Boy took his weapon, snuck out of Yokwat, and found Malahas, the Woman of the Woods, up the Mowinis. Snot boy hid in a tree above a quiet pool of the river.

Malahas saw his reflection in the water, and exclaimed, "What a beautiful face!" But when she looked up, Snot Boy hid himself. He continued the ruse three times. The fourth time Malahas turned, Snot Boy showed himself. The Woman of the Woods was smitten.

She said, "Come be my husband, beautiful one."

Snot Boy answered, "I cannot, for you are ugly."

"What did your mother do to make you so beautiful, young man?" asked Malahas. Snot boy shrugged his shoulders. Malahas persisted.

Snot Boy relented, "Very well. I will tell you. She positioned my head on a flat rock and smashed it with another. Then my mother artfully remolded my head, and brought me back to life. She taught me her secrets."

Malahas frowned.

Snot Boy said, "I could do this thing for you, if you can find the courage. Once you are beautiful, then we can marry."

Malahas hesitated, but then found two stones of sufficient size. She laid her head on the biggest flat one.

Snot Boy lofted the other stone, but Malahas jerked back.

Malahas asked, "Are you sure you can make me alive once again after you have made me beautiful?"

Snot Boy sneered, "I thought an old woman like you would lose courage. Stay ugly. I will not marry you." Snot Boy stomped off. But the Woman of the Woods begged. She fell to the ground, groveling. Snot Boy waited, pretending to be undecided. Then he consented. The Woman of the Woods squealed with glee.

She put her head on the flat stone and closed her eyes. Snot Boy smashed her skull to bits.

Snot Boy walked to Malahas's house. He heard a man's voice calling. It came from the pot in which the old witch crapped at night. It smelled terrible. Snot Boy smashed the pot. Each piece of the broken pot called to Snot Boy, making a racket.

There was a voice at the door. There stood the Woman of the Woods. Her head was roughly pieced together. She roared her evil laugh. Snot Boy notched an arrow, and shot Malahas through her heart. Now she was really dead.

In the rafters of Malahas's house, over his head, Snot Boy found two desiccated lads of the Mowachaht. Dried, they dangled. Snot Boy laid the victims on the floor. He pissed on them. Their thirsty bodies drank up his urine. They regenerated.

When their senses returned, the three boys paddled back to Yokwat. Small Clam Boy's mother was most grateful. She kissed Snot Boy.

The entire village celebrated his valor.

Tootoosch and Yachakas neared the spit that made Yokwat cove. Their songs had sufficed. Mink had spared them. The storm lashed. Thunder broke, ricocheting off rock cliffs. But two fishermen rounded the jumbled rockery to Yokwat's safety. They had escaped Old Man's indigestion.

"Well done, Yachakas. You stroke well." His uncle offered praise freely. For that, Dogfish was grateful. He smiled, and splashed a little brine back toward Tootoosch. They laughed.

Yachakas, however, could not shake the ravens from his mind. Nor their hill across the open water. The island called to him, in the dark of night as he huddled beneath animal hides which warmed him near the communal hearth.

PENNY AT YELLOWSTONE, WITH MOM, DAD, AND JILL

31
SUICIDE

Friends, an elderly couple I will call Buck and Pearl Greenwood, died, he of Alzheimer's in 2005, she of a broken heart and multiple organ failure in 2006. Greenwoods planned their deaths. Each made an advance directive to their physician instructing that no heroic measure be taken to prolong their lives, if terminal. Each selected a trusted family member to make end-of-life decisions, if Greenwoods were incapable of doing so. Each expressed to family and friends (me included) that they did not wish to linger in their twilight months. Greenwoods did what Washington law allows to avoid dawdling death. Greenwoods even hatched a private compact of mutual suicide assistance, which Washington law does not (and should not) permit. Still, Buck and Pearl suffered exactly the prolonged deaths they sought to avoid.

Buck's short term memory faded. One day, Buck accidentally knocked frail Pearl down. Osteoporitic bones fractured. Pearl healed, but Buck spiraled downward. During their last day at home together, panicked Buck flagged down traffic to warn of dangers apparent only to Buck. Buck entered Alzheimer's care. Buck's ability to recognize loved ones deteriorated. Months later, I found Buck smooching another resident at a communal movie in the locked living room. I asked him to introduce his friend. He said, "This is Pearl, my wife." Finally, all recollection departed. Buck died from an intestinal bleed after a year.

Pearl visited Buck daily at first. As he declined, as he ceased to recognize Pearl, her heart broke. The stress of caring for Buck, combined with Pearl's own failing health, sapped her. She elected to stop eating, which is an option open to Washington residents. It turns out that intentional starvation is harder than one might imagine. Hunger induces weakness and delusion. Delusional starving people lose resolve; they eat. So Pearl started her own grinding demise.

> **SURRENDER LIFE ONLY UNDER DIRE PROTEST.**

She died in the company of her valued Ethiopian caregiver, after months of semi-consciousness.

Suicide is complex, both ethically and socially. I cannot presume to tell you how, or whether, to live. In my view, life is generally worth living. Life should be surrendered only under dire protest. Depressed persons should be medicated and loved. Despairing persons should be encouraged and helped and loved. Ill persons should be treated, their pain addressed, and loved. Nevertheless, I am not competent to ask terminally ill persons to persevere despite their pain, or emptiness, or fervent wish to flee life. Nor do I believe you are competent to do so.

Can a preference for death be, under certain circumstances, reasonable? R-1000, the death with dignity act, preserves to the terminally ill individual, with appropriate review and counsel, choice about ending one's life, with the skilled assistance and comfort of one's physician. Thanks for voting for R-1000. I did.

**GRANDFATHER BILL, WHOM I NEVER KNEW,
WITH HIS DOGS, WHOM I NEVER MET.**

32
DISPUTE WITH AN ABSENT FRIEND

My friend Arthur has passed. We, his friends, grieve. We imagine his end. We shudder. We sob. We find ourselves impotent, just when we would act. We sigh and inquire, of ourselves, of the universe, of gods. We ponder fruitlessly. We suffer a splinter none can pull. Arthur's departure makes us, for a time, unwell.

Arthur's absence decimates his spouse. We share Evelyn's pain dimly, like the whisper of a distant cataclysm of thunder. We hold her in our hearts; we honor her need for solitude. When she is able, we will embrace her. During her pained absence, we bank the fire of our affection for Evelyn, keeping its embers lively.

Arthur's death erases from our futures his quirks, his affections, and funny little trinkets. We shall not again enjoy Arthur's strong helping arms, his silly boots, his contrarian views, his oddness. Arthur shall never again plummet us into boisterous laughter. For Arthur is gone. Our lives are diminished by subtraction. A piece of us has perished.

Arthur died by his own hand, I am told. Some of us, in important dialogues of the past, have asked Arthur to decline such action. Many of us believe such action wrong. Arthur has voted against us in that regard.

For me, after Arthur's act, I restrain judgment. I do not know Arthur's pain. I do not know what particular problems he sought to remedy by suicide. I do not know what he deemed essential in those critical moments of decision. I do know that, for Arthur, his reasons were sufficient to himself. I do know Arthur suffered neuro-chemical imbalances. I do know Arthur, in his great intelligence, found much in our culture insufferable, things most of us simply ignore. Most essentially, I know that I do not know the deep inwardness of others, including Arthur. I see that many are hounded by feelings

> **WHAT LIES IN THE INACCESSIBLE DEPTHS OF OTHERS?**

of inadequacy, by life puzzles they cannot solve, by the limited remediation love offers. For all, life contains suffering. For some, living becomes torment. Death provides a lasting analgesic, the pain-killer that one day relieves every agony. Arthur needed relief; he found it.

Arthur's solution to his pain increases ours. For those who remain in the wake of death, questions linger. When we are done denying that death has touched us, we progress to regret. We speak within. We could have done this. We should have done that. "If only I had…," one thinks, imagining, like a child, that good behavior inoculates against bad outcomes. To all who read this page, I say plainly: Arthur did not die of our deficiencies.

We suffer many flaws. Our defects do not, however, explain what overtook Arthur. Arthur's departure is a mystery shrouded in the inaccessible depths of Arthur's essence. Even Arthur himself grasped only a portion of what moved him to act. We would appreciate a simple answer to Arthur's death. None exists.

ARTHUR

33

ARTHUR THE ROTARIAN

EULOGY FOR A FRIEND

Rotary International is a group of 1.2 million do-gooders. Rotarians have no creed, other than to help others locally and internationally. Rotarians, on the whole, are a staid bunch. Most Rotarians tend toward conservatism. Because of this, Rotarians can be—well—boring and excessively earnest. Still, Rotary is a remarkable organization. I am proud to be a Rain City Rotarian. I was also proud that Arthur was a Rain City Rotarian.

In some ways, Arthur broke Rotary's mold. He was not conservative in either soul or opinion. Arthur liked to shock people. Arthur's vocabulary was often better suited to a crab boat than polite society. Rain City Rotary established a special weekly award, called the Tawdry Trout, for that Rotarian who during our meeting cursed or injected topics more appropriate for taverns. Arthur was frequently awarded the Tawdry Trout. Evelyn blushed more than once. Arthur had the checkered past one might expect of a brash Alaskan crabber. Arthur survived the Bering Strait because he was just plain tougher than those seas. Arthur lost digits, fingers and toes, to the battle, but not his sense of humor. Few Rotarians bring their parrots to meetings. Fewer still wear dead fingers around their necks or carry toes in their pockets. Arthur is the only Rotarian who ever gave me a switchblade. Arthur thought I needed one.

In my view, Arthur was a perfect Rotarian. His idiosyncrasies were a front. Arthur's oddnesses hid a great heart. Arthur gave to others. Arthur cared more than most of us. These traits are the essence of Rotary. I should be specific. Arthur loved our service projects, especially when he got to cut things down with his chainsaw, blast things clean with his pressure washer, and haul other people's garbage to the dump in his giant white truck. Arthur bought all the bowling

> **WORRY IS A MISUSE OF IMAGINATION.**

shoes from Leilani Lanes when it closed its doors. He threw them in his truck and took them to a homeless shelter. Our little dog Lucy died slowly of complications from a brain tumor. Arthur offered to put her down for us, knowing what a great grief that day would be for Kim and me. Arthur brought a piece of homespun wisdom to each Rotary meeting for Arthur's Words of Wisdom. One night he recited the King James Ten Commandments from memory. Arthur chided us that "Worry is a misuse of the imagination." On Arthur and Evelyn's tenth wedding anniversary, Arthur told us: "When you draw the Queen of Hearts, put down the deck and play the hand." He also shared this fisherman's gem: "Before you drink water, remember that fish mate in it."

We go on. Arthur does not. We will heal. There will be a scar where Arthur was excised from our souls and our community. When we rub that indelible mark, we shall fondly recall the exuberant uniqueness of Arthur the Rotarian.

34
ADIPOSE OSCILLATIONS

I am a sixty-six year old, 350 pound, obese male. I first experienced dramatic weight gain at age nine, which subsided. I was again overweight at age twelve, which also subsided. At age eighteen, I weighed 195 pounds and was fit. At age forty-three, I weighed 378 pounds and was fit. My diet history, in pounds lost, is: 1973: 30, 1974: 30, 1976: 58, 1980: 75, 1982: 50, 1985: 30, 1991: 25, 1995: 35, 1996: 107, 2004: 90, 2005: 22, 2011: 44, 2015: 23, 2018: 38, 2019: 27. There were other less significant weight loss efforts as well. Aggregately, I have lost more than 674 pounds and gained more than 900. I have presently regained 153 pounds from my post-law school low weight of 197 pounds. I conclude from these facts that I am a slow learner, and doomed to suffer a "pounding" in fat school.

I studied and followed the Atkins low-carbohydrate diet with success. I studied and followed a version of the LEARN (lifestyle, exercise, attitudes, relationships, nutrition) calorie-restriction diet with success. I did intermittent fasting for a year; ten days was my longest continuous fast. Every diet, even inane ones, has succeeded. My attempts at weight maintenance, in multiple theories, have failed. I lose weight (with great effort and no small measure of suffering), but reliably. But I regain lost pounds readily and reliably. I have grown food neurotic in the process.

My parents were obese. One sister is thin; she, unaccountably, does not like dessert. A second sister would be obese but for constant dieting. My genetic grandparents were either large or obese.

I draw the following conclusions regarding obesity, which have been influenced by my science reading of the last forty years, as well as *Rethinking Thin* by Gina Kolata (2007), and by my life experience and knowledge of other obese persons.

Obesity is genetic. Hunger fundamentally drives behavior, like thirst. DNA determines body weight, as it does height. Intention is no match for predilection.

CONCLUSION #1: Many obesity commonplaces mislead us:
1) *Fat people suffer psychological dysfunction.* This is wrong. Thin and fat people experience identical psychological dysfunctions. No psychopathology unique to weight gain exists.
2) *Fat people are immoral.* This is wrong. Fat people are not lazy, weak-willed, doltish gluttons. Dieting obese persons behave as do starving thin people. Hunger trumps intention to lose weight, in the long run. Thin people are not necessarily good; they are lucky by birth.
3) *Good parenting prevents obesity.* This is wrong. Adoption and twin studies show that, regardless of home environment, fat people gain and thin people do not. Fat people seldom lose; thin people seldom gain. Parental models matter little.
4) *Changing behaviors changes obesity.* This is wrong. No behavioral changes decrease body mass more than ten percent for obese persons. Obese persons never, over a period of years, maintain stable body weight; they gain.

5) *Fat people can become thin people.* This is wrong. Thin obese people are starving; they exhibit behaviors identical to starving thin people. Fattened thin people lose automatically; thinned fat people gain automatically. The tiny fraction of dieters who achieve permanent thinness almost always obsess about fat (deprivation neurosis).

6) *Regarding food, people are the same.* This is wrong. Fat people differ fundamentally from thin persons in genetics, brain architecture, satiety, fat cell count, and set point. Fat people eat more because they experience more hunger.

7) *Fat is unhealthy.* This is wrong. Overweight persons have lower mortality than thin or obese people. No one knows if overweight is intrinsically unhealthy, though one would never surmise such from listening to doctors. Correlation is not causation. Americans are taller than one hundred years ago. Americans are also fatter. Obesity may indicate improvements in national health care and nutritional success.

CONCLUSION #2: **People, thin and fat alike, persecute fat people.** Society permits (or encourages) fat prejudice. Fat persons are no more likely than thin people to be lazy, stupid, gluttonous, uncaring, self-centered, or uncontrolled. Obese persons frequently suffer impaired self-image, poverty, dearth of social relations, lack of credibility, social rejection, and self-deprecation due, at least in part, to societal prejudice toward and incomprehension of their obesity. Americans view fat people as aesthetically defective, and America loves beauty. America hates fat people, though most Americans are fat. Americans should reconsider.

CONCLUSION #3: **Some battles cannot be won.** A tiny minority of fat people permanently lose more than ten percent of their weight. A fraction of those victors do so without fixating, without making weight loss the core of life. The critical question is: Am I part of that minuscule fragment who become non-obsessed fat people of normal weight? What path lies open to perpetual semi-starvation without deprivation neurosis? At this late date, I have arrived at answers to these two questions: No and None.

SOFIE

35
INTIMACY

Sharon, an educated and professionally successful woman, stood five foot five and weighed as much as a Seahawk lineman. Despite her many professional accomplishments, Sharon's self-image resembled 1946 Hiroshima. Sharon despaired. Her doctor advised: exercise, reduce portions, eat foods higher in water volume, lower in fat content, maybe an antidepressant. But Sharon's primary problem was not obesity. She was starving relationally. Sharon was an intimacy anorexic. Sharon refused to date or relate. She abstained from her loving family. Sharon practiced unhappiness, and had a knack for it. Hating herself, Sharon insisted all others should hate her also. People who valued Sharon were, in her view, profoundly mistaken.

Aristotle (Athenian, 4th century B.C.) insisted: "Man is a social being, and designed by nature to live with others; accordingly the happy man must have society, for he has everything that is naturally good" (*Nichomachean Ethics*, Book IX, §ix). Cicero (Roman, 1st century B.C.) went further: "The effect of friendship is to make, as it were, one soul out of many" (*De Amicitia*, §xxv). A human alone is a jagged fragment of his or her real self. Sharon was alone.

With considerable persistence, friendship grew. Our hope and esteem infected Sharon. She concluded she might be able to lose a little weight. Haltingly, she reduced her size and confronted self-loathing. Sharon struggled through the protein diet, then transitioned to Weight Watchers. She lost about half her body weight, and has heeded all her physician's advice. Sharon still wars with both weight gain and her emotions. Pounds return, inexorably. But she now trains herself in the skills of well-being. Aristotle urged that "Happiness is a form of activity" (*id.*). All must learn the art of felicity. Sharon is getting the knack of it, with some trepidation.

> **A LONE HUMAN
> IS A JAGGED FRAGMENT.**

Sharon had professional photos taken recently. Her eyes twinkled. She thinks, but cannot yet voice, that she may be loveable. She may date. She may become a mother. She may be beautiful.

To us, she has always been so.

LUCY ON HER BIG OUTING

36
JOHN HENRY: ELEGY

Among American tall tales, John Henry was an African American steel-driver, a towering railroad man. Henry pitted bone and sinew against steam drilling hammers of profit-crazed railways—and won. To confront worker displacement, Henry challenged his mechanical replacement to a steel-driving contest, crushing holes in granite, blasting, gouging rail tunnels through bedrock. Prevailing, Henry's heart quit. The machine triumphed, *sans* glory. Transcontinental commerce coursed through Henry's veins; America's economic titan leapt from his loins. American workers in every age are John Henry.

Tall tales enshrine ideals. Real people shrink by comparison. Most of us are, frankly, Lilliputians astride mythic Gullivers. Nevertheless, Shoreline boasted its own John Henry. John Henry of Shoreline was a lawyering man. He pitted brains and street saavy against human nuttiness—and won (sometimes). Wisdom pulsed in John's veins. Fragments of the best of Shoreline sprang from our John Henry.

John Henry excelled at law. To my knowledge, only John possessed a Superior Court judge's epistle, penned after trial, commending lawyerly courtesy and efficiency. Colleagues sought John's guidance, I in their number. John delivered insight with growl and grin, as pontiffs issue bulls or saints beatitudes. John erred, but never thoughtlessly. John castigated foolishness and petulance. John hoped for better than America gives most days. Nothing escaped scrutiny. Our Henry slung cross-examination as his

> **ENJOY YOUR FRIENDS GREEDILY.**

mythic counterpart wielded a hammer. He drove penetrating, impertinent questions. He was good at it.

To know John as lawyer missed the lion's share. Carolyn, John's widow to whom he was immensely devoted, is a national treasure; were she bullion, America would deposit her in Fort Knox and return to the gold standard. That portion of his great heart not expended on family and hearth, John Henry lavished upon Rotary. On a bad day, Rotarians lunch, laugh, and leave. But on good days (and there are many such), Rotary creates human peace and promotes personal and communal goodness. John treasured this latter Rotary; he ridiculed the former. John pressed Rotarians to build relational bridges to odd, foreign, uncomfortable places--in our hearts, in Shoreline, across oceans. He promoted peace, not by yammering platitudes, but by making friends of persons who were not.

I know John Henry had to leave us; it was his time. Seneca (Roman, 1st century A.D.) said: "To me, the thought of my dead friends is sweet and appealing. For I have had them as if I should one day lose them; I have lost them as if I have them still. . . . Let us greedily enjoy our friends, because we do not know how long this privilege will be ours" (Epistle LXIII, *On Grief for Lost Friends*).

I hold John Henry in my heart. I miss his growl. And that is no tall tale.

SAM AND ANOTHER BAILEY

37
KIDIST

My petite, bristle-haired bride flew halfway around the earth, and changed my life for (at least) eleven years. Once home, Kim laid a photo of a beautiful seven year old African girl on our office counter. *This is Kidist; she needs tuition. For more than a decade.* I gulped.

Kim traveled with seventy-five Rotarians to Ethiopia to help that nation administer Salk polio vaccine to its fourteen million children. (Rotarians do amazing things.) While in Ethiopia's capital, Addis Ababa, Kim visited the German Church School. The organization, funded by Finns and Germans, serves Addis's poorest children. Each year, 400 interviews yield eighty admissions. Those children enter first grade, each sponsored by a German, Finn, or (now) American. The modest monthly sums sent are split between the child and her family--kids must eat at home to learn at school. German Church School curriculum integrates blind and sighted students. All learn not only numerical and textual literacy, but also karate and character. In the midst of Ethiopia's grinding poverty, in a culture that undervalues women, Kidist might have a chance.

I did not leap to support Kidist. I have reservations. Why cannot Ethiopia nurture Ethiopia? Are we creating a continent economically addicted to foreign largesse? Will education dollars be squandered instructing a girl in a culture that suppresses women? Does German Church School teach Ethiopian children to be good Europeans? Are there no children in need of education in Shoreline? I struggled, conflicted. As Goethe (German, 19th century A.D.) complained, "Two souls dwell, alas! in my breast" (*Faust*, Part I). When my skirmish subsided, I consented.

ENLARGE THE CIRCLE OF CARE.

I needed to consent. Kidist is no macroeconomic microcosm; geopolitical conundra must desist. Kidist needs help. I also consented *for me*. My soul is small. It needs stretching, like sore muscles before a jog. Thighs complain when stretched; so too my heart. There are great spirits for whom vast compassion appears effortless: the Gandhis, the Schweitzers, the Mother Teresas. Their hearts enfold the planet. Not mine. I care at home. Most days, my soul extends to Shoreline. Few days does it reach across America. Never has it extended beyond oceans. So, little Kidist scares me. I may learn to care about someone on the other side of the planet. I might have to visit. I might grow.

Spooky girl, that Kidist.

SOFIE

38
TEACHER

The best teachers speak little. They scout poignant, instructive moments and shepherd pupils to them. Fine educators midwife pregnant events. Silent experience writes young minds, indelible.

So my Father taught me. His course book was veterinary outings. "Son, get in the car. First autopsy." Dad's white Volkswagen bug bounced down dirt roads trailing a storm of dust. A rancher's corral held the bloated corpse of a prized cow. Dad murmured with the cattleman about contagion. They shook hands. The farmer ambled off. A scalpel slid down the bovine belly. Tugging pulled aside the beast's hide. Tissues shone, pink and white and yellow. Fluids leaked. "Move away, son." I stepped back. "Farther. Over there." Howard Lancaster pointed to the distant side of the corral. I slid through the rails into a field. A scalpel edge glistened in late morning sun, then nicked the pressurized abdomen. Whoosh! An emerald stream jetted from the wound, arcing across the corral, a firehose of grassy glop. The vaporous mess landed on my feet, painting sneakers and shins green and putrid. "Not quite far enough," Father chuckled, and beckoned me. Methodically, the cow dismantled. As hours passed, parts spread across the enclosure: intestines, heart, liver, lungs. All good. Then, working inside the neck, dad grunted. He excised a large artery impaled by rusty wire. "Careless barnwork," he whispered. Some hand lost baling wire while breaking bales of winter feed. The cow ate it. That metal strand crept from a stomach through bovine flesh until fatally situated. The farmer nodded and sighed. At least his herd faced no epidemic.

> **SILENT CLASSROOMS TEACH MUCH TO THOSE WHO LISTEN.**

My middle sister tells a calving tale. Father roused Karen in the wee dark. (Why do cows always birth at ungodly hours?) The distressed heifer lay exhausted from long labor. Donning an armpit-length glove, he probed the birth canal to his elbow. The calf lay wrong. Dad could not grasp its feet. His arm was too big. He hatched a plan with pre-teen Karen. My skinny-armed sister reached into the cow's birth canal, seized the calf's legs. Dad pulled Karen and Karen hung on to the calf until it came free. The steaming, slimy newborn slid onto the stall floor. The cow grunted relief, and licked her baby.

My youngest sister, Jill, was Father's prize student. She too pulled calves and de-horned steers and autopsied victims. She helped spay dogs and cats and de-scent skunks. Jill watched giant pills threaded down horse gullets, and pondered the plight of listless goldfish. But, unlike Karen and me, Jill learned Father's trade. At seven, she cleaned kennels. She advanced to reception. But she kept going. Jill learned everything else. She assisted surgeries, billed, ran the front office, screened problem cases, herded the staff. She still does, though the clinic passed hands since Dad retired. Among his brood, Jill learned most in Father's silent classroom.

Horace (Roman, 1st century B.C.) wrote: "Deep in the cavern of the infant's breast / The father's nature lurks, and lives anew" (*Odes*, 4.4). We three children of Howard hope so. Howard Lancaster turns eighty years of age on July 2, 2008. It is a privilege to be his child.

[Howard died of Parkinson's at age eighty-eight.]

RUBY

39
MENTORS

John Terris invaded Dalton Gardens in a dying Volkswagen, ink still drying on his music education diploma. Coeur d'Alene School District assigned John six elementary music programs. One was Dalton. I sat in John's first band class, an undented rental trumpet in my hand. Our herd of noxious sixth graders made stupid blats and giggled wildly. John pattered in, unnoticed amid childish cacophony. His baton timidly tapped the conductor's stand. Nothing happened. Louder he rapped. Two of thirty heads turned. We limped through the lesson. "This is a clarinet. That is a note." John urged daily practice; few obeyed.

By next lesson John changed. He barked. He broke a baton on his stand. Twelve year olds cowered, instruments in laps. John tossed a non-compliant few out of class. One at a time, John listened as we butchered the week's assignment. He reassigned seats based on our performances. One girl wept silently. John offered free tutoring on Saturdays. I came. It was a price my family could afford to pay. My parents compensated John in the coin of the poor; he was invited to dinner.

Saturdays held wonder. John taught me instruments and music. That, however, proved the smaller part. John taught life. He spoke as a peer, the first adult to treat me so. John entertained my ideas and confusions seriously, and criticized them seriously. He nurtured a kernel of maturity in me. Our dialogue rambled: politics, pain, girls, death, science fiction, beauty. John did not lecture. We conversed. He told me

> **INVESTING IN YOUNG MINDS IS TIME WELL SPENT.**

more of his life than I knew of mine. John taught me that a man's dearest friend is himself. And that investing in young minds is time well spent. I taught John to ski and goof around.

Xenophon (Athenian, 4th century B.C.) said: "Socrates spent his life in lavishing his gifts and rendering the greatest services to all who cared to receive them. For he always made his associates better men before he parted with them" (*Memorabilia*, Book I). So too John Terris. May you have or be, at least once in your life, a mentor.

ANOTHER KATIE

40
TEAMS

"Big Daddy" Rasmussen taught me football.

I slouched into the first practice, ambivalent. At fourteen, books, not blocking, fascinated me. It showed on the field. I rapidly earned the sad distinction of slowest man over forty yards. Fifty push-ups defeated me. August scorcher two-a-days doused my wan enthusiasm: sore muscles, dehydration, exhaustion. Big Daddy saw. He demoted me to junior varsity. I was "black dog," as Winston Churchill (English, 20th century A.D.) called his despondencies.

Just before our first game, things changed. Big Daddy had a birthday. The coaches promised festivities. I, being a fool, anticipated short practice followed by cake and juice. Hell broke upon me. Big Daddy barked. We ran, did push- and sit-ups, leg lifts, then ran and vomited and started all over again. After two hours, all bodies screamed for water. Big Daddy brought out a hose, turned it on, and let us watch. No drinking. Then we ran and puked and ran again. At the beginning of the third hour, something glimmered within. We smashed into one another. "Learn pain," Big Daddy mumbled. More illumination dawned. Grass drills—kick

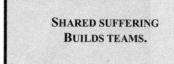

SHARED SUFFERING
BUILDS TEAMS.

your legs behind you, land on your sternum, get up and do it again. After that hour, I (and others) got it. Insight trumpeted. We suffer together. We achieve together. We might win together. We were a team.

I improved. The Japanese say that defeat teaches better than victory. My football skills remained modest on a good day. But it turned out I could remember what every player was supposed to do on every play. I became our huddle's walking encyclopedia of what Big Daddy wanted. Muscles grew. Confidence followed successes. Award time arrived. I received "Most Improved Player." Read that "not as bad as when he began, but not that good either." As a team, we won, mostly.

My reward came. I got promoted to the varsity squad for one play in the last game of the season. I ran onto the field. A lumbering defensive tackle crushed me into a puddle of protoplasm. I was ecstatic.

Give them what they need, and boys become teams.

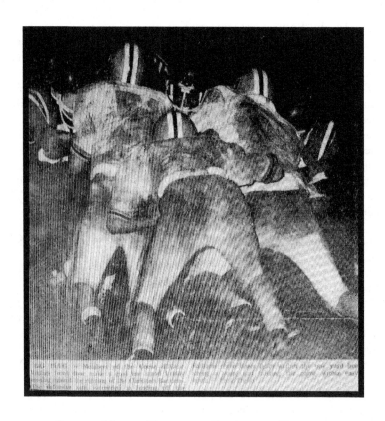

**COEUR D'ALENE VIKINGS V. CLARKSTON BANTAMS
OCTOBER 1970**

41

CHILDLESS

"Are you sure?" asked my urologist, inquisitive professional wrinkle in his brow. "Thirty is young. This procedure is probably irreversible." I nodded: "Knew since I was eleven. Snip on." The doctor shaved me where I don't shave. He made an incision, retrieved two half-centimeter sections of vas, and threw on a stitch or two. Weeks later, I gave a sample. A bored nurse peered in her microscope. "Zero count. Good to go." It was 1984. I was sterile.

I have no children. Yet, I love children. I have spent years educating, playing with, and parenting children—the children of others. Some big reasons I chose childless parenting are:

First, overpopulation. In 1800, the planetary population reached a bit less than one billion persons, twice Earth's carrying capacity, apart from mass production of grains and livestock. Today, almost seven billion humans live; population has more than doubled since my birth. Crowding hobbles humans. Problems wax: poverty, disease, deforestation, pollution, species extinction, unsustainable economies, military adventurism, resource depletion and scarcity, to name a few. Thomas Robert Malthus (British, 18th century A.D.) believed that population waxes inexorably to the limit of sustenance, at which limit follows misery in premature death (*An Essay on the Principal of Population*). Ingenuity forestalls Malthus's dystopia. But his vision grips much of Africa.

Second, freedom. Procreating is not mandatory. Every human needs to parent. Not every human needs to copy herself. Oral contraception (and vasectomy) makes childlessness a serious option. Many imagine fulfillment lies in child-bearing. For some, it does. Others (far too few) imagine living without offspring; they embrace riches beyond gamete mix and match. Still others never consider childlessness, but should. I am no mathematician (so, doubt this calculation). If only one in every ten couples rears two children to adulthood, human population would plummet under one billion, a sustainable number. Biological parents could then open their families to parenting support from others. Every child might have three or four or five parents. Raw arithmetic demands we open the arms of family wider than genetic contribution.

Third, responsibility. Many, including many with children, do not want children. They bore babies because their parents wanted grandkids, or their spouse sought pregnancy, or their contraception failed, or they never really considered alternatives. Persons who yearn to parent and have capacity for parenting should bear children. Peter De Vries (American, 20th century A.D.) said, "There are times when parenthood seems like nothing but feeding the mouth that bites you" (*The Tunnel of Love*, 5). Parenting is a decades-long, often unrewarding, road. Parenting requires all day, every day attention. Those devoted to other endeavors should not procreate.

I have not mentioned government; laws won't help. Rather, we need parenting conversation. Habits change when values change. Our values grow when we ponder possibilities in fond friendship. Population control is on the horizon, a few billion conversations away.

LUCY AND KIM IN HAMLIN PARK SNOW

42
BEAR CHILDREN ONLY IF YOU MUST

SECTION 7.16 OF *CULL: CHOOSING WELL*

7.16.   *Fecundity.*   **Simple Rule: Bear children only if you must.** Runaway human reproduction threatens human well-being. Communities and members, as well as the human species as a whole, suffer from overpopulation. Please grip firmly in mind: your decision whether or not to make babies is the stuff of which our overpopulation problem consists. Curbing human reproduction is a primary challenge. Historical human events have been driven by the scourge of exploding population. In the deep past, dramatically fewer humans strode the planet. But their survival, despite their relative sparseness, lay in peril, for their technologies were primitive. Technology has averted apocalypse under the burden of bloated human numbers, but cannot dodge the ultimate debacle.[67]

7.16.1.   *Population Numbers.* We lack perspective on overpopulation. Perhaps some numbers help. The entire population of humans on earth derives from a few thousand individuals (perhaps only a few hundred) clinging to the southern tip of South Africa approximately 164 thousand years ago during a terrible global glaciation-induced drought.[68] Before the invention of agriculture, human population growth approximated zero. In 8,000 B.C., there were around 6 million people globally. In 1 A.D., perhaps 250 million persons existed. In 1600 A.D., there were about 500 million persons on earth. In 1800, one billion humans inhabited the planet. In 1930, the population of earth reached two billion; in 1960, three billion; in 1974, four billion; in 1986, five billion; in 1999, six billion; in 2012, seven billion. To the present, the human population has doubled once per millennium on average, but the population more than doubled

---

[67] Gwynne Dyer notes that overpopulation created the State, government coercion, loss of personal freedoms, poorer life, class distinctions, and seething resentments that permeate modern cultures. She says, "The human race had dug itself a very deep pit, and we would be living in it for a very long time." Dyer, *War: The Lethal Custom*, 145-146.

[68] Marean, "When the Sea Saved Humanity," 55, and [♪] Wade, *Before the Dawn*, 52.

twice in the last 200 years and once in the last forty years.[69] Numbers, unfortunately, seldom persuade most people of anything whatsoever.

7.16.2. *Population Propositions.* Joel Cohen adds sobering propositions to the statistical circumstance: 1) stopping population growth without coercion will take, at a minimum, decades, 2) if birth rates do not fall, then death rates will inevitably rise, 3) governmental edicts do not work to reduce birth rates (though some forms of government assistance seem to be of some effect), 4) parents cannot on average bear more children than required to replace themselves due to the limited resources of the earth, and 5) the limits of earth's resources to support our present technological and institutional structures will be reached within the next 100 years, barring a dramatic change in human behaviors.[70]

Thomas Malthus, in his famous nineteenth century essay, stated his dour moral assessment that, because food is necessary and sex unavoidable, when sufficient resources exist, men and women will breed heedlessly, until they again lack resources, and are once more mired in misery and vice.[71] Malthus certainly underestimated the ingenuity of thoughtful men in avoiding disaster, and has also overstated the compulsive imperative of child-generating sex. Malthus drinks deep nineteenth-century England's putrid class bias and seems convinced that hyperpopulation results from abject dearth of self-restraint in the lower classes. Perhaps we have had enough of blaming the poor for their plight, and so can spit out Malthus's class prejudice in the same gob with his unbridled pessimism. Despite the flaws of Malthus's argument, one still must account for the fact that human coitus appears to have none but the most tenuous nexus with calculations of global well-being. The horrid net effect of pregnancy in the hyperpopulous twenty-first century is that the birth of this woman's baby insures the death of another woman's baby elsewhere, usually in the Third World. That dark soot besmirches every newborn.

It would appear that women of many cultures, often abysmally poor, are learning that one benefits one's existing children by declining to add to their numbers. One doubts that humans are having less sex. We do seem to be having less sex that leads to pregnancy. That trend corresponds directly with the meaningful education of girls and women.[72] We can augment the trend,

---

[69] These population numbers derive (with the exception of the estimates of population in 1999 and 2012) from Joel Cohen's definitive work on population. Cohen, *How Many People Can the Earth Support?*, 32, 76-77.

[70] Cohen, *How Many People Can the Earth Support?*, 11, 16.

[71] Malthus, *The Principle of Population*, 11, 37.

[72] Cohen, *How Many People Can the Earth Support?*, 65.

creating controlled population deflation without coercion and without famine, plague, or war. Teach women. Offer them and their children better, more stable lives. One can also attempt to teach men, but many among them may prove ineducable.[73]

One draws a conclusion from the statistics and perspectives mentioned above. Future humans will, either by choice or compulsion of circumstance, breed less frequently or expect much less than do earth's present denizens. One way or another, the human population will have zero growth in the near future.[74] We should breed less frequently because we choose to do so. Humanity should hope for a life ever so much *better* than do our contemporaries. To accomplish this delightful outcome, I ask you, Kate, and every couple undertaking the joy of coitus, to bear children only if you must.

7.16.3. *Moral Decision.* The conviction that earth is overpopulated with humans is a moral, not mathematical, proposition. Any opinion of the realistic carrying capacity of the planet expresses deeply held values and assumptions.[75] This fact grows clear when one learns that some thoughtful people estimate the optimal human population to be mere millions, while others assert that a possible human population might be one trillion.[76] In determining that number of inhabitants the earth should bear, one deliberates a host of specifically moral considerations that serve to sketch limits to human population.

One weighs, in proposing an optimal population, the following:

7.16.3.1. *Quality of Life.* For populations over one billion (an equivocal number), population and quality of life are inversely proportional. As population increases, quality of life decreases, and vice versa. One requires sufficient human numbers to maintain redundancy of economic specializations and to

---

[73] An expedient so simple sounds preposterous, when arrayed against a reproductive plight so out of control. Yet, the same conclusion was reached by early feminist author, Charlotte Gilman. In her 1915 utopia, asexual propagation sustains a population comprising only women. These grand creatures, sequestered from masculine depredations, restrain their reproductive impulses by education and reasoned care for the children who do exist and who will come to exist. Gilman, *Herland*, 58-61. Though I find Gilman's sexism unwarranted and hyperbolic, her confidence that women devoted to parenthood will curb natural impulses to insure the well-being of their children and long-term community is heartening. Robert Engelman warns that Africa's population, currently 1.2 billion, could mushroom to 6.1 billion by 2100 A.D. His solution is not coercive government interventions, for in population control, one must push without pushing. He prescribes, rather, a broad program that aims to improve the lot of women, educating them, and offering them the technical means to control family size. Engelman, "Six Billion in Africa," 63. It appears I am not alone in being a population simpleton.

[74] Cohen, *How Many People Can the Earth Support?*, 154.

[75] Cohen offers a helpful analysis of assumptions and issues in assessing earth's human carrying capacity. Cohen, *How Many People Can the Earth Support?*, 261-296.

[76] Cohen, *How Many People Can the Earth Support?*, 177, 212.

weather unanticipated insults to the human community (say, plague or meteor devastations). One wishes at all costs to avoid a global Tasmanian Regress.[77] But beyond mere sufficiency, additional humans degrade quality of life, rendering our existence an unrelenting monotony of outfitting one more member with essentials we just supplied to his predecessor, *ad infinitum*.[78]

7.16.3.2.   *Non-Human Species.* Non-human species deserve space to prosper and resources to consume. Their ranges support non-human lives, and are savaged by deforestation and plowing. Humans are members of a global biome, and dramatically dependent upon it. No other biome can conserve us, or our vegetable and animal and microbial companions. Conserving our living companions conserves humanity. Further, other species deserve moral status. Our interpersonal relations exceed the merely human, including, analogically, all living things. Human altruism should extend to the weal of our non-human companions.[79] As we expand the list of "isms" we wish to excise from our collective soul, speciesism should go the way of racism.

7.16.3.3.   *Other Endeavors.* Surely we shall always invest some effort merely sustaining human biofunctions. What portion of human effort should be directed to that end? To what extent should we be diverted from other efforts? Shall arts and sciences and explorations be abandoned to the extent incompatible with the demands of producing as many persons as possible? Producing sustenance for life is laborious and often boring. Where one labors over nothing but primers, one seldom exults in masterpieces. He who plows seldom sculpts. Excessive sweat of the brow drowns creativity. Life can, and

---

[77] [♪] Ridley, *The Rational Optimist*, 80-83. Ridley details the "Tasmanian regress." Tasmania is an island off southern Australia. People walked there during lower Ice Age sea levels, but were marooned when sea levels rose. The Stone Age immigrants to Tasmania suffered a loss of essential technologies already in their possession due to lack of outside infusion of ideas and insufficient numbers to specialize all the critical skills. The Tasmanians degenerated from fishing and maritime sufficiency to clubbing seals.

[78] In hyperpopulation, other endeavors starve (or, at least, should starve). But the arts and sciences live. They prosper by selective attention. We have carved well-being for the fortunate gated cultures of blessed life. In so doing, we have wrongly relegated most of humanity to an impoverished ghetto. We err. This moral error deadens the ethical existence of the blessed, feeding them the false tale that the dying babies of the ghetto are not their problem, or at least not a solvable problem. From the perspective of the ghetto, our morality is sociopathic. Were we less willing to acquiesce to the deaths of millions of outsiders to preventable scourges, over-population would squeeze to the front of civilization's agenda. Albert Weisman proposes that an optimum human population for the planet is the "number of humans who can enjoy a standard of living that the majority of us would find acceptable." That is something like the lifestyle of Europeans. Weisman, *Countdown*, 43.

[79] Peter Singer would extend moral consideration (and exclude mere instrumental use) to all sentient creatures, those who experience pain or pleasure, and, therefore, have interests. Singer, *The Expanding Circle*, 123. Albert Schweitzer seeks an ethic that reverences all life of whatever sort, with special emphasis on sympathy for animals. Ethical humans, according to Schweitzer, help all life, including leaves, flowers, and insects. They shrink from injuring any living thing. Schweitzer, *The Philosophy of Civilization*, 296-297 (Chapter 25), 310 (Chapter 26).

should, consist in more dynamic enterprises than merely insuring that every ill-deliberated birth reaches nurtured adulthood. Do we not seek a human presence that blossoms and flourishes, not merely wilts and goes to seed? For flourishing, one requires liberal leisure and some unassigned resources. Surely, there must exist alternatives other than coercing celibacy or rearing the tiresome fruit of unbridled promiscuity.

One occasionally meets people so ignorant they could not recognize excellent life if it stood before them. None, however, do not want a good life for themselves. Perhaps we should ask everyone politely not to bear children unless they must. We could explain to all exactly what we mean and why we ask. We could even offer every human the tools and procedures that a person might require to avoid bearing unwanted children.

7.16.3.4. *Freedom to Procreate.* According to prevalent views, western "freedoms" reside in individuals and constrain public interventions. One possesses freedom from government intrusion into essentially private decisions and life choices. Nothing could be more private than procreative choice, so the story goes. No government should trample such sacred ground. This popular story has such widespread support that its net effect is to forbid discussion of decisions to procreate. Freedom-mongers fear justly; coercive governments regularly intrude wantonly. The meager list of intrusions forbidden to states should be defended. However, "individual freedom" to procreate is a relatively modern invention. Marital fertility did not drop globally until around 1970. The first inklings that factors had conjoined to make family limitation feasible arose in Europe and Japan in the eighteenth century. There exists no predictive socio-economic pattern to family limitation. Generally, family limitation must be socially acceptable, confer an advantage, and be feasible due to fertility reduction techniques.[80] In the end, families make choices about their size, or fail to do so.

Viewed from the vantage of the breadth of human existence, no decision is less private than making babies. Making babies makes the public. Children become members. Each should be entitled to a well-nurtured life of great possibility amidst a meaningful community. This fact alone makes breeding an object of common scrutiny, since it necessarily involves all members in caring and providing.

Every community needs privacy boundaries across which it shrinks to venture. Quad sociality asks members and their cadres to factor the well-being of future humans in today's family calculation. The rule "bear children only if you must" creates ethical family limitation borders for members and

---

[80] Cohen, *How Many People Can the Earth Support?*, 54-63.

for communities. No member should bear children absent strong personal motivation and sufficient resources in her cadre to nurture her child (I include fathers in this "her.") No community should impede a cadre member's natal decision once these questions have been meaningfully answered within that member's cadre.

The cadre of a potential parent consists in that person's closest friends. These have been granted permission to address all of a person's life, to intrude without rebuff, for the lives of friends are shared in common. Friends will be those who are likely to become alloparents to the child, who may provide financial support to the biological parents, who adopt the child as their own when parents perish. It is these persons who deliberate birth-decisions with anticipatory parents. Can the cadre provide needed support? What is the population of the cadre's community and what is its population trend? Are the many communities of earth managing their own population stability? Potential parents and their cadres deliberate, then decide.

Communities must note the natal decisions of their constituent cadres. Are their deliberations meaningful?[81] Are they choosing those persons best able to parent from among persons willing to bear children? Are those parents deeply motivated? Are the cadre's children being deeply nurtured? If not, why not? If not, the community must intervene to remediate the ill-deliberate child-bearing decisions by irenic means. A community may not coerce a cadre or, worse, particular parents into avoiding pregnancy. Neither may a community stand silently by, disapproving.

In the end, in a deeply interpersonal world such as Quad sociality envisions, no member has individual freedom to breed. Nor would any member desire such freedom. For life is shared. Humans, to survive as a species, must reproduce themselves each generation. No person, however, may arrogate to themselves the decision that all must suffer the depredations of hyperpopulation so that he or she may breed heedlessly.[82] The desire to have a little Tom or Susie who looks "just like you" is the self-indulgent protrusion of a deeply narcissistic iceberg in the ill-deliberate parent's heart.

---

[81] A "meaningful deliberation" is one in which those factors that generate meaningful community are embraced, and the erosions that etch meaningful community are eschewed. See Sections 1.12 and 1.13 for a description of more, and less, meaningful communities.

[82] Alan Weisman argues there are four questions that we must answer to evade a hyperpopulation disaster: a) How many people can the earthy really sustain?, b) By what nonviolent means might we convince all the various peoples of the earth that bearing many fewer children is in their best interest?, c) What other species and ecological processes are essential to human survival?, and d) How do we design an economy for a shrinking population, and, ultimately, for a stable, much smaller population? Weisman, *Countdown*, 10-32. I believe that hyperpopulation cannot be addressed without boosting the self-reflective planning capabilities of most of earth's women. That means we must invest dramatically in ending oppression of females, in their education, and in making women players in our cultural decision-making.

7.16.3.5. *Transgenerational Horizon.* What planet do we deliver to our descendants, especially our distant-in-time descendants, by the population size we elect? No component of this deliberation about population proportion deserves more attention, and none receives less. Our distant grandchildren will deem us self-absorbed moral midgets for declining to insure their needs. That we do not know their names does not render them less our own. They too are our children. They are the part of us that lives on in our absence, just as we now, for a moment, live on in the absence of progenitors. With respect to delimited resources, our consumption today benefits us, but projects most costs to our descendants. We avoid transgenerational myopia by making the weal of our future offspring a part of present identity. Every human undertaking should express our affection, concern, and commitment to unborn generations of the distant future.[83] When we consider our children's children's children and their descendants to the horizon of human existence, smaller populations appear desirable.

To return to this simple rule, "bear children only if you must," one takes as a provisional waystation the idea that a desirable human population hovers somewhere under one billion members.[84] This number is equivocal. All the functions required to generate meaningful life in Quad communities could be well supported, with cautious redundancies, by a population of that size. This estimate could be wrong. We should calculate carefully, based on our well-deliberated preferences about shared moral values. The benefits would be staggering. We might, by depopulating to mere hundreds of millions, evade our hysterical drama of attempting to produce survival infrastructure for a human population that doubles every handful of years on an accelerating treadmill to nowhere. We might, by dramatically paring our numbers, sidestep debacles of collapsing social systems crushed beneath the terror of starving, diseased billions. But my proposed number should be scrutinized for its adequacy with withering intensity. Humanity needs only that number of members that protects the human legacy into the deep future. Any greater number imperils that legacy at its root.

As a rule for member life, one should bear children only if one is inclined to and able to focus one's attention on nurturing children for the first three to

---

[83] Cohen details the thought of John O'Neill of University of Sussex, who argues that the earth is a temporal commons, even if none is owned collectively, for future generations depend upon that which we have not presently consumed. To avoid the tragedy of the commons, considered temporally, we must make the chain of generations part of present identity. Cohen, *How Many People Can the Earth Support?*, 259.

[84] Such was the conclusion of H. R. Hulett in 1970. He calculated the optimal population of the earth based on assumptions concerning the desire of many people for lives approximating those enjoyed by First World inhabitants. Though his conclusions are equivocal, they address likely preferences of most: high quality lives in sustainable social structures. Cohen, *How Many People Can the Earth Support?*, 179-183.

six years of each child's life. What's more, the infant being nurtured needs a mother who is attentive, resilient, and sensitive to the infant's communication and needs. Infatuation with one's infant appears to be necessary for secure attachment of that infant. The bored, distracted, anxious, or unwilling primary caregiver may cause anxious or avoidant attachment in their charge. Mother's absences for work shifts injure very young children. If you lack resources sufficient to enable your constant attention to your infant(s), you should reconsider making babies. By this, one does not mean that mothers cannot work. The mother's work needs to include her baby, on a hip or back, while mother attends to employment tasks.[85] The workplace can tolerate the interruptions that babies create. There are, after all, matters more important than maximizing efficiency and pecuniary return. If a mother must be absent from her child, then she must provide consistent, responsive, caring alloparents to attend the baby.[86] Absence-injuries to infants ring through life, and injure subsequent generations as well. We are appalled when babies starve. Inattentive or absent nurturance by half-hearted or much-distracted parents starves infants just as surely, and whittles the child's horizons.[87]

Procreation is a calling, not a birthright.[88] Most members lack that vocation, and should avoid pregnancy. Mere possession of ovaries and the propinquity of a willing set of testes are insufficient conditions for parenthood. Parenting well demands substantial social, emotional, psychological, and financial capital. Parenting well demands a wealth of supportive friends committed to alloparenting. Undercapitalized procreation issues those train wrecks of failed attachment and nurturance that plague present societies. Atrocities ensue. Jails flood. Frankly, many children induce great joy in

---

[85] So, our attitudes toward mothers, babies, and crying in the workplace must shift toward greater tolerance and welcome. The workplace might shift from male task-fixation alone to include a greater measure of female nurturance concern.

[86] Hrdy argues that human babies best prosper when they have *three* secure relationship on which to rely, each of which offers the intense attention and unlimited care provision the infant requires. Hrdy, *Mothers and Others*, 130.

[87] I rely on the results of attachment investigations for this bright-line rule. See [♪] Karen, *Becoming Attached*, Chapters 22-23, pages 313-357.

[88] I am asked who might be voicing such a calling, since god, in my treatment, is a monotone nullity hidden behind an impenetrable metaphysical barrier, and kithdom would seem to permit no enduring human hierarchy. Life calls people. One's circumstances summon a person to her task in life. We perceive our gifts in a matrix of persons and happenstance in which we find ourselves embedded. We recognize, if we look, that purpose for which we were born, the way we fit. One discovers purpose not in asking, What do I want?, but rather in asking, What deep need of others can I meet with my gifts and joy? David Brooks offers a nice discussion of calling. Brooks, *The Road to Character*, 21-26.

parents, but they also deliver substantial grief and suffering.[89] Children stress one's ability to befriend others, including a spouse. Children impair one's ability to care for oneself. Ill-nurtured children make parental life a living hell. Disabled children may demand unlimited and ultimate devotion. Every instant one spends parenting is an instant not otherwise invested. If you well tolerate such efforts, then you may make a good parent. If not, you may prove a lackluster caregiver. Every child deserves more. If you lack a vocation to procreate, devote your energies to an endeavor that thrills you.[90]

Those other endeavors are a second progeny. Man, considered as a member in community, propagates not only by the admixture of genes in children, but also in the creative work of fashioning the communal future and enriching the communal present.[91] Each is critical. We nurture children. We nurture communities. Without either, the human adventure grinds to a halt. Presently, humankind teeters overbalanced. We breed prolifically. Our vision of our own possible futures, however, suffers a ghastly deficit of attention. We are functionally blind to our possibilities. The number of life experiments dared by adventuresome communities wanes to a trickle, throttled by the well-intentioned regulations of coercive governments. Our technologies fascinate us. So thin is the gruel of the life pots in which those technologies stew, that the technologies often appear the stock of culture, rather than a seasoning of it. Human essence is to recognize oneself in the stream of life,

---

[89] Tolstoy offers (perhaps hyperbolic) counterpoint to the child-adulation talk that permeates our (and his) culture. Children torment parents, poisoning parents' relationships, inducing extreme anxieties, and impoverishing many. Tolstoy, *The Kreutzer Sonata*, Chapters XVI-XVIII.

[90] Thomas Andrews complains that I have failed to define the critical language of this section: "only if you must." I suggest that some parents are well-positioned to nurture children, and should be encouraged to do so. Others are less well-positioned, and should be discouraged from making babies. I answer Andrews that in this section of *Cull*, I address Kate (and persons positioned like Kate at the inception of adult life). When I consider the circumstances of mankind, which I have described above, I find that few should reproduce. "Only if you must" has, in my mumbling, a subtext that could be put, "Well, if you have considered all I have said about overpopulation and your role in human misery, and you still think it best for you and all the humans yet to be born that you should reproduce, then proceed, you foolish person." Perhaps that overstates my sentiment, but it gives a gist. I value Kate, but stand at the periphery of her cadre. I do not know what is best for her and her intimates. I oppose creating a regime in which parental fitness of members is assessed and ranked. Nor do I hope for a lottery in which everyone, except winners, is compelled to avoid pregnancy. I address Kate. I offer Kate, and the Kates of mankind, reasons not to bear. If, after substantial deliberation, Kate and her cadre find it reasonable for Kate to procreate, I am ill-positioned to gainsay their choice. Our first moral task, after nurturing ourselves, is to nurture earth's babies. In kithdom, there are no ill-nurtured babies, for mankind has put its hand to that plow in a way that now seems impractical or impossible. Andrews, in private correspondence with the author, June 5, 2016.

[91] Gustav Landauer argues for our transgenerational connectivity with past and future. He says that we, despite death, live on in the human community by our children and our deeds. Human nature consists in consensus and community, which is just where the divine lurks. Landauer, *Through Separation to Community*, 104-105.

awash in human community, wedded in one's genes and culture to all that has come before and all that will come to be. Our many babies mature in a cultural barrens. Enriching the human loam launches experimental creativity. For the possibilities of humanity depend upon the richness and depth of the cultural soil in which each generation is planted.

Our culture, and the host of folkways that have preceded our own, glorify child-bearing. Children, many argue, prove one's health, wealth, and normalcy. Children have been deemed the crown of success. Some imagine that, apart from procreation, little else matters. They link child-bearing to family itself, arguing that children make a family.[92] Some ardent proponents claim theological justification for their views.[93] Influential others (Malthus among them) believe that procreative restraint simply lies beyond human capacities, and should.[94]

Given the coercive miseries of our global human adolescence, perhaps it is understandable that parents might project upon their children their hope for simple decencies denied them in their own youths. Given the historical death rate for children, it is perhaps understandable that mates generated the maximum number of offspring, in the hope a few might survive to adulthood. Given the novelty of contraceptive technologies, one grasps that, before 1970, where mates loved, children ensued. These predicates no longer pertain. Contraceptive technologies wait on store shelves. Unwanted pregnancies are terminated. Vasectomy is simple and cheap. Most babies survive. Nurture of each is possible. And one can safely enjoy sex without procreating.[95] So, bear children only if you must.

Behaviors surrounding child-bearing have deep evolutionary roots. You harbor compulsions, of which you may be scarcely aware, to make babies.

---

[92] Day, *The Long Loneliness*, 135-136.

[93] For example, *Genesis* 1:28.

[94] Darwin argues that struggle makes man resilient, and ease makes him indolent. "Hence our natural rate of increase, though leading to many and obvious evils, must not be greatly diminished by any means. There should be open competition for all men; and the most able should not be prevented by laws or customs from succeeding best and rearing the largest number of offspring." Darwin, *The Descent of Man*, 618. Perhaps Darwin could not foresee the social mores and technologies that restrain evolutionary culling from its natural operation among humankind. Darwin's over-emphasis on competition, to the neglect of human cooperation, mars his work. In seeing the competitive engine of evolution, Darwin downplayed the tangible result of evolution in humanity: shared parenting and hyper-cooperative eusocial communities.

[95] Singer notes that we have successfully sundered sex from procreation, and so extricated ourselves from the necessity of having children. But the sundering may only be possible because evolution itself has worked indirectly in relating sex and procreation, a fracture we have exploited. Singer, *The Expanding Circle*, 132 (Chapter 5).

Making copies of itself is what DNA does. Reproduction carries life forward, and bears the deviations that aggregate into new species. Brain function, some argue, merely regulates behaviors that amplify the frequency of copying one's genes into offspring.[96] This view is unwarranted reductionism. Brain function, at least as evidenced in human consciousness, undertakes tasks other than copulation and the justification of it. But sexual selection certainly waxes large in human behavior. Let me explain some common features of human child-rearing from the perspective of evolutionary biologists:

7.16.3.5.1.   From a gene's perspective, the goal (though, of course, genes are subsentient and therefore lack thoughts or purposes) is to propagate into the next generation. Given the likelihood that any gene that makes its bearer unfit in his environment is likely to result in childlessness or pre-reproductive death, the gene wants to have no impact or a positive impact. Where a gene renders its bearer even slightly better adapted to his environment, the gene strikes out on a path to rapid (in a genetic timescale) replacement of individuals lacking the gene and species-wide replication of itself. Psychological traits of male and female humans have been evolutionarily selected for their tendency to maximize fit gene transmission. These psychological traits differ between men and women.

7.16.3.5.2. From a gene's perspective, women must be highly selective in mate choice. Producing a gene carrier (baby) is an expensive and debilitating event from a female vantage. A woman has a delimited number of eggs, and a short window of opportunity for using those eggs to make gene carriers. Female selectivity in choice of mate drives the evolution of males, since the female bottleneck in reproduction determines the number of opportunities males have for loosing their abundant sperm. A woman looks for a man who can protect her, since she will, for several years during pregnancy and while nursing, be quite vulnerable. A woman looks for a man who can help feed her and her child. So, a woman looks for a man who will stick around, who is sympathetic enough to help, and will make substantial paternal investment in her children.

7.16.3.5.3.   From a gene's perspective, men must employ a strategy to breach the female reticence barrier. One strategy for the male gene to propagate is to spread itself into every willing ovum, encouraging copulation as frequently as opportunity permits. This low paternal investment strategy creates many copies of a male's genes, but each carrier (baby) has a relatively low likelihood of survival because of the father's lack of investment and protection. Another strategy is to capitulate to female sensitivities, to limit

---

[96] Wright, *The Moral Animal*, 53-54.

oneself to a single female during her reproductive years, and insure, to the extent possible, that the mother and those offspring prosper to reproduce themselves. This high paternal investment strategy reduces the number of copies of a gene effectively transmitted into a child likely to itself breed, but also dramatically increases the likelihood that any such child will survive to breed. Men's brains contain periconscious programs that seek women with breasts adequate to feed babies, and hips wide enough to expel infants without injury. Hence, the hourglass female contour men find so alluring. Men, encountering female selectivity, suffer an evolved psychological mechanism that views a sexual prospect as either Madonna or whore.[97] In courtship, a man assigns a sexual prospect to one category or the other. If the woman surrenders too soon, she does not merit ongoing devotion, after sexual encounter. The woman who expresses reserve, but then embraces a man at just the right moment, becomes to that man a sacred thing.[98] Each category exceeds what the woman's facts warrant, and serves for the male as blinders to keep him on one sexual strategy or the other with regard to a particular female.

7.16.3.5.4. From a gene's perspective, when a man overcomes a woman's wariness, love ensues. Love, from a gene's perspective, is a relatively brief period of infatuation with the sexual partner that insulates the messy, vulnerable, and emotionally stressful business of new coitus from near-term relational collapse. Where the woman once fled, she now clings. Where the man once wandered, he now attends. When infatuation fades, many find themselves linked to partners deeply different than they had imagined. There follows the crucial choice, where one, in a better-deliberated state of mind, elects to persevere with or depart from the now-better-perceived mate.

Evolutionary pressures favored humans with these psychological traits, and extinguished those who lacked them. Our dispositions cumulate the psychological results of such survival pressures in the Pleistocene environment. Considered from the vantage of genes, we are convoluted transmission devices. We live to breed.

Humanity, however, has departed the veldt. In thousands of particulars, we have deflected our Pleistocene psychological traits where they prove disadvantageous, by culture, by thought, by habits. With respect to our breeding habits, deflection is itself a survival trait. If every child matures with the expectation that he or she can and should procreate, it will soon be the case that

---

[97] Wright, *The Moral Animal*, 72-74.

[98] For an entertaining, if grim, example of this psychological event, see Tolstoy, *The Kreuzer Sonata*.

no family can flourish, without employing deeply self-interested coercion to insure one has sufficient resources for one's own offspring, while others suffer fatal deprivation.[99] So, undeflected procreation demands a stark and ugly rule: kill some babies to preserve others. Repress and deny as we may, this rule governs human procreation at present. Swedish babies survive in vastly greater percentages than those of northern India. American infants survive more often than Malawian. First World babies prosper while Third World babies perish.

We can, with hundreds of millions of members engaged in childless nurture of children (alloparenting), alter and evade this bitter calculus. Humankind's task is to revise its culture of child-bearing, family, and the social scope of parenting. We have no alternative but to celebrate meaningful nurturant childlessness and to support the fecundity of that minority who were born to the task of bearing the next, smaller generation.

To survive, mankind must elect a course at odds with the mechanistic reproductive urgency we inherit from the tangled trajectory imposed by ancestral African savannahs. We must, as we have done so frequently since we abandoned tropical nomadism, cull our own hearts.

Objection 21: Presumptuous Parental Puffing. *Another protests that the author is himself childless, and yet presumes to offer parenting advice. One imagines it preferable to have an experience before instructing others about it.*

Response: I am no parent. I have been a step-parent and alloparent to friends' children. As a thoughtful alloparent, I offer a viewpoint that may warrant the attention of some who are engaged in parenting. The unfortunate fact is that bearing children does not guarantee parental insight or the adequate nurture of children. Would that it were so.

---

[99] This unconscionable prospect already pertains on one-half of the planet, which is incomprehensibly neglected by the other, richer half.

SOFIE AND ANOTHER ANNIE

43

PERSEVERANCE

Kirk bought Mali B, his sailboat, on Lake Union. The hull needed work, as did interior hardwoods. Mali B was more Kirk's therapy than transportation. The vessel promised escape—from America, from expectations, from his life. Kirk sought release from work, from parents, and (I hate to admit this) from me. Kirk wanted ultimacy, not penultimacy. Kirk longed to voyage around Vancouver Island, down the west coast, past Mexico, then to parts yet undetermined. Kirk fought to haul anchor and vamoose if the locals started bugging him. Kirk's bottom line bothered me most: Kirk had no intention of returning. He was going for good. Leaving.

For two years, I reasoned with Kirk over beers and breakfasts. I emphasized connections and our twenty years of friendship. I advocated the social and psychological importance of work. I criticized American mobility. I chastised his self-indulgence, perhaps too frequently. I described the pain of Kirk's plan—for Kim and me, but also for himself and his spouse, Lisa, even his cat (Mali, for whom the vessel is named). Kirk humored me. He defended his dream. He tolerated my dissent, even toyed with staying. But Kirk kept sanding and varnishing. Mali B took shape. I helped, not because I approved, but because Kirk was part of me.

IMPROVE PEOPLE, OR TOLERATE THEM.

I scraped hull. I painted. One afternoon, I helped liberate Mali B from a vengeful shipyard. I observed, but failed to share, Kirk's exuberance. Lancasters threw Kirk a *bon voyage* party. I penned him a poem rhapsodizing the safe harbor of home.

In the end, Kirk stowed his gear. He christened Mali B; her sails caught wind. I stood on the beach at Shilshole as breeze pushed Mali B out of sight toward Port Townsend. In the first few years, we visited where they landed. Over years, Kirk's local "family" withered, as he had wished. Kirk never returned. We don't write any more.

Marcus Aurelius (Roman Emperor, 2nd century) asserted: "Men exist for each other. Then either improve them, or put up with them" (*Meditations*, Book 8). Kirk imagined a third alternative. I doubt he found it. We are stuck. We must help people or tolerate their inanity. Regardless, we must persevere. I hope Kirk prospers, wherever the breeze has blown him.

MALI B, DEPARTING

44
SHIP-SHAPED
1996

Ocean: Sculptor.

Nothing comes from nothing.
What-will-be is chipped from what-was and -is.
Tomorrow is today tweaked by yesterday.

Seas carve continents, but rock resists wave.
Salt corrodes. Sacrificial metals, doom-intended,
Divert the onslaught, delay water's triumph.

Land-Kirk, scabby with alienations inflicted, imagined.
A flint pocked with softest weathering talc.
Wholly holy. Resisting the sea.
To evade, to heal, to become.

Metal-Lisa, pinned in the full-nelson of love, sweaty.
Wrestler, overmatched, pretzeled. Ionizing.
Wholly holy. Lifeline to land.
To preserve, to heal, to become.

The Sea. Imperious. Keeping its Own counsel.
Kirk stuff. Lisa stuff.
The Sea erodes, corrodes, sculpts.
Sea-Kirk. Sea-Lisa
Culture delicatessen? Hull and drown? Writer's orgasm?
Unknown.

A Prayer.
May the Sea erode Kirk toward us.
May the Sea corrode Lisa sparingly.
May adventure be healing.
May love prevail.

Bon Voyage
The wind at your backs.
The best harbor is our hearts.

KATIE

45
PRESIDENT WITH A MIRROR

JULY 2008

National elections loom. Politics as usual threatens. Our quadrennial season of mutual distortion draws nigh. Rightist pundits rant: "Obama, weird Christian with Islamic leanings and America-bashing wife." Leftists spit: "McCain, reactionary Bushist at death's door married to Barbie." These are dog days of talking heads and bombast.

How should Americans choose a national government? The politically astute answer, Platform. Choose candidates who advocate sensible policies. That sounds good. Yet, normal Americans spare little time sorting budgets, weapon systems, or proposed bureaucracies. We want to hire someone we trust to do that for us. That is the point of elections, is it not? Common citizens exhaust their time working to pay bills, patching up Johnny's broken arm, and getting mom to cataract surgery. We in life's trenches need a succinct marker that identifies preferable candidates.

We need leaders with mirrors. We need candidates who inspect **themselves** and are secure enough to tell us what they see. We need presidents who know themselves well enough to shore up their weak spots, who know what they can and cannot do as individuals. Mencius (Chinese, 4th century B.C.) noted well: "Only when a man will not do some things is he capable of doing great things" (Book IV, part B, §8).

The weakness of Presidents defines presidencies. Recall recent administrations. John Kennedy, the brash philanderer, almost started a nuclear war. Lyndon Johnson's pride made Vietnam an enduring misery. Richard Nixon's paranoia convulsed the nation. Gerald Ford's niceness let him pardon Richard Nixon. Jimmy Carter's unctuous handwringing left Americans captive. Ronald Reagan's growing dementia threatened constitutional crisis and permitted Iran Contra. The elder George Bush's caution failed to finish Saddam Hussein. Bill Clinton's womanizing and prevarications gridlocked years. The younger George Bush's education gaps tolerated a defective war rationale and a passel of poor English.

McCain or Obama? What are Obama's flaws? Only he can tell us; he holds his mirror. How does McCain fall short? Does he know; does he peer within? We need to know. Our next decade will be defined by the shadows John or Barack see in their respective reflections. John Locke (British, 18th century A.D.) said, "It is of great use to the sailor to know the length of his line, though he cannot with it fathom all the depths of the ocean. It is well he knows that it is long enough to reach the bottom, at such places as are necessary to direct his voyage, and caution him against running upon shoals that may ruin him. Our business here is not to know all things, but those which concern our conduct." (*An Essay Concerning Human Understanding*, §1.1.6).

Keep us off the shoals. Make the man who knows his limitations president.

SOFIE'S SLUMBERING SNOUT

46
TRUTH-SPEAKING

Nate came to me the troubled father of young Jana. Jana's mother had recently died of overdose. Nate's own mother now challenged Nate's custody of Jana. This grandmother believed herself a more able parent than her son. She belabored Nate's misdemeanor joyriding conviction years ago; he unforgivably embarrassed her.

During deposition break, Nate confided, "I have another conviction. An assault felony in Colorado." I withered. Opposing counsel had asked, not ten minutes before, if Nate had any criminal convictions besides the joyride. Nate answered plainly, "No."

What to do? I sucked my teeth. I advised Nate to correct his misstatement. I also advised him that doing so would reduce his chances of retaining custody of Jana. My advice resembled that of the King of Hearts to the Mad Hatter at the trial of Knave of Hearts for stealing some tarts: "Give your evidence, and don't be nervous, or I'll have you executed on the spot" (Carroll, *Alice in Wonderland*). Nate muttered, "There are truths and there is truth." I hung gored on the horns of my renegade ox: the horn of confidentiality through my liver, the horn of transparency threatening my heart.

I speak truth for a living. That is not how most people see lawyering. Thoreau (American transcendentalist, 19th century) scoffed: "The lawyer's truth is not Truth, but consistency or a consistent expediency" (*Civil Disobedience*). Facts arrive on my doorstep, dirty and disheveled. I clean them up and buy them a tuxedo. But a pig in a tux is still a pig. All judges are farmers; they know their beasts. A warning from Confucius (Chinese, 6th century B.C.) lingers: artful words ruin one's virtue (*Analects*, Book XV, §27).

> **HOW DOES ONE
> ESCAPE FROM
> DOING WRONG?**

Nate never corrected his deposition lie. Opposing counsel never checked Nate's criminal record. Ultimately, the Court left Jana with Nate. That grandmother faded from both their lives. For that, I am glad.

Speaking truth perplexes me, balancing truths and Truth. Socrates (Athenian, 5th century B.C.) held, while on trial for his life: "The difficulty is not so much to escape death; the real difficulty is to escape from doing wrong, which is far more fleet of foot" (Plato, *Apologia*). I sometimes feel like a weekend jogger being run down on the savannah by a cheetah.

GRAMMA EDE

47
TRASH

Shoreline may soon boast a third Rotary Club. Its prospective members have begun meeting weekly. The fellowship is a family of Rotary families serving humanity locally and internationally. Bring your spouse and kids. Let Mitch and Mom (Grinder's proprietors) cook you some dinner. Come serve with us. Help shape the heart of this new Rotary venture. Good-will put to action makes a difference for others—and for you.

To be true to our charge, we did an initial modest service project on Saturday afternoon. We picked up trash on Aurora and the Interurban Trail for an hour and a half. I had expected to fill a few bags in about an hour. But as we walked, the crush of highway trash came clear. In ninety minutes we filled a pickup truck, and completed less than one-half of the twenty blocks we set ourselves.

The trash itself was a welter. We anticipated beverage bottles and cigarette packs, paper scraps and cigar butts; we also found condoms, surgical gloves, soggy books, shoes, six-pack rings, socks, plastic vehicle bumper parts, and children's toys. Kentucky Fried Chicken detritus bedecked the roadway near KFC. Starbucks cups and lids and little brown straws decayed into wind-blown sculptures. We encountered muffler fragments, bolts, washers, styrofoam cups and packing blocks and peanuts. Cigarette butts spattered asphalt, myriad like winter stars. Smokers blight landscapes as do they their lungs. Several trillion cigarette butts get flicked every year. Butts are the most littered item in America. Apparently, drinking beer in a vehicle (which is illegal; RCW 46.61.519) induces an involuntary elbow reflex that ejects cans out automobile windows. Flattened empties were legion.

> **DO NOT LITTER.**
> **REALLY.**
> **JUST STOP.**

Where old garbage piled, littering increased. Litter ignored authorizes littering. Washington law dings trash-tossers. Littering is prohibited (RCW 46.61.645), subject to a fifty dollar fine (RCW 7.80.120). If one drops sufficient volume, littering is a crime (more than one cubic foot is a misdemeanor; more than one cubic yard is a gross misdemeanor. RCW 70.93.060).

Some weeks ago, a sleek black 2008 Cadillac sedan parked near North City's HotWire coffee house. As I admired it, a young joyrider pressed a button. His window retracted, and a drink cup, some sloshy icy concoction, splatted on the pavement. Silently, the window closed. The two boys stared. Concerned how teenagers came to be driving a fifty thousand dollar vehicle, I said nothing. I tried to recall, had I littered as an adolescent? Memory fails me.

The litterer slaps our communal aesthetic. He blemishes, sows toxic hazards, and bedevils wildlife. Then, with a shrug, he careens down the road.

For what it is worth, it did me good to pick up some up trash. But Don Quixote ambled through my mind, wobbling toward a wind mill.

LUCY, BLAZING ON A LOW-TIDE SAND SPIT

48
NEWS

I walked the Interurban bridges. No reporters scribbled. No photo flashes blinded me. Lucy, our little dog with the big attitude, towed Kim and me down the newest section of Interurban Trail, over those lovely pedestrian bridges, and up to the dignified bronze raven that graces the Interurban's southern terminus. We pulled a few weeds and sequestered some windborne trash. No one died. The SWAT teams stayed home. Our saunter was not news.

A genuine news victim strolled with us: Judy Nicastro (and her paraplegic mutt, Ruckus). Judy, my law school buddy, served Seattle as a city council member. The Seattle Times and Post-Intelligencer guillotined her political career with Strippergate hoopla. Now *that* was news. An Italian family (with Soprano overtones) sought a zoning variance for business parking. The *famiglia* gave campaign money (possibly, in an impermissible manner) to candidates who might vote for their variance. The candidates, of course, knew nothing of contributor shenanigans. What made this news, you ask? The Times and P-I needed a big story, and so insinuated mob vote-buying (for which the P-I offered no evidence and the prosecutor acquired no conviction). The Times and P-I editorial board disfavored the council members involved. And, most critically, the Italian business was a strip joint (not named Bada Bing). Sex, the "mob," and media bias: now that's news.

Back at the "not-news" bridges, we walked. Thousands collaborated to create the spans: visionaries, engineers, contractors, politicians, interest groups, taxpayers, bikers, dog-walkers. Dedicated citizens opposed the bridges, concerned their construction diverted funds from more pressing social needs. I thank dissenters. Physical and social infrastructures counterbalance. We must constantly revisit their delicate scale. In the end, mammoth joists lofted and asphalt lay. On our afternoon stroll, we bet our lives upon the collaborative competence of

> **WHAT'S IMPORTANT IS OFTEN NOT NEWS.**
>
> ---
>
> **WHAT'S NEWS IS OFTEN NOT IMPORTANT.**

thousands. William James (American pragmatist, 19th century A.D.) noted: "A social organism of any sort whatever, large or small, is what it is because each member proceeds to his own duty with a trust that other members will simultaneously do theirs" (*The Will To Believe*, §IX). On the bridges, our faith was not disappointed. Such is the daily experience of tens of millions of Americans. Every flight. Every commute. Every time a light switch is flipped, faucet turned, or hamburger eaten. And, certainly, every time one crosses a bridge.

But, oddly, that is not news. When a bridge collapses, that is news. Witness the media frenzy over recent Minneapolis suffering. Failure or perversity (even substantially fabricated perversity) is news. The semi-miraculous coordination of societal success is not. Odd. Very odd.

GRAMPA RHYNARD AND GRAMMA EDE

TURK RHYNARD
Great Grandfather
Oklahoma
Circa 1925

49

GOD TALK: TRUTHS

A friend, and infrequent detractor, who claims to know God, demanded I write all the truths I know about the Divine. I comply with the symbols contained in the following box:

With respect to God, reliable utterances require generous restraint. Ludwig Wittgenstein spoke well of deep language: "Whereof one cannot speak, thereof one must be silent."[100] Here, I speak truly.

---

[100] Wittgenstein, *Tractatus Logico-Philosophicus*, 7 (page 108).

LUCY, READING TO KIM

50
GOD TALK: ENCYCLOPEDIA

A friend, and occasional detractor, proud to know God, asked me, given my theological training, to express my encyclopedic comprehension of the Divine. I comply nonsensically with the symbols in this box:

- Aardwolf at abject; and abhor ambivalent aborigine, Azazel. Abridgment aboard abscond; abstinent about acerbic. Acrimony among ado,
- But banish botulism behind. Barren bastion below bedim, bodacious by bullock.[101]
- Cassowary, caustic cavalcade, centrifugal chameleon, coalesce criminogenic coagulants.
- Dark dazzle debauch deprecation; detestable dither during diocese—drudgery down dreamland.
- Either earmark egress, Eor emblazon except espouse expiation.
- Fallacious fiasco for fiddle-faddle. Finis. Forthwith, foist forlorn foursquare foundlings. Frolicsome fuzzy.
- Gaiety gall; gargantuan gargle. Gastronomy gelds giddy gesticulations. Goldbricking gripes gyrate.
- Habitation hence haggle. Hamstring handkerchief harmonica. Hassock hatred, haversack heckle. Heretical highbinders hoc hoggish hoot. Horrendous! Humdrum hyaline. Heretofore hysterical.
- Idiosyncratic ilk. Illegitimate is imbue. If imbroglio impedimenta, impious imponderables. Improvised in inappeasable incarnation. Incongruous incredulity, indefatigable, indefensible. Indolence… Infinitesimal inside inundation. Inveigh ironic.
- Jackanapes jabber jitter jolt jollity; jurisprudence joined jugglery. Juxtapose
- Kidney kinfolk knit knickknack. Knurled kosher kudos. Kowtow.
- Labyrinth lip liqueur litigious, loadstone lone loquacious lower, loveless. Lubricity lumber luria: "Luxuriant lyricism."
- Maddening machinist. Maggot majesty malcontent. Malediction mammoth meditation, melodrama mesmerize mildew. Minx modulation. Morgue. Mutilated mystique.
- Narcotize necessitous negligence. Newborn niggard nonessentials, notwithstanding nudist nutrition nymph.
- Oafs obeisance, objectivity off obfuscation. Obloquy of oddballs. Offhand onset ooze. "Open opprobrium ordeal; on orchestral orgy." Overhaul ox.

---

[101] Bullock: Duluth drag does doppler dong ding.

- **P**acific padding paint. Panegyrical panhandling paraclete; paranoid parliament partition. Parley passage pastel. Patsy pawn pedestrian. Peccant pelt pension, portending perfume perky perpetuity. Perturbation pious platitude pococurante pointer. Pope [potpourri] precarious. Profuse propitiation pucker puss.
- **Q**uarrelsome quandary qualm. Quench quintessence. Quizzical quotidian quiver. Quiz quota.
- **R**acketeer raincoat. Ratiocination realm. Recantation recluse remonstrate rhythmic ribaldry.
- **S**atanic savor. Scintilla secretion segregate sentimentality. Show-off spoilage.
- **T**eetotaler tetradodecahedron tizzy tuppence. Telepathy thoroughbred tonic.
- **U**lcerate until umbrella. Unclothe urbanity uttermost.
- **V**acillate vacuity. Venom vehemence. Voluptuous.
- **W**alkabout. Weakling whirl whoremonger.
- **X**anthous xenophobic xylophone.
- **Y**ak yokel.
- **Z**aftig.

Note, as you read these words, your struggle to invest gibberish with meaning, though forewarned. One stutters: That might mean...? The punctuation indicates... Unknown words suck meaning from fractured neighbors. Is this a puzzle? A cypher? A poem? A bad joke? One exults: I see! But then, No, no. Despond skulks back. One shakes a weary head. She retreats to less abortive tasks, wondering how nonsense differs from meaning.

Your troubled reading mirrors the theological impetus—inquiry smashed upon ignorance. To verbalize of ultimacies and intimacies: one utters mostly nothing. This, the bastion of theologians and wordsmithy tormentors (say, lawyers). Rendition without content: frankly, harder than it looks. Here, I speak impishly.

51
GOD TALK: *VIA NEGATIVA*

A friend, and frequent detractor, demented about God, adjured me to tell him what ultimacy is not. I comply alphabetically with words in an apophatic[102] box:

God is **no aardvark**, for mammals know pain. The Divine is **not beauty**, for beauty juxtaposes human perceptions. Yahweh (Hebrew) is **not callous**, but oft tolerates the intolerable. Allah (Arabic) is **not disengaged**, yet neither does he brood upon human minutiae. The Supreme is **not equitable**, for the wicked prosper. Shiva (Hindu) is **not flippant**, for gravity always sucks. Bog (Slavic) is **not grand**, for she lacks size and valuation. Aum (Buddhist-Brahmanist) is **not hysterical**, for panic preserves the precarious. Numen is **not intelligent**, for it has no brain. The King is **not jaded**, for weariness follows impotence. The Creator is **not kaput**, for it lacks beginning, middle, or end. Hu (Egyptian) is **not lingual**, for he lacks tongue, lung, and dung. El (Mesopotamian) is **not malign**, for goodnesses proliferate. Krishna (Hindu) is **no nihilist**, for the sun rises afresh. The Avatar is **not otiose**, for she neither works nor rests. The Formless is **not powerful**, for power compares relative weaknesses. The Prime Mover is **not querulous**, for heaven hovers in utter silence. Joss (Chinese) is **not reliable**, for it knows neither time nor obligation. The Sovereign is **no shibboleth**, for its many names are nullities. Vishnu (Hindu) is **not timid**, for the term disparages pantywaists over blatherers. The Infinite is **not unkempt**, for time tidies things. Brahma (Hindu) does **not vacillate**, for it lacks a mind with which to dither. Spirit is **not whiskey**, for one is reliably soothed by that spirit. The Eternal is **not x**, an unknown variable, for here I sit writing of its none-ness. The Ultimate is **no zombie**, for to die, one must have lived.

Via Negativa: no concept describes God. One could say "not cosmos." Of what is not cosmos, we know nothing. Ultimacy defies humanity. We would say that God is Wholly Other; yet, we then abuse the words "wholly" and "other." Humans imagine they know God. They are wrong. I am wrong.

In contentless contemplation, one might encounter the Nameless. Do not hold your breath. Here, I speak to amuse.

---

[102] Apophatic: knowledge of god by means of negation.

SOFIE AT THE BIG CEDAR

52
MACK FOR JUDGE

My first jury trial was a shambles. The courtroom was August hot. Courthouse air conditioning faltered, so windows were thrown open. Trucks roared past on Fourth Avenue, intermittently drowning the proceedings. Insulating obesity conspired with nervousness to drench me in perspiration. Perversely, the district court judge kept counsels clad in wool suit jackets. I mopped myself with a washcloth. One cuff of my slacks unhinged. I kept tripping on the loose hem. My trial notebook, neatly organized, cascaded from the prosecutor's table, splattered across the dusty floor. A juror sighed. Panic gripped me.

A small hand found a place on my shoulder. I turned to Barbara Mack, my supervisor at the King County Prosecutor's Office, a big person in a small lady's body. "Take a deep breath, Brad." I had not noticed I was not breathing. "You are doing fine," she optimized. I doubted her, but calmed myself and returned to my duties. Instead of lunch, I loitered in my skivvies while the local tailor repaired my "costume malfunction." That afternoon, the jury deliberated, then convicted. A domestic abuser got well-deserved censure. Barbara sat through the entire sweatfest. I survived.

Throughout that year, I worked as a rule nine intern for the fraud division. Barbara Mack mentored me, soothed my litigation woes, and strategized my nits and inanities. I discovered a remarkable, patient human being.

On your November ballot, you will find Barbara Mack, a candidate for King County Superior Court Judge, Position 37. Barbara is thoughtful, tough, compassionate, experienced, deserving. Please vote for her.

BREATHE.

Nationally, Barbara Mack has co-founded The Environmental Policy Center, testified before Congress, organized grassroots environmental coalitions, worked in the bowels of the Carter Administration (Interior Department), and taught at Harvard. Locally, Barbara Mack has prosecuted felonies and complex financial fraud for more than twenty years, argued before the Court of Appeals and Washington Supreme Court, taught lawyers law, taught police officers courtroom skills, and served on boards of charitable foundations. Personally, Barbara Mack has a life, parenting her son, watching the Mariners struggle, and enjoying hikes, racquetball, her garden, birding, and music.

Often, come ballot time, people cannot recall who they wanted for judge. Let me help you with that. Barbara Mack. Like Mack Trucks. Like Mack n' cheese. Like Mack-aroons. Mack-num opus. Mack-nanimous. Mack-nificent. Elect Barbara Mack a Superior Court Judge. We will all be glad you did.

Join me: Mack for Judge.

JESSIE ON KALALOCH BEACH

53
DRUG DIVERSION COURT

Rain City Rotary, the new evening Rotary club in Shoreline took 100 doughnuts to Presiding on the ninth floor of the downtown Seattle courthouse. Presiding is a gigantic courtroom. Around 200 gathered there to celebrate drug diversion court graduation. I think we brought too few doughnuts. The audience heard twenty-seven graduates speak, tales of failure and redemption. Judges St. Claire or Inveen introduced each, with obvious personal knowledge. Many stories of hope and gratitude moved me.

Drug diversion court addresses the systemic futility of imprisoning addicts. Incarcerating drug abusers imposes cold turkey withdrawal in the company of offenders far more corrupt. Jail becomes an academy of addiction with a faculty of felons. Hardened recidivists mentor newbies, herding their stampede over moral precipices. Prisoners learn ugly lessons. Once released, they re-offend. So whirls the revolving door of drug justice.

Drug diversion court offers an alternative for some. People who commit relatively minor drug possession or delivery offenses, or the crimes that support these habits financially, can opt into diversion. Divertees suffer the direct supervision of a superior court judge and drug rehab counselors. Tough love abounds. Rules are plain and vigorously enforced. Noncompliance reaps days in jail. Many divertees drop out; they are sentenced on their original charges. Divertees may well spend more time in jail than the drop outs. But divertees get treatment and support. Graduates get their criminal charges dismissed. A significant fraction abandons drug world and joins the rest of us, struggling along, mostly sober.

> **INCARCERATION COSTS MORE THAN TREATMENT.**

A few influential King County Superior Court judges oppose drug diversion court. Budgets squeeze tightly. Diversion costs money up front, and innovatively conjoins social services with judicial administration. It is a rule of government that any program conjoining tax dollars and change attracts opposition. American justice, true to its medieval English roots, aims at retribution, not rehabilitation. King County's naysaying judges reason that drug diversion has no part in the judiciary's mandated role. And, they note, budget limitations make drug diversion inexpedient. Theirs is a narrow, hidebound conception born of another century, another continent. They are wrong.

Though American courts do mete out justice, those same courts are charged to deliver *equity*, fairness tailored to individual circumstances. An irked W. Somerset Maugham (American, 20th century A.D.) said, "The most useful thing about a principle is that it can always be sacrificed to expediency" (*The Circle*). When treatment is appropriate, failure to deliver treatment is unfair and irresponsible. Ultimately, incarceration costs more than treatment. Our jails brim. And the human toll is unconscionable. Fund drug diversion court. Please ignore any judge who argues otherwise.

SOFIE

54

PACIFIST ASSASSIN

Decades ago, I passed some years happily incarcerated in Fuller Theological Seminary's deepest basement. There, among fine minds living and dead, I encountered Dietrich Bonhoeffer (German, 20th century A.D.). Concerning his earliest works, I wrote a half-dissertation in my abortive doctoral studies. From Bonhoeffer, I learned a lesson. Right conduct frequently confounds our ethical ideas about right conduct.

Bonhoeffer seminally revised the concept of the church. When Lutherans collaborated with Hitler's Reich, Dietrich jumped to the Confessing Church, which castigated German Lutherans. Bonhoeffer advocated the pacifism of Jesus (Roman, Province of Judea, 1st century A.D.). He corresponded with a genius of nonviolent protest, Mohandas Gandhi (Indian, 20th century A.D.). Bonhoeffer prayed that God would give him strength not to take up arms. He joined Brothers House, a monkish pacifist community.

The Nazi SS forbade Bonhoeffer to speak or write. But as World War II dragged on, the anti-Semitic Holocaust progressed. Bonhoeffer had written, "The great masquerade of evil has played havoc with all our ethical concepts" (Essay: *Who Stands Fast?*). Despite pacifist convictions, Dietrich joined a military intelligence conspiracy to assassinate Adolf Hitler. The *Fuehrer* survived their July 20, 1944, bomb. Bonhoeffer's involvement surfaced. The Reich hung Dietrich Bonhoeffer on April 9, 1945, at Flossenbürg Prison, as the Allies pressed into the heart of Germany.

> **RIGHT CONDUCT FREQUENTLY CONFOUNDS OUR ETHICAL IDEAS ABOUT RIGHT CONDUCT.**

For years, several friends have gathered Saturday mornings to read philosophical ethics at Third Place Books. We call our enterprise the Witless Protection Program, a poke at ourselves. Witless struggles with history's great minds deliberating human conduct; we share our ethical puzzlements. Mine are most often bonhoefferian. The resolution a client hires me to fashion demands legal battle. I become a warrior peacemaker. The joy I wish a friend requires I make him cry. I become a torturing comfort. I need to lose weight, which urges me to savor food with friends less exuberantly. I become an ascetic celebrant. I watch others; this is not my dilemma alone. Muds of complexity stain the linen of ethical clarity. Deserving goals may recommend means which give pause.

We walk an ethical razor, in the good company of Dietrich Bonhoeffer, pacifist assassin.

LUCY, IN KALALOCH'S DRIFT LOG PILES

55
TONE POEM[103] FOR THE DEAF

Preface to *Tone Poem for the Deaf: Amity at Law*

Many years now I have declined to address the Bar.[104] Reform sounds implausible, even corny. Who would listen if I spoke? The offer to aspire together presupposes collegiality conspicuously absent from my relations with many lawyers. Sowing hope in the field of law yields a harvest of discord. Rationality flowers in soils of shared values, that elusive and earthy "we" eerily absent from life in law.[105] The task of waking American jurisprudence, even locally, seems a windmill at which only the quixotic might tilt. So, I have said nothing, and practiced, and grieved.[106] Grief should end. Joy, or at least forgetfulness, in the normal course, surmounts tragedy. Rhapsodies, once mired in muds of melancholy, should lilt free to drown the dirge.

My legal despondence, however, lingers, its dark flame fanned by the withering sirocco of court houses. Disputing legatees claw for testamentary cash. Pyrotechnic dissolutions, detonated upon babies, fragment childhoods and lacerate attachment. Parents forget their young, lusting after intimate vengeance. With Solomonic logic, the time of minors is sundered, like bucks and bills, as divorce booty. None among criminals, their victims, law enforcement, prosecutors, judges, or parole officers, when candid, view their system as adequate. Some believe that judicial retribution wounds society so deeply that it is hardly preferable to self-help vendetta. Attorney entrepreneurs sell injury-outrage to juries, their windfalls funded by everyman's insurance. Juries are sidestepped by plea bargains that hardball prosecutors zing at society's errant members, enforcing ill-born statutes, bequeathing jails frothing with struck-out felons, often convicted by uncriticized evidence. Incarcerated, cellmates teach amateurs the professional standards of larceny. We transform drug dabblers into hardened menaces. Courts mandate rules which those same courts decline to

---

[103] A "tone poem" is a single movement of orchestral music, which illustrates in sound a non-musical theme or sentiment. In this book, the musical themes are a sharp trill at the Bar's insensitivity to the social carnage it fosters, and a somber dirge that the Bar spurns amity as the profession's core rationale, preferring to fight.

[104] The "Bar" is a metonym for the institutions of law and associations of lawyers. The term particularly refers to the physical partition in some courtrooms that segregates members of the public from direct participants (such as lawyers and claimants).

[105] From my vantage, much of American life has misplaced its sense of communal solidarity. We are much degraded by this paucity. If flourishing coexistence stands nowhere near the apex of our values, how could we cherish peacemaking?

[106] About a quarter century ago, while contemplating whether to enter law school, I wrote admonitions to myself. One read: "Law is a mess. Just practice. Don't fix. They'll punish you for trying. Swallow your idiosyncracy. Just hide." I find, now decades later, I cannot restrain myself. Apparently, I surrender to old age and hubris.

enforce, emboldening corrupt lawyers while hobbling diligent ones. Fairness is hijacked. In my subterranean heart, and in that of many attorneys, a magma plume of frustration simmers just beneath our carefully-manicured topography. Our inwardness is a Yellowstone hot spot, awaiting some triggering seismism to erupt. Some disagree. Those are not paying attention to themselves or me. Even as I speak, most dysphoria lingers unspoken.[107] So, grief endures.

One cannot expect systemic change. When the alarm of first stampeders over a cliff rings back through the onrushing herd, there ensues yet greater haste to the brink. Lawyers, ever obsessive-compulsive, sense something awry in their ceaseless hand washing. They feel an urge to give their digits yet another thorough metaphorical scrub. Confronted with law's shortcomings and misdirection, the legal community proffers what it knows: more distinctions, another rule, more procedure, another tax, more this, another that. Scrub, scrub, scrub. The more we offer is more of the same. Most scarcely consider that we might restructure our life together. We might reorganize our inwardness. We might become something fundamentally better. We seem incapable of even attempting those conversations.[108]

Most judges are good people working hard, making tough decisions. Their tough decision-making is part of our problem. Most attorneys are good people working hard, advocating intelligently. Their intelligent advocacy is part of our problem. Have we been seduced? Character, the homely but chaste cousin of that painted looker, law, dies an uncourted spinster. Shall we rediscover deeper truths and begin afresh, in our courts, in our culture? Can we abandon at least some laws in favor of a resurgent bloom of self-restraint? Can we fashion some better way to relate to one another than as strangers? Is friendship no longer an option? A dispirited voice inside me laments,

The answer is "No."

Fundamental change waits, not gouts of hopeful collaboration, but, rather, disturbing derailments of disasters and demolitions.[109]

The Oracle at Delphi named Socrates the wisest man in the world for knowing he knew nothing. That old gadfly spent his days pressing questions, living provisionally, and savaging the haunch of Athenian normalcy. Socrates never knew. For him,

---

[107] You may think me prone to clinical depression. Neither that, nor its weak sister, situational depression, are characteristic. I prefer to think that I am *awake* to law. The experience is somber. Which is not to say that I am never depressed.

[108] I have mulled, at some length, deliberated societal and personal change in my books, *Cull: Choosing Well*, and *Cull: Epitomes*. If you have read this far, you might like those works.

[109] The restorative justice movement, focused mostly on criminal activity and victim restoration, has been yammering away at courts and their denizens for many decades. Still, efforts to redirect jurisprudence have had little (but not no) effect. See Zehr, *The Little Book of Restorative Justice*, 74-76. David Gil chastens me. He says: "Moving toward structurally just societies by nonviolent, rather than violent means—the only strategic mode likely to be effective—requires transformation of status quo-reproducing consciousness into status quo-challenging critical consciousness. . . . When people speak and act in accordance with 'normal' expectations, they reinforce, by implication, the existing social order and its 'common sense' consciousness. On the other hand, when people's words and actions 'transgress' the ranges of 'normal' communications and behaviors, by questioning and challenging the status quo, they create opportunities for reflection and for the emergence of critical consciousness on the part of others with whom the interact." Gil, "Toward a 'radical" paradigm of restorative justice," 508-509. I should speak.

uncertainty broadcast the virtue of epistemological humility. Lao Tzu advocated letting people rule themselves from below, intuitionally ferreting the Way. To his lawyers and kings, Lao Tzu advocated non-action, abandoning coercion, recognizing that inherent contradictions riddle truth. Verity is ever a punctured fabric.

But we attorneys spit out Socrates and the Taoist masters. We know. We act. American jurisprudence springs from opulences of purported knowledge, erected upon dunes of oft-unexamined supposition. The word "jurisprudence" means the wisdom of law. Is law wise? Our halls of law tackle fathomless problems. Court rooms ring with din barked by people more studious than educated. Those women and men execute plans and remove obstacles, intervening from above, making themselves a sorrow to Lao Tzu. Attorney "knowledge" is a concrete that defies jackhammers, grieving Socrates. Attorney suppositions, ever shifting yet masked, castrate needful change. We peer to the past, to precedent. Attorney action dismays and disappoints; its rudiment is coercion. Attorney mindsets induce skeptical politicking where spin savages scruples. Our juridical administration lies locked in a thousand minds too exhausted to learn ignorance-in-principle. Our courtrooms are peopled by humans too jaded to ask what would happen if we did nothing, if we let matters unfold and resolve themselves. Jurisprudence trundles onward, suspecting its futility, but hawking its necessity. Socrates and Lao Tzu weep.

So why break silence? Why indeed. To what end?

Perhaps there is some point. The hoary medieval walls of our imported English jurisprudence trap a horde of uncomprehending litigants, and, perhaps, more than a few attorneys clutching after sanity.

As to the litigants, who suffer the misfortune of paying the invoice, financial and emotional, for our misguided system, they may find relief in hearing it said, "Peace is banished from courtrooms." Perhaps, then, litigants can file their encounter with courts in that mental bin which contains road rage, bar fights, and war. Jeremiah, the eighth century B.C. Jewish prophet, criticized his "lawyers." He said, "They have healed the wound of the people lightly, saying 'Peace, peace,' where there is no peace. Were they ashamed when they committed abomination? No, they were not at all ashamed; they did not know how to blush."[110] I do not blush in courtrooms. I see no others blushing either. I do, however, feel redness creep up my neck, late at night, when assessing my day. I suffer, as do many of my colleagues, courtroom chagrin.

As to the attorneys who may share my concerns, who are taxed as officers of courts in the coin of equanimity, they may find solace in hearing Cicero say, "Laws damage us." *Summum ius, summa iniuria.*[111] Perhaps, then, we can set aside our denial and be reconciled to our role in the suffering that our legal dynamic creates. We might whisper that other, better ways to arrange ourselves may exist. We who share these concerns might even talk face-to-face; the timid among us could email; those agoraphobic or inarticulate could text or tweet. In the end, breaking silence may help rescue my own sanity, which is always at issue. And perhaps peril awaits

---

[110] *Jeremiah* 6:14-15 (Revised Standard Version).

[111] Cicero, *De Officiis*, Book I, X, 33. Free translations of this Latin saw might be: "The more law we make, the more injury we cause," or "Maximum justice is the greatest injury."

your equipoise as well. I occasionally doubt your normalcy. I lie when I say "occasionally."

My singing voice is crap. I am better lip-synching Gregorian chant than crooning Taylor Swift. So, I sound scratchy, out of tune to ears accustomed to a different register and catchier rhythm. My jeremiad rings doleful. Still, I harbor, in a secluded vestibule of my heart, more hope than my words trumpet. I write to invite you to peek in my seldom-revealed closet. For I know you hide such a covert closet as well.

I bray my lament. I sing this *tone poem for the deaf*.[112]

You clap trembling hands over tortured ears.

You resist my ragged rendition.

I sympathize utterly.

So once did I.

Years ago.

Then…

SIL

---

[112] Deafness may be congenital or acquired, partial or complete. All deafness is not physiological; some suffer aural incapacity for psychological reasons. Metaphorical deafness (that is, acquired partial psychological inattention) may emerge from religious conviction, inveterate opposition, exhaustion, ill-marriage, or hubris. Life at law would seem to be another of the syndrome's risk factors.

56
RABUOR

Loyce Ong'udi's mother, Rosemell, lives, as has she throughout her life, in the small west Kenyan village of Rabuor, three kilometers up gentle hills from Kisumu highway. My friend Loyce recalls an idyll of childhood, playing in the security of Luo tribal life, sheltered in the bosom of Rabuor. Poverty did not grind Rabuor. Villagers ate and bore young and grew old and died, as had Rabuor families for generations. Loyce's grandfather, an Anglican priest, valued educating children, including girls. Loyce left Rabuor for Maseno Girls Anglican School, then high school in Nairobi. Marriage brought Loyce to San Diego, then turned ugly. Divorce left Loyce in the American dilemma of single motherhood. Loyce persevered. She studies at the University of Washington, her daughter at Seattle University.

While Loyce struggled, so did Rabuor. HIV crept through the population. AIDS struck able young men and women. Rabuor teetered toward social collapse, slowly crumbling into a region of old people and babies. Not individuals alone, but communities also, may die, withered in hopelessness. Herodotus (Greek, 5th century B.C.) said, "Calamities fall upon us; sicknesses vex and harass us, and make life, short though it be, to appear long. So death, through the wretchedness of our life, is a most sweet refuge to our race." (*Histories*, VII, §46). Despair is death's handmaiden.

> **INNOVATE
> IN THE FACE
> OF DESPAIR.**

Rosemell resisted. She fanned Rabuor's ember. Rosemell sheltered area AIDS orphans. Their numbers kept growing. East Africa's familiar story began a new chapter in Rabuor: disease created poverty, poverty assisted disease, unstable and ineffective government bolstered both. Kenya is only recently unstable. Still, Rosemell was awash in needy kids. She called for help, and many answered, Loyce among them.

Rabuor Village is determined to survive HIV-AIDS. The villagers have taken steps. They have planted sunflowers, pressed them for oil to sell. They feed the husks to hybrid goats, milk producers, of German stock. Men make bricks from local soils. In their new coop, Rabuor raises chickens for ready protein. American friends help Rabuor build recovery. Rabuor Village Project is a Washington non-profit 501(c)(3) entity that supports these west Kenyan efforts. Rabuor has erected a nursery school for the orphans, a pharmacy, and works toward securing a steady water source. Rabuor has broken ground on a vocational center, located on the valley highway. They will teach marketable skills and sell local products. Rabuor spreads its successes to adjacent communities. Some fifteen hamlets are affected at present. Village by village, Rabuor exports its model of sustainability, straight in the teeth of the HIV-AIDS epidemic.

Octavio Paz (Mexican, 20th century A.D.) said, "Political crises are moral crises" (*Postscript*). Political crises I leave to our State Department. But the moral crisis of east Africa troubles me. Rabuor Village Project helps, both me and west Kenya.

PAUL LANCASTER, AND PUPS

57
FORBEARANCE

I flew Horizon Air from SeaTac to Spokane. My father celebrated his eightieth birthday in Coeur d'Alene, Idaho, with family and friends. When boarding was announced, two flights were called. We hundred passengers walked onto the tarmac toward two identical turboprop aircraft. I stopped, backing up the line for a moment. Unobtrusive hand-scrawled signs said, "Portland" with an arrow pointing right, and "Spokane" with an arrow pointing left. I veered left. I put one foot on the stair, then boarding traffic began debarking. Seven people clambered down, dragging carry-ons. The last, mumbling, eyes downcast, fled to the other plane. We reboarded. I got to the forward bathroom this time, then retreated to the tarmac again. My third embarkation succeeded. I sat. The ritual, however, continued. One after another, passengers smirked at the plane-swap dance. Mirth turned to grimaces for some, as they realized the error was theirs as well. Twenty minutes passed before all mis-planed passengers sorted themselves out. The cockpit chimed, "It is a beautiful day in Spokane, 83 degrees the expected high. It's beautiful, unless you were expecting to be in Portland. No day in Spokane seems beautiful, when you expect to be in Portland." Everyone laughed. Many nervously checked their tickets one last time.

The public forbearance impressed me. Jockeying back and forth was difficult for some, frustrating for all. People, really, could have paid attention. And Horizon Air could have jumped for legible, well-placed laser-printed signs on colored papers. Still, no one bitched. No steward was browbeaten, no passenger belittled. Puget Sound politeness prevailed. Rabbinical scholars (1st-6th century A.D.) wrote: "Deeds of kindness are equal in weight to all the commandments" (*Talmud*). We were, publicly and collectively, beatific.

LEARNING PATIENCE REQUIRES PATIENCE.

Privately, I was otherwise. I doubt I was alone. Faced with two mirrored airplanes, the question of which craft was which seemed pressing. What happened to the twenty percent who mis-planed? How many others got on the right plane by accident, without recognizing the puzzle? I felt impatient. Waiting, especially if tired, chafes me. Critical monologue kvetches in my head. A Yiddish proverb runs, "If you're out to beat a dog, you're sure to find a stick." I had mine. Stanislaw Lec (Polish, 20th century A.D.) noted: "You have to have a lot of patience to learn patience" (*Unkempt Thoughts*).

The pilot proved right. It was a beautiful day in Spokane.

PUPPY LUCY WITH HER PACKMATE

58
THICKET

Harry Truman taught me a lesson. Not President Harry S. Truman, but rather headstrong Harold Truman, incinerated at Mount St. Helens in May 1980. I know Harry only from newspapers and television tidbits. Still, his stories stuck with me. Harry fixed and flew Army aircraft. His WWI troop carrier was torpedoed. Harry ran rum to brothels during Prohibition. For decades, Harry Truman owned Spirit Lake Lodge on Mount St. Helens. Harry was the resort hallmark, curmudgeon in residence.

In the 1970s, geologists swarmed over the volcano, embedding instruments, lasering bulges, scribbling temperatures. Academics predicted cataclysm. Mount St. Helens would erupt, as do her siblings Shasta, Hood, Adams, Rainier, and Baker, regularly, in the parlance of geological time. Vulcanists spun a theory. Residual heat from earth's formation and radioactive decay spawn dense mantle convections on which float continental froths of lighter rock. Mantle friction pushes these massive plates around, driving them past, over, or under one another. At the United States northwest coast, the Pacific plate plunges beneath the North American plate. When crust reaches melting depth, balloons of molten light rock rise to the surface. These magma pockets emerge as the Shasta to Baker string of volcanoes, with occasional spectacular pyroclastic belching.

Harry Truman would have none of this heady blather. Spirit Lake slumbered in the bosom of Mount St. Helens, as had she for millennia. Trees towered. Snows fell. Harry would stay. The federal government ordered evacuation. Harry planted his boots. Finally, Mount St. Helens did what volcanoes do. Her north face exploded, Spirit Lake vanished in plume of steam and gout of mud. The 230 square mile blast zone became Harry's headstone, and the spewing cauldron scattered ash, possibly Harry's, eastward across America. I admire Harry's independence, but he slid silently into ruinous recalcitrance.

I see Harry in myself and my clients. We know the score but desperately plug our ears. A languishing marriage, long dying, disintegrates into litigious cacophony. Simmering antipathy for a brother bursts into flaming recrimination at the last parent's death. An unwise, but profitable, manufacturing shortcut injures consumers. Closer to home, my obesity little deters overeating. My consumerism hastens others' starvation. My roof is worn; I dither, praying for stormless winters.

We are frequently Harry. We cannot excise desire. Without desire, mankind would notice peril, then nap. Yet, desire distorts. Aldous Huxley (British, 20th century A.D.) said: "We don't know because we don't want to know" (*Ends and Means*). Harry's fate teaches the risk of pigheaded yearning. Demosthenes (Greek, 4th century B.C.) saw: "Nothing is as easy as deceiving yourself, for what you wish you readily believe" (*Olynthiaca* 3.19). Even as we choose rosy paths to oblivion, we sense our delusion, and scoff. Joseph Jourbert (French, 19th century A.D.) notes: "Half myself mocks the other half" (*Pensées*). We are a thicket, aren't we?

SOFIE

59

TRUBBLE TALK

Ima N. Trubble
123 Everyman Lane
Elysium, Eldorado 00001

RE: Life Lived Well

Dear Ima:

THE OCCASION OF THIS LETTER

Kim and I were deeply concerned about your life after talking with you and Cynthia last night at the Space Needle. Before I address a person's life, I prefer to converse at length. The purpose of this long question and answer prelude is to insure I possess all the relevant facts, to give me a chance to reflect and imagine, and to convince the person with whom I am speaking that I am hearing their view of matters, not merely imposing my own. Your inability or unwillingness to endure such a protracted exchange cut short the process of my education and your unburdening.

Normally, I would take your abrupt departure from our dinner table at face value and assume that you do not value my counsel or, at a minimum, do not want to take the (often bitter) pill of my analysis just now. But your description of your circumstances strikes me as so exigent that I cannot in good conscience stand silent. Nor can I in good faith convince myself that you will be safe until such time as your efforts to work out your problems on your own have resolved. So, I am writing to you—now. When I err for lack of information, forgive me. I also ask you to take responsibility for your part in my ignorance.

EXAMINING YOUR LIFE

Socrates asserted that "the unexamined life is not worth living." (Plato, *Apologia*). By this letter, I invite you to examine your life. You can do so alone if you please. You will have greater success if you do so with another, especially a wise other. Cicero advises: "[D]are to give true advice with all frankness; in friendship let the influence of friends who are wise counselors be paramount, and let that influence be employed in advising, not only with frankness, but, if the occasion demands, even with sternness, and let the advice be followed when given." (Cicero, *Laelius de Amicitia*, 157).

You will not much like what I have to say, Ima. Ralph Waldo Emerson encouraged men to "speak the rude truth in all ways." (Emerson, *Self-Reliance*, 123). He further said of intimacy that for persons who care about one another it is "better [to] be a nettle in the side of a friend than his echo." (Emerson, *Friendship,* 198). This letter is both rude and nettlesome. Learning, especially learning about your own soul, is difficult. Aristotle said, "Learning is no amusement, it goes hand in hand with pain." (Aristotle, *Politics*, 226). I invite you to learn.

"Make your rules of life brief, yet so as to embrace the fundamentals." (Marcus Aurelius, *Meditations*, 63). At the end of the journey described in this letter, should you decide to undertake such a journey, Ima, you may grasp your life with such clarity that you can make a list of the rules you believe govern life. With luck, they will strike to the heart of the fundamentals of human existence.

EXIGENT CONCERNS

1. **Depression.**
   As Seattle rotated slowly past our view last night, you acknowledged that you are depressed and in pain. You attribute that depression to the collapse of your relationship with your recent boyfriend and his family, domestic violence, loss of your job at the local restaurant, the provincial culture of your small town, conflict with your parents, and lack of friends beyond Cynthia.

   Depression is a life-threatening medical condition. The person least able to know how to cope with depression is the depressed person. Your psychologist is correct about your treatment. You are wrong about what you need.

   Depressed people must deal with the underlying physiological problems antecedent to their disturbed psychological states before they are able competently to be led to insight about their dysfunctional mental states. Put simply: fix the body, then address the mind. Your counselor is right that you need to get rested, straighten out your blood chemistry, ameliorate your brain neurochemistry, remove the stress-inducing stimuli, and heal yourself. That means go to bed at the same time every night (I suggest your retire nightly at 9:00 p.m. and rise at 6:00 a.m.), eat properly and take a good (expensive) multivitamin and other needed supplements, take an appropriate antidepressant, lose your boyfriend and his family, separate yourself from your mother (with whom you seem to be in a running battle), establish a meaningful routine, balance your life (work, self-nurture, meaningful relationships), and learn to provide for yourself.

   After you have spent a few months getting physically stabilized and beginning to learn how to talk about your life constructively with another person, then you may be ready to begin the hard work of restructuring your attitudes and thoughts. I attach an excerpt from *A Guide to Rational Living*, which is a simple book about self-therapy for people whose problems are not too complex. This book employs a "rational-emotive" or "cognitive" approach to dealing with neurosis and dysfunctional thinking processes. It is the most widely used approach among psychologists in practicing therapy. Reading this excerpt might help you identify some of the issues involved and the "feel" of psychotherapeutic talk.

   Your problems, Ima, are not the sort that should be approached on a self-analysis basis. Your problems are too complex, and your analytical skills too feeble. Your mind and emotions and will pose to you a maze from which you will find no exit. You need a competent psychologist to assist you, one that you trust, and one with whom you are willing to spend a great deal of time over a long period. That person will help you straighten out your body, and ultimately your attitudes and thoughts. If you will embrace the process, you will become both more productive and less self-destructive. In the long run, those characteristics will translate into happiness and a profound sense of well-being that you can savor for the rest of your life.

If you choose to "treat" your depression yourself, you will fail. Worse, you could end up dead. Suicidal ideation (recurring thoughts about killing oneself) is a symptom of depression. The urge to end the pain of depression can lead one to dramatic action. For some depressed people, that means suicide. Those persons do not "decide" to kill themselves. All of a sudden, depressed people just find that suicide seems to be the only appropriate option. To the depressed person, it all seems so plainly logical. Then they are gone, leaving their loved ones in a sticky soup of grief and second-guessing from which it is difficult ever to extricate oneself. This could happen to you, Ima, and to us who love you. I ask you to take my words seriously.

You expressed concern about the amount of money it might cost to rectify these problems you are suffering. Your family, whom I know, will all step up to take care of the cost of treating these problems. You, too, will be able to contribute, because an important part of healing yourself will be to find meaningful work. Take the months required to heal your depression. Be patient.

2. **Anger and Domestic Violence**.

Many people, both men and women, suffer domestic violence in their intimate relationships. We Americans have long taken the position that hitting is an acceptable form of dispute resolution. People can "just take it out back" and the matter will be resolved with a broken nose or two and some skinned knuckles. We are, as a culture, only now beginning to insist the hitting stop and that other forms of dispute resolution replace the fisticuffs.

The focus in American jurisprudence on domestic violence has fallen squarely upon male hitting. American jurisprudence has sorely neglected female provoking. Women strike with their mouths, men with their fists. Women often think they can strike men (verbally or physically), and expect those men to behave chivalrously in declining to strike back. Those women are wrong. Some such women suffer broken bones; others die. You have learned that fact personally and painfully.

Kim and I deal with domestic violence routinely in our work. We know that the reason your boyfriend was not prosecuted for domestic violence was one or both of two issues: either you refused to bring the matter to adjudication by testifying against him, or you also committed domestic violence against your boyfriend and gave as good as you got. When either or both of these events happen, the judicial system throws up its hands and waits for the problem to escalate to coherence and clarity. That means something bigger happens. Then the bench belatedly puts someone in jail for felony assault or murder. That solves the problem for everyone except the victim.

I do not know your boyfriend. He obviously has problems, and those problems find one root in his family. I do know you. One of your problems is anger. You do not know how to manage your anger and vent it constructively. Your anger problem, like your boyfriend's, has roots in your family.

Ima, you were ill-parented. You describe them as people who have struggled long and successfully against daunting obstacles. They prospered financially and carved out for themselves lives they find generally meaningful. As you will discover, that is not so simple a task as many people would have us believe. Your parents deserve your respect. They are, as you describe them, honorable people, hard-working people. They are not, however, perfect people.

Your mom and dad did not parent you well. They worked too much. Maybe they ran out of ideas or energy. Perhaps they cared too little. I do not know. I imagine that whatever the problem was, it was generally diminished, obscured, and wallpapered over. You recount people expressing concerns about your development. Those delicate words met steely denials and recriminations. As a child, you tell me you were farmed around between daycare providers, school teachers, grandmas and grandpas, parents, your great grandma, and any other convenient caregiver. Each cared for you as best they could, but the overall result was that you lacked coherent care and carefully delineated boundaries. Your parents had neither the time nor energy nor the educational resources to cope with your problems as those quandaries developed.

You say you did not eat well. Your childish fits were tolerated. Your poutiness was poo-pooed. Your adolescent inanities were ignored, or in the alternative, countered with angry outbursts. Your life was not given a structure upon which you could rely. You were not taught intimacy and communication. You were not taught problem-solving, especially for your own psychological needs. You were left in the educational wastelands without the nourishment your mind required. These deficiencies were not parental abuse. This was parenting shortfall. Every childhood suffers some degree of parenting insufficiency, since no parent possesses all another human being needs. As an adult, it is your job to take up where your parents left off or failed, to parent yourself, to elect to grow and fill in the coping skills you missed or your parents failed to communicate.

As a result of defective parenting, you experienced frustrations consequent to your problems, and those frustrations went unremedied. You got angry. A deep-seated long-smoldering anger about everything and nothing in particular took root in you. You developed some dysfunctional self-talk that you are probably little aware of at this juncture. Further, you unreflectively drank in the attitudes and perspectives of your psychologically dysfunctional classmates and their crippled families. Then, at seventeen or eighteen, you began to interact with the panoply of complexities which constitutes adult American life. You were ill-equipped and have swamped rather badly in your maiden voyage into adult waters.

The appropriate aim of parenting is to equip a child to meet the challenges of forming for herself a meaningful, socially-connected, and socially–responsible existence. Life construction does not come naturally to humans; we have to be taught the skills. This is especially so in highly differentiated cultures like western civilization. In such cultures, there are high degrees of specialization and deferral of rewards and postponed entry into adulthood. For many persons, whether due to youth or immaturity or lack of native intelligence, finding a place for oneself can be bewildering and fraught with dangers. Parenting is supposed to ease the shock of transition from the protective umbrella of hearth and home to slogging forward under the persistent drizzle of American adulthood.

When I say that you were ill-parented, what I am saying is more in the way of an observation than a criticism. You are not equipped to make your own good life. I know that because I see that your efforts are misdirected. You eat poorly. You sleep at the wrong times. You communicate ineffectively. You ignore the wrong people. You heed the disastrous people. You have failed to sustain a productive work environment. Most, you have not achieved a vision of your own personality and future that is workable. How can you turn things around? I shall have more to say about rightly directing your efforts below, when I address concerns that are less in need of immediate remedy.

Ill-parenting has exacerbated your anger. That cauldron of antipathy now bubbles barely beneath the surface, waiting merely an inconvenience or slight to boil over. It sloshed forth when your car burst a radiator hose. It spilled again when Kim contradicted you last night at the Space Needle restaurant. I can only imagine how your igneous pot of anger erupted when your boyfriend crossed you and wrongly harmed you. You have also let your anger sting your boss at the restaurant from which you were fired, your mother, and, I am sure, your former friends. Last night you boiled over on Kim. "Your mind will be like its habitual thoughts; for the soul becomes dyed with the color of its thoughts." (Marcus Aurelius, *Meditations*, 84).

There are means to dampen anger, to grasp its origins, to redirect it, to avoid it, generally, to manage it. You can learn these approaches. You must learn these skills if you want a good life. Anger will poison not only your relationships with others, but also your everyday consciousness. It will make your life unpalatable if it remains unmanaged. Even you will spit yourself out.

3. **Hubris**.

The word "hubris" is a Greek term. It means "overweening pride or arrogance." Usually, the word "hubris" conveys the idea that the pride in question is wholly unwarranted. Hubris is not the justifiable pride one feels at a job well done or the confidence one feels when one has acquired skills upon which one can rely comfortably. Hubris is the pride one asserts when unreflectively rejecting another's challenges to you or your actions. Hubris is a defect of character, an impediment to maturity. Hubris loves the company of other killers of the good life: denial and anger and defensiveness and pointless self-justifications and revisionist histories and bitter resentments. In the mouth of Socrates, Plato puts the words, "And is not this the most reprehensible form of ignorance, that of thinking one knows what one does not know?" (Plato, *Apologia*).

Ima, you suffer hubris. You are not listening, except to persons whom you should never heed. You suffer from delusions of adequacy. You think you know much more than you do; you consequently welcome incoming wisdom too weakly. Some of your selective deafness is adolescent rebellion. About this transitory state I am little worried, because it will moderate as your hormonal structure achieves adult stability.

About the character issue your hubris betrays, I have great concern. If you notice, I am putting this in the section of my letter entitled "Exigent Concerns." "Exigent" means "requiring immediate action or aid." In my view, your hubris is a pressing danger. I will speak obliquely of hubris again in the second section of this letter, where I discuss issues of character development generally. But here I want to address the issue of hubris not as a general defect of character, but as an exigent danger.

Hubris seals one's ears; it inoculates the mind from intruding wisdom. Cicero said, "Now we must despair of the safety of the man whose ears are so closed to truth that he cannot hear what is true from a friend." (Cicero, *Laelius de Amicitia*, 199). You stand at the embarkation point of your adult life. The skills you lack are numerous; those you possess are few. More importantly, you have little idea of who you are or what you might be able to accomplish in life. You meander, or worse, lie fallow. You tell me you have inherited or been taught your mother's pigheadedness and disdain for learning. There are few spectacles more disheartening to me than that of an uneducated troglodyte shouting down the quiet wisdom of an informed and willing counselor.

If you do not like my counsel or Kim's, that is fine. As an adult, you choose those who advise you. But you must seek some counselor, for you are suffering a dire scarcity of wisdom. Where will you find the wisdom you lack? Bleak nihilism (the belief that nothing matters) is vogue among people your age, Ima. Refuse their march. The world contains not only ugliness and futility, but also beauty and possibility. Reconcile yourself to the battle between nihilism and utopianism (the belief that a perfect society can be achieved), and choose to be hopeful rather than despairing, so long as there exists some reasonable basis for hope.

The inoculant for the disease of hubris is humility. Humility is a habit, and not an especially difficult one. Humility amounts to an accurate and forthcoming self-appraisal; in this context, reality is ever pressing upon us opportunity to state accurately our deficiencies in the form of humility. When confronted with his ignorance, the humble man says "I need to learn; please teach me." When confronted with her errors, the humble woman says "I am sorry about my actions; please let me repair what damage can be repaired." Even when confronted with his knowledge, the humble person says "I am glad I know, but greater wisdom lies deeper still, and just a bit beyond my reach at present; I shall continue to grasp after it." Epictetus, a Roman slave and philosopher, captured well the attitude of humility: "If a man has reported to you, that a certain person speaks ill of you, do not make any defense (answer) to what has been told you: but reply, the man did not know the rest of my faults, for he would not have mentioned these only." (Epictetus, *Enchiridion*, 33)

Our culture often equates humility with a soggy, milk-toast compliancy. Some imagine that humility means that the humble man senselessly depreciates his capacities and cowers in the bushes when human lions prowl onto the scene. This denigrating perspective is inaccurate. Humility makes people strong because it makes them adaptive. Humility coexists comfortably side-by-side with great confidence, and in fact builds confidence. Humility obviates the need for denials or backpedaling explanations or outbursts of assertiveness.

Humility is the natural state of the human ego. When a person is not distorted by fictional mythologies or diseased ideas or neuroses or debilitating trauma, when a person is surrounded by loving and supportive intimates (very close friends) and has meaningful work and gives to others in preference to taking from them, then a person naturally becomes humble. When we eat, our bodies naturally convert those substances into the stuff of our existence. When we chew upon reality, we naturally become humble.

Hubris is a state of confusion and unreality. The person of precocious pride conceals a sorely damaged self-concept by his or her hubris. Hubris is therefore a mask; its purpose is to hide from oneself and others the vision of the damaged and incomplete person that each of us is. Hubris is therefore a form of lying— to oneself, to the world. Hubris deludes oneself and attempts to mislead everyone else.

Hubris makes an intelligent person stupid. Here, by "stupid" I mean not lacking in native intelligence, but inclined, even compelled, to repeat past errors. A too-proud person sees the errors of others, but denies, after reflection, her own complicity in problems. Consider yourself. What is your part in the domestic violence with your boyfriend? What is your part in your unemployment? Why did you flunk out of high school and then fail to complete your graduation requirements at the alternative high school? Why were you willing to accept a diploma without simultaneous commitment to complete the requirements for graduation? What is your part in the fragmentation of your relationship with your mother? What fault in your soul sent you fuming from the dinner table last night? If you feel your anger rising about now, or if you cannot answer these questions sensibly and specifically, hubris dims you.

Ima, you lack humility. Hubris cuts off people. Your intimates **are** you. [I will explain more about this below.] When you cut off people who care and are supportive, you are cutting off a piece of yourself. Hubris is a kind of spiritual anorexia. The person possessed of hubris refuses the very sustenance that might nourish and heal and preserve her. Thus, considered spiritually, hubris is a disease process.

Ima, take the inoculant. As you grow honest with yourself and others, you may be momentarily embarrassed. But the blush of cheek will pass quickly and you will be refreshed by the great freedom and transparency that humility affords its beneficiaries.

NON-EXIGENT, BUT NEVERTHELESS PRESSING, CONCERNS

Life is mostly habit. Habits include not only physical acts, but also mental acts. We have habits that incline us to turn left at certain corners when driving, and to click on our seatbelt without thinking "I am going to put my seatbelt on now." We also have habits of thought, such as a penchant for adding two and two and getting four, or the habit of thinking well or ill of oneself. When you add up the sum of a person's habits, along with the sum of the person's relationships, you have the person. "Character is the interpenetration of habits." (John Dewey, *Human Nature and Conduct*, 38).

In contrast to habitual thought, humans also think substantively on occasion. Humans think substantively only when pressed by a novel problem or circumstance. The result of substantive thinking is that we make changes to our habits or institute new habits. So, the big issues in moral life are these: what habits shall one seek?, and how can one change the habits one already possesses? The first issue is philosophical; the second is practical and technical. I will address each in turn.

A. Which Habits Are Best?

"The really important thing is not to live, but to live well, . . . to live honorably or rightly." (Socrates in Plato, *Apologia*, 33). How one goes about living well is not immediately apparent. Plato writes: "It is our duty to do one of two things, either to ascertain the facts, whether by seeking instruction or by personal discovery, or, if this is impossible, to select the best and most dependable theory which human intelligence can supply, and use it as a *raft to ride the seas of life*, that is, assuming that we cannot make our journey with greater confidence and security by the surer means of a divine revelation." (Plato, *Phaedo*, 68).

Aristotle wrote of the good life: "The best life, both for individuals and for states, is the life of virtue along with such external goods as suffice for the performance of good deeds. . . . A man's felicity [happiness] is in exact proportion to his moral and intellectual virtue, and to his virtuous and wise conduct." (Aristotle, *Politics*, 192).

The classical world (from the rise of Athens to the fall of the Roman Empire, approximately one thousand years, from 500 B.C. to 476 A.D.) formulated a view of habits that demonstrates enduring value. Several hundred generations have benefited from the classical formulation of the virtues. This question about virtue, which means morally good action, boils down to what habits one ought to seek.

The four classical virtues are wisdom, self-control, justice, and courage. Wisdom pertains to insight about the meaning and import of events as they unfold, and often includes prognostication about where present events might lead. Self-control is also called temperance, and it includes the Greek ideal of seeking the mean, avoiding the extremes in all things. Justice pertains to our relationships with others both personally and in society; it aims to insure that each individual receives what his actions and character deserve. Courage is the only virtue that directly pertains to an emotion. The emotion of courage means the ability to face danger without shrinking, and to be confident in the face of uncertain outcomes.

I decline to explain further these classical virtues because that job has been done so much better than I can manage by Marcus Tullius Cicero, a contemporary of Julius Caesar in the first century B.C. Cicero's son, also Marcus, was an underachieving youth who avoided work and lingered too long in Athens. Cicero was concerned that Marcus lacked all the moral direction he required, and so Cicero set himself the task of explaining moral virtue to Marcus. The result was *On Duties* (translation of *De Officiis*), an essay for the benefit of Cicero's son.

There exists widespread modified endorsement of this four-part structure to moral virtue. It is the starting point for most discussions of the moral good. Of course, many people, including me, would put his or her own spin on each element of classical moral virtue. Christians would emphasize that wisdom entails humility, and justice should be shaded strongly by the demands of love. Buddhists would emphasize that self-control and justice should be tempered by the knowledge that this world is transitory and reality lies beyond things visible. Ghandi would alert us to the fact that courage consists mostly in the quiet strength that undertakes moral challenge, and not in battlefield heroics. Friedrich Nietzsche would put the whole scheme on its ear, creating anti-classical and specifically anti-Christian virtues. The canvas of moral virtue has been decorated by many shades upon virtue, painted there by intellectual artists, literally thousands of them, each with distinctive brush and style.

You too are an artist of this sort, Ima. You get to decide what counts as a habit worth having. You get to reject some habits and endorse others. You get to grow, which means you do not have to reach ultimate conclusions--ever. You will nevertheless have to make interim decisions and act upon them. You will enjoy the benefits and suffer the consequences of those decisions. You get to advocate. Everyone else gets the same privileges of moral artistic expression and endorsement. The only differences among people in this regard is the care with which they make the decision about what habits to have and what habits to eschew, and why they endorse or reject those particular habits.

What is at stake here is not some minor matter. The issue is what sort of person you want to become, what sort of self you are making you into, and what sort of world you hope you and others can live in.

What follows are some general thoughts and admonitions to keep in mind when selecting the habits you prefer.

A. 1. Communal Identity.

You are not alone. You were created when a germ of tissue from your father swam up a fallopian tube in your mother's belly to meet her germ of you. You first learned that you were you when you recognized, at about six months of age, that your mother was something separate from you. Since that moment, your learning has consisted in differentiating what is inside you from what is outside you. So where is the "you" that is Ima?

Our culture answers the question succinctly: Ima is what is inside Ima's skin. Ima is an individual and a repository of certain "inalienable" rights. Ima is ultimately created alone and remains alone. Ima is on her own, left to her own devices. This answer, which summarizes American individualism, does not satisfy me.

"Ima" exists as a a shifting set of relationships, some close, some distant. Psychologically, you extend beyond the confines of your body and "self." Your consciousness of others invades your consciousness of yourself. In fact, you are you only insofar as those intimate relationships exist. You are not YOU alone; "you" are the intersection (a nexus) of all these relationships. The person closest to you is an overlapping nexus of relationships, similar to yours but different. You reflect them to themselves. They do the same for you. We find ourselves in one another's responses. At some point, you might want to read a book by a Jewish theologian, Martin Buber, called *I and Thou*. It is the wellspring of this way of understanding individuals and communities.

That is why friendship matters so much. Aristotle says that man is essentially a social being. That means that we cannot live without others, not only physically, but also psychologically. This relationship, or rather set of relationships, is difficult and requires careful attention. "It is not possible to have many friends in the full meaning of the word friendship . . . [F]or perfect friendship you must get to know a man thoroughly, and become intimate with him, which is a very difficult thing to do." (Aristotle, *Nichomachean Ethics*, 473).

One upshot of this way of understanding yourself is that in taking care of your intimates, you are in fact taking care of yourself. This way of thinking expands the "you" to include the intimate others, and blunts the imperative of selfish action. It encourages openness and generosity toward others. It restructures the ego.

A. 2. Criteria for Habit Selection.

Before you even begin to decide what habits you want to choose, you have to decide what sort of person you want to end up being. This is a matter of vision, of looking into the future imaginatively.

With this purpose in mind, John Dewey urged us to be loyal to what makes excellent life possible. (John Dewey, *Human Nature and Conduct*, 21). He went on to suggest that, overall, we want to seek an essential openness to the world. "The important thing is the fostering of those habits and impulses which lead to a broad, just, sympathetic survey of situations." (John Dewey, *Human Nature and Conduct*, 207).

I would add the following to criteria for selecting one's habits. Your habits should:
- Make you physically healthy;
- Make you happy in the long run;
- Enable you to endure short term pain and difficulty;
- Help you do what you think is best;
- Foster relationships with other people;
- Make other people's lives better;
- Help you face challenges squarely;
- Lead you from mistakes to better future decisions;
- Keep your life balanced;
- Help you sort the more important from the less important;
- Provide guidance in the face of difficult decisions;
- Let you die with dignity.

A. 3. The Problem of Priorities.

Adult American life often becomes a morass of competing urgencies. It grows difficult for adults to sort out what is more important from the welter of less pressing matters. "Wisdom . . . is the ability to foresee consequences in such a way that we form ends which grow into one another and reinforce one another. Moral folly is the surrender of the greater good for the lesser; it is snatching at one satisfaction in a way which prevents us from having others and which gets us subsequently into trouble and dissatisfaction." (John Dewey, *Theory of the Moral Life*, 60).

Your life should have priorities, Ima. Make a list—one to whatever. You should be at the top of the list. Your first job is to take care of yourself. "[F]or a man is his own best friend. Therefore he ought to love himself most." (Aristotle, *Nichomachean Ethics*, 551). This is not to say that a person should be essentially selfish. First, the "self" is bigger than just your consciousness of your body. Second, life is seldom so pressing that the only item permitted is care of your self.

Next on your list should come your intimates. They, after all, are parts of you. Then comes those persons to whom you are close, but they are not the two to seven people with whom you share everything (your intimates).

After that, your priorities should include other persons and events, but the order differs among individuals. Family, work, your social periphery, your hobbies and interests, and your involvement in society generally should be on the list, but you should order them to fit the life you want.

Here are my priorities:

1. Me (rest, exercise, diet);
2. Kim and Lucy;
3. Intimates;
4. Family;
5. Lancaster Law Office and clients;
6. Enrichment: writing and reading, guitar, Rotary;
7. Shoreline;
8. The United States;
9. The world.

The big danger in priorities is letting the loudest demand take first priority. Americans frequently let work drown out all else. We then suffer the spectacle of fathers who seldom see their children. Low priorities can also get top billing too. I have seen marriages damaged beyond reclamation by a love of golfing.

The point is this. You have to know what is most important, and keep it that way overall. Minor deviations are sometimes necessary, but long term deviations will destabilize your life.

A. 4. The Problem of Emotion and Impulse.

Your brain has a three part hierarchical structure. We share a brain stem with all vertebrates, from salamanders to gorillas. It controls autonomic functions like heart rate, respiration, secretion, and other matters of which we are barely aware. Overlaying that portion of the human brain is the limbic system. We share those brain structures with higher mammals, from rats to chimpanzees. The limbic system is the seat of emotional response. It gives us our "fight or flight" capacity, our human bonding, our sense of well-being or lack thereof. Capping the human brain structure is the cerebrum, a great mass of gray matter deeply implicated in higher consciousness and abstraction, human vision, perception of time, and other higher functions.

Problems arise because, although all these brain structures communicate with one another and are integrated, they do not function identically. In essence, these three levels of the brain give competing, and sometimes contradictory commands. Consider happening upon a hungry grizzly bear alone and far from your campsite. Your brainstem will raise your blood pressure, increase your heart rate, and prepare you for battle. You limbic system will scream "Run!" and command you to seek help of other humans. In the alternative, under the right circumstances, the limbic system might ready you to fight (futilely) for your life. Your cerebrum says, "I read a book about bear encounters. It said to back away slowly, don't run, and stay calm. I also have a hatchet." What will you do? It depends on your habits.

In ethical thought, there has been a millennia-long strain that emphasizes that human emotion is fundamentally unreliable as a basis for decision-making. In recent history, however, emotion has been better received, and thinkers and scientists alike have recognized that one cannot merely suppress such an important portion of human consciousness. Emotion provides motivation, insight into social interactions, and constitutes an "intelligence" of a different sort.

There lie dangers in emotion. Our self-talk can be truly life-affirming, but it can also destroy us. Please consider the admonitions of *A Guide to Rational Living*. Those authors assert that we largely create our negative (and positive) emotions by the self-talk we promote. The importance of reining in emotion and impulsive action, and moderating its grip on life cannot be overestimated. "Happiness is a matter of the disposition we actively bring with us to meet situations, the qualities of mind and heart with which we greet and interpret situations." (John Dewey, *Theory of the Moral Life*, 46.) What will you do with your emotions, and how will you manage them? Your happiness hangs in the balance.

A. 5.   The Problem of Evil and Stupidity.

"Evil" is a theological concept much maligned in the last fifty or more years. In academic circles, for many decades to speak of evil was to invite scorn. Yet, evil humans have never been more prominent and destructive than in the last century. Consider the Nazi Holocaust, the killing fields of Pol Pot, the Stalinist purges and the Gulag archipelago, the Cultural Revolution in China, the African tribal genocides, and the Balkan atrocities.

One thinker has defined "evil" as malignant narcissism, and proposed the scientific study of the phenomenon as such. Narcissus was an especially handsome youth in Greco-Roman mythology who caught sight of himself in a mirror, fell instantly in love with himself, and ultimately died of longing because his love was unrequited. Narcissism is a habit that makes the self the all-absorbing center of attention and importance. Conjoined with the idea of malignancy, the evil person is one whose conviction of self-importance is exported to others, who themselves act in the thrall of the evil person's narcissism.

Evil comes in small packages as well as large ones. The effects of "small evil" are less newsworthy, but no less damaging at the personal level. Evil in the individual life can best be characterized as bad conscience or bad faith, upon which the Danish thinker, Soren Kierkegaard, ruminates extensively. When one lies, for example, he disrupts relationship with the person to whom he lies, as well as with himself. Distrust spreads. "The difficulty is not so much to escape death; the real difficulty is to escape from doing wrong, which is far more fleet of foot." (Socrates, in Plato, *Apologia*, 24).

Habitual personal evil, such as prevarication or substance abuse or violence, is closely linked to the phenomenon of moral stupidity. By "moral stupidity" I mean not general dullness or incomprehension, but rather the propensity to repeat evil behaviors without regard to their negative consequences. Moral stupidity is not an inability to learn, but a concerted refusal to do so.

A. 6. The Problem of Authority and Dissent.

We live in a day when distrust of societal authorities seems well warranted. Wall Street cheats, the President lies, charities pay their CEOs unseemly salaries, and the Catholic Church hides sexual predation of minors by its priests. To question authority is healthy and necessary. Conforming to sick institutions can make one sick, and condemn one's society to a slow death by lethargy. Nietzsche said human cultural institutions all want the same thing: "All dogs nicely on a leash." (Friedrich Nietzsche, *On the Genealogy of Morals*, 87). At least some of us need to run free, to keep our systems honest.

Despite the downside possibilities, "authority" is frequently a repository of wisdom. The structures in which we live and the rules by which we govern ourselves often reflect painful learning of prior generations from which we can and should benefit. To fail to do so is to relearn every lesson every generation. That is a fool's errand.

The problem comes to a head when society's institutions are vacuous or corrupt. What should our habitual response be then? Dissent is appropriate under such circumstances. The "right" then lies elsewhere than in the edicts of the empty or perverse institution, be it a church, a government, or a bridge club. "Any man more right than his neighbors constitutes a majority of one already." (Henry David Thoreau, *Civil Disobedience*, 259). Differentiate yourself; stand apart from the offending institutions. "To refrain from imitation is the best revenge." (Marcus Aurelius, *Meditations*, 91). Or, from that iconoclast, Ralph Waldo Emerson, we hear: "Insist on yourself; never imitate." (Ralph Waldo Emerson, *Self-Reliance*, 142).

When selecting your habits, question institutions. Embrace their good acts. Criticize them from within and without. Hope for the best, but watch them as an enemy lying in wait. We cannot live without institutions, but living within them can injure you grievously. If an institution is a blessing, give thanks. If it is wrong, speak out. If that institution is intransigent, depart.

A. 7. The Problem of American Consumerism.

Corporate America has decided that the public exists to purchase its goods. It spends billions annually brainwashing us to do just that. Aristotle addressed the problem, long before America was anybody's dream, in the fifth century B.C.: "Some people, therefore, imagine that to acquire wealth is the object of household management, and their one idea is either to grow increasingly rich, or at any rate sit tight on what money they have. This attitude results from their being so intent upon living rather than upon living well. They are anxious to possess unlimited means for the gratification of their unlimited desires." (Aristotle, *Politics*, 19).

The wisdom of most of human history contradicts American sentiment. "A good life requires no unlimited amount of property." (Aristotle, *Politics*, 16). "Nature herself, as I have frequently remarked, demands not only that we should be able to work well, but also to make right use of leisure; indeed, this latter power is the basis of all human activity. Occupation and leisure are both necessary; but leisure is preferable to and the end of occupation." (Aristotle, *Politics*, 222). By "leisure," Aristotle does not mean sun-tanning and lazy strolls. He means freedom to pursue virtuous activity. He means opportunity to read a good book, volunteer at the YMCA, or parent a child in need.

The American "good life" requires so much labor that little energy is left to expend on self-nurture, or the nurture of others. One wage earner was not adequate; our toys and extravagances have required that every family have two adult wage earners. Nevertheless, bankruptcies have reached epidemic proportions. We go on buying. One recalls Jesus' admonitions regarding rich men and needle eyes.

I encourage you, Ima, to think consumerism over carefully. This habit, once encouraged, can overwhelm all others. Reconsider your wardrobe.

A. 8. The Problem of God.

Theological ethics are much simpler than philosophical ethics. In theological ethics, God speaks, then believers do as they are told. If the Bible, or some other good book, is finally authoritative because God said so, then that really settles the matters of morality once and for all. Nietzsche contemplates this possibility and ridicules the possibility of "some spider of finality and morality which is supposed to exist behind the great net and web of causality." (Friedrich Nietzsche, *On the Genealogy of Morals*, 90). Nietzsche is plainly not a proponent of theological ethics.

After many years thinking about theological ethics, I have come to the conclusion that God wrote no books. And so, I do not believe we can settle the issue of which habits one should prefer by asking, "Well, what does the Koran say?" Many books contain valuable insights. I have quoted some of my favorites, and entirely neglected others I hold dear.

Though the problem of what habits to choose is difficult, I encourage you to make your own decisions on a case by case basis, rather than adopt a prefabricated ethical structure "off the shelf" from some religion or guru.

Those are my thoughts to date on selecting what habits to promote in yourself. I'll turn now to the second, less complex, issue. How does one change one's habits?

B. Changing Habits.

Habits, once established, become ingrained. Often drivers make their usual turns at a corner, despite the fact they intend to go the opposite direction. Often one calls a woman by her maiden name, even after one is fully aware that she has married and taken her spouse's name. Habits have a life of their own. That is good, because that is their benefit. Habits keep us on a good path, when those habits are good.

When, however, our habits are undesirable or have become less useful than they once were, how do we break a habit? In my experience, the strength of a habit is directly proportional to how early in life we learned the habit and how frequently we exercise the habit. The time to change a habit wholly can be roughly equivalent to the time it took to acquire it in the first place. "Ends contemplated only in thought are weak in comparison with the urgencies of passion. Our reflective judgment of the good needs an ally outside reflection. Habit is such an ally. And habits are not maintained save by exercise; they are not self-generated. They are produced only by a course of action which is persisted in, and the required persistence cannot be left to chance." (John Dewey, *Theory of the Moral Life*, 53-54).

To change your existing habits, you must:
- Conceive an alternative path of behavior;
- Consciously force yourself to follow the new path you have selected;
- Consciously refuse to follow the habitual path;
- Persevere until the new habit is firmly established.

This can be easier said than done. The habit of smoking can be decades old. Will you have to live with cigarette craving for decades to be free of the habit? Not necessarily. But many people find that instead of ridding themselves of a deeply-ingrained bad habit, what they end up achieving is effectively stalemating the undesirable impulse. This can be almost as good as establishing a better habit, if the matter is one of mere abstinence. If, however, the matter entails continued interaction with the subject matter of the extinguishing habit (as, for example, in eating), stalemating the undesirable habit can leave one with a burden of perennial conscious deliberation before each act. And that is exhausting.

PRACTICAL CONCERNS

You have practical concerns. How can you change residences? How can you get into a school of your choice? How can you pay for these events? How can you deal with your feelings? Where will you find new friends?

I encourage you to be patient, Ima, and to treat your life with greater seriousness than you have to date. Educate yourself. "The less a man knows of the past and the present, the more unreliable must his judgment of the future prove." (Sigmund Freud, *The Future of an Illusion*, 2). Learn not only at schools, but in the lessons life brings each day.

There are people in your life who will help you deal with your problems, Ima. Kim and I are two such persons. You will have to trust us and those others. You will have to face and embrace some pain and disappointment. You can do it. Things will turn out well.

I remain your friend,

Brad Lancaster

RETICENT BIKE DOG

60
FEAR

Kim and I, before we became a law office, were paint and wallcovering contractors. In 1990, a Japanese firm invited us to work on a Virginia colonial mansion in Omotego, Japan. The "Amelican" house boasted four sixteen-foot Doric columns and a Gone-With-The-Wind staircase; it nestled into a steep hillside. The rear foundation lay seventy feet below the chimney cap. Laborers accessed these heights from scaffolding built for Japanese laborers. I was overweight, about two Japanese workers big. The scaffold complained beneath my clomping. Its moaning stoked my acrophobia. I (probably unfairly) blame Grandmother Lancaster for my fear of heights. She discovered that if she changed squirmy Brad's diaper by placing him on her lowboy freezer, the hell-on-wheels toddler lay perfectly still. Over the years, I learned to restrain, but not defeat, my fear of heights. With sweaty palms, I climbed that rickety scaffold's reaches to paint chimney caps.

An early-winter morning brought frost. A final task remained. Up the scaffold, over the gutter, onto the frosted roof, along the frosted peak to a chimney cap requiring a final coat. I climbed like a monkey. I put one foot on the slick roof. I froze. Terror made me stupid, inept. After ten minutes of silent war, fear won.

Safe below, I reported; the crew laughed. After the frost melted, I took my bucket and brush up again. The only way to spit back at fear is to aim straight into its teeth. To my astonishment, that nemesis chimney cap had been recoated. I retreated, relieved but puzzled. Inquiring, I learned that John, my friend and boss, had scampered up that frosty roof and finished my bit. He eventually confessed: "You couldn't; I could. We all do our part."

> **WE ALL DO OUR PART.**

Seneca (Roman, 1st century A.D.) said: "Friendship produces between us a partnership in all our interests. There is no such thing as good or bad fortune for the individual; we live in common" (*Epistle XLVIII*). I was grateful to avoid that roof. I am more grateful for a friend like John.

ANNIE

61
GOOD

I shuffled into Hotwire coffee house, damp from drizzle, to meet two teenage friends, sisters. Tweedle Dee and Tweedle Dum, locked in sibling intensities. I smiled. "Good to see you two."

Then began trouble. Dee piped, "Why do you think you know what is good? Goodness is prejudice. The world is always going to be a mess until old people stop imposing their values on everybody. People must do what they want, without censure or praise." I gaped, and started to respond, but Dum jumped in. "Dee, it's just the way old people are. They grew up thinking wars are inevitable. Make judgments; kill those who disagree. Right, Brad?"

"Well," I began. "My generation made its judgments and wars. I was conceived during Korea. Raced Soviets to the moon. Got my first kiss during Vietnam. Finished graduate school before the Berlin Wall fell. Then came Iraq 1 and Balkans and Somalia and Afghanistan and Iraq 2. Maybe Iran and Korea 2 next." I paused, frowning. "Wars are generally bad ideas."

Dee's arms shot up like a referee signaling touchdown. "There you go again! You don't know what is good or bad. There is no such thing as virtue. Evil is a projection of infantile insecurities. 'Goodness' is you coercing me to agree." I zagged and got us all another cup of coffee.

Rich aromas and a brief respite tamed frothing waters. I had responses. Humans are unalterably moral creatures. Voltaire (French, 18th century A.D.) described virtue as "doing good to one's neighbor. ... I am poor, you are liberal; I am in danger, you come to my help; I am deceived, you tell me the truth; I am neglected, you console me; I am ignorant, you instruct me" (*Philosophical Dictionary*, Virtue). And consider Jesus. But I dropped it. The Wonderland twins suffered selective deafness that afternoon. After a twenty minute yammer about life's inanities, time was up. I hugged Dee and Dum. Dum said sheepishly, "We needed to vent." I nodded and smiled.

Dee took my hand and whispered, "Thanks. It was *good* of you to listen."

> **VENTING IS GOOD.**

CAMP UNITED WE STAND

62
IN MY BACK YARD

Two storms struck in late fall of 2015. One was meteorological, the other sociological. Both were bad. The sociological tempest spun up from America's persistent neglect of its poor. Increasing prosperity bulldozed cheap housing. And high tech workers kicked the unskilled to the curb. Homeless people proliferated, squatting on freeway fringes, in empty buildings, in wrecked RVs, on sidewalks, and, most pertinent to us, in church parking lots. To paraphrase George Will (American, 20th century): Homelessness is a sidewalk spectacle of disorder, a contagious decay; none has a reasonable right to live on sidewalks (*Hartford Courant*, 19 November 1987). We ask George, But where then?

A homeless group, Camp United We Stand, moved into vacant space outside Bethel Lutheran Church, across the street from our law office. Many helped feed them. We did some legal problem-solving for campers, and felt connected. Bethel Church, long struggling, sold their premises to a Buddhist group. Despite promises the Camp could hunker a few more weeks, the Lutheran pastor demanded the Camp clear out in forty-eight hours. The new-neighbor Buddhists proved likewise unhelpful, their compassion lagging that of the Enlightened One. The disorganized camp found nowhere to land. The Camp's Board contacted us. Camp United We Stand comprised, among others, two pregnant women (one with advancing cancer), a family with four children under twelve, two sorely challenged mentally ill men, a sociopath, and one inveterate smoker suffering advanced emphysema. Perhaps we could have ignored the camp's plight were it peopled by drug-addicted men of foul mouth and aromatic hygiene. But that was not the Camp's composition (which is not to say the Camp had no substance abuse problems). With many reservations, Kim and I decided that the Camp could settle in our back yard for the winter. We expected two sorts of problems: first, legal challenges to our decision; second, adjustment to sharing our private little world with sixteen strangers. Both materialized rapidly.

The first of November's gullywashers arrived. As the Camp loaded trucks, the downpour began. When the trucks had departed, our yard was a mudpit. Exhausted, sodden campers huddled on our covered patio. We ushered the terminally ill, pregnant women, and children indoors. Then we and they started solving problems. In a couple weeks, matters stabilized.

All the adjacent neighbors had consented to the Camp's presence. Others, more distant, were less accommodating. One family complained that they could see a tarp in my back yard. Another expressed anti-homeless sentiments succinctly: "I don't want to see them. I don't want to hear them. I don't want to smell them. I don't want them anywhere in Shoreline." For that neighbor, malice savaged sympathy. No less a luminary than Abraham Lincoln (American, 19th century) shared that Shoreliner's sentiment: "You are destitute because you have idled away all your time. Your thousand pretenses for not getting along better, are all nonsense—they deceive nobody but yourself. *Go to work* is the only cure for your case." (4 November 1851). In Shoreline, NIMBY (Not in my back yard) neurosis prevailed. Complaints to the City brought code enforcement to my door. Those minions asserted my use did not comply with my parcel's zoning. I asserted that, to the extent a zoning regulation inhibits practice of my religious faith, that regulation is unconstitutional. We haggled with the City Attorney, and danced around lawsuits. Eventually the City let the Camp stay until spring, provided I did not again make such an invitation.

Some NIMBY opponents rediscovered empathy. Delegations brought used items and food for the Camp. At Christmas, a few delivered toys for the children. Most remained adamant: homeless people, even those who have lived in Shoreline all their lives, do not belong in Shoreline. Vagrants impair aesthetics; bums depress property values; hobos offend morality. We Americans *work*. Whoever doesn't can eat dirt, these neighbors reasoned.

All our campers, in the course of four and one-half months, found more stable housing. All got health care when needed. All ate regularly. But there was no formula. The twenty-five people who rotated through the Camp needed twenty-five different solutions to improve their life circumstances. If there were a formula, it consists in a nebulous conviction that compassion trumps terror. I estimate these campers expended hundreds of thousands of public dollars during their winter at our residence, mostly for emergent health care for indigent pregnant women and the chronically ill. But the City also spent substantial funds attempting to placate Shoreline's well-heeled conservative rancor, and to wrangle us. One may well doubt the wisdom of these approaches to homelessness, both mine and the NIMBYs'. I do.

People ask why Kim and I welcomed the Camp. At some level, we do not know. It sounded right. We could. The need was heart-wrenching. As an experience, the Camp helped us. Relationships coursed deeply, as they tend wherever friends live together or face exigency. Our acts, and theirs, infused meaning, ever scarce in skin-deep American culture. But more. Deep in chartless wilds of consciousness, Isaiah (Israelite, 8th Century B.C.) beckons. To Isaiah, pious Israelis complained that Yahweh ignored them, despite fervent prayers and scrupulous fasting. Isaiah erupted, to this effect: "Your petty piety lacks the compassion Yahweh seeks. Your stunted spirituality stinks in God's nostrils." Eight centuries later, Jesus (Judean, 1st Century A.D.) adopted Isaiah's disgust with pretense religiosity. Isaiah's rant shaped the Galilean's gospel, and so, rings through time.

> "6 Is not this the fast that I choose: to loose the bonds of injustice, to undo the thongs of the yoke, to let the oppressed go free, and to break every yoke? 7 Is it not to share your bread with the hungry, and bring the homeless poor into your house, . . ."
>
> *Isaiah* 58: 6-7a (NRSV).

Welcoming the camp seemed right. It was right. Or so we hope......

63
YAMMER AT SHORELINE CITY COUNCIL

In support of Shoreline's homeless population, I spoke to the Shoreline City Council for a number of months. Here are most of those three-minute exhortations..

NOVEMBER 23, 2015

Honored members of Shoreline City Council, friends and neighbors who have come to watch the council work, and citizens of Shoreline. My name is Brad Lancaster.

I ask the Council to declare homelessness in Shoreline an emergency. A number of people are trapped outdoors with no realistic prospect of finding housing in the near future. So, these folks are faced with the prospect of fragile shelter, or no shelter at all, during the storms and cold of this winter of 2015-2016.

It is difficult to know just how many homeless people are struggling in Shoreline. Shoreline School District defines a homeless student as one who lacks a fixed, regular, and adequate night time residence. Recently, a representative of the District reported that 355 Shoreline students are homeless. That is 4.4% of Shoreline's more than 8,000 students. Let's just say the number of homeless persons in Shoreline is hundreds.

Cities and counties and states in the western United States are declaring homelessness an emergency. Los Angeles, Portland, Hawaii, Seattle, and King County have declared homelessness a state of emergency. Utah declared no state of emergency, but took gutsy steps, with the LDS church, to give every homeless person a residence and a case worker. The federal government has released many millions of dollars to end veteran homelessness. Local governments declare homelessness a state of emergency by stretching their powers to declare emergencies when earthquakes, terrorists, or rioting strike. These mayors and executives do so to make a formal plea to the state and federal government that homelessness is a growing problem that exceeds the resources of the local community. Mayor Murray of Seattle intends to use the declaration to bypass zoning restrictions and create new sites for homeless encampments.

When the Oso landslide struck in 2014, 43 people died and 30 families were displaced. It was declared a disaster. We all grieved. When Mount St. Helens erupted, 57 people were killed and more than 200 homes were destroyed. It was declared a disaster. We knew that was the right thing to do. Homelessness differs. It is a slow motion plague. Homelessness in King County rose 21% in the last year. So is there an emergency? Consider the numbers. If one counts only the homeless persons in Shoreline, more people are exposed this winter to tremendous danger than died in the Oso landslide and the eruption of Mt. St. Helens combined.

I ask the Council to declare Shoreline homelessness a state of emergency.

NOVEMBER 30, 2015

My name is Brad Lancaster.

Last week I asked the City Council to declare homelessness in Shoreline a state of emergency. In that declaration, the Council would be following the lead of several west coast governments. I recited some sad statistics about the relentless increase in homelessness in Shoreline and King County. I thank you for the funds you dedicated in your budget decisions last week for helping low-income persons.

So, why should the Council declare homelessness an emergency? Will not the poor always be with us in their suffering? Is not homelessness a complex cultural and economic problem that exceeds the capabilities of small cities? I offer three reasons to declare homelessness an emergency.

First, the Council should support Seattle, King County, Portland, Los Angeles, and Hawaii in their attempt to move homelessness up the list of government priorities. Supporting this change of priorities is an emergency because this winter is very cold so far and the number of homeless persons is swelling. It matters, morally and historically, to be on the right side of this issue.

Second, declaring homelessness a state of emergency can serve as a premise for making changes to the zoning code and zoning enforcement in Shoreline. I would ask that the Council consider a simple directive that no zoning enforcement action that negatively impacts homeless persons shall be undertaken during the months of December 2015 through March 2016. At a later date, I will speak of what actions I hope the Council will take in 2016.

Third, caring for homeless persons is a moral imperative. America has long struggled with what to do with those citizens who lack political power. We fought a revolution to gain our own freedoms when it appeared we had none. We endured bitter civil conflict to free America's slaves. We gave women the vote and political equality, after considerable political agitation. We perform a massive wealth transfer through social security to avoid elder poverty. Even now, we struggle to confirm in our policing that black lives matter. The underlying fact is simple. We judge cultures by the way they treat their weakest members. If that is the standard, we have much work to do.

Shoreline is a vibrant, wholesome place to live. Let us treat our homeless with the respect they deserve. To do so, we must all change our priorities. Including this Council.

I thank you for the often thankless work that you do on our behalf. And I thank you for listening.

Please address homelessness.

DECEMBER 7, 2015

My name is Brad Lancaster. I live in Shoreline. I ask the Council to make homelessness a high priority. Tonight, I ask the Council to look at the Shoreline zoning code from the perspective of a homeless person.

Imagine you have become homeless yourself. Unexpectedly, you suffered some setback. You develop a chronic disease or disability. Or your spouse or child did. Your sanity might have fractured. Or you found yourself addicted to some substance, and in trouble with the law. Maybe you suffered domestic violence, or your child was abused. Perhaps you became unemployable because you never finished high school, or you speak English poorly, or you cannot read well enough, or you just got out of jail, or you have been bouncing from job to job for years. So, now you are homeless and broke, in Shoreline.

Where, in Shoreline, should you live? In the parks. No. On the sidewalks. No. In an apartment? You cannot afford one. On the beach? No. With friends? Not if you have worn them out. In a tent? No. That's not permitted. Shoreline contains 12.3 square miles, 413 acres of parks, 191 miles of streets, and 3.4 miles of beautiful shorelines. But there is not one square inch available to you and your homeless children. Not in Shoreline.

If you live in a tent city, you might get a church to take you in. To make that legal, the church will need a temporary use permit. That permit costs several hundred dollars and takes weeks. And you will have to move again in ninety days. How do you keep your new job when you might be moving from Shoreline to Renton? What kind of education are your children getting when they bounce from school to school every ninety days? Regardless, the Shoreline zoning code says, "Sorry about that. Move along."

Oddly, cats, dogs, chickens, rabbits, bees, goats, and sheep can live in Shoreline without a permit. People who are dead, golfing, running a business, being sick, gambling, doing theater, selling marijuana, or living in an RV (briefly) can locate themselves in Shoreline. But if you are poor and homeless, there is no legal place for you. Not in Shoreline.

We each stand but a few terrible events from being homeless ourselves. I know you care about these suffering citizens. Each of you is a good person. I know. Because I live here and I watch.

Please address homelessness.

DECEMBER 14, 2015

My name is Brad Lancaster. I live in Shoreline. For the last month, I have been speaking to the Council about difficult circumstances for Shoreline's homeless people.

I want to thank the Council for devoting time tonight to homelessness in Shoreline. I do not know what you should do about homelessness. I do not even know what I should do about homelessness. I have ideas. I will wager you and the city staff do as well. I hope we can start exploring ideas that address homelessness, together with the citizens of Shoreline. We must stop ignoring this problem.

I value what All Home is doing to address homelessness. So long as we persist in very large groups, like King County or Seattle or even Shoreline, we shall need coordination and overview like that provided by All Home. But the answer to homelessness, I believe, lies in a different direction. It lies in caring. It lies in human affection taking a few well-calculated risks. It lies in personal relationships. The answer to homelessness is one family taking in another. The answer to homelessness is caring people making room for neighbors during difficult transitions. The answer to homelessness lies in knowing and welcoming placeless strangers. If I am right, Shoreliners do not need their City to solve homelessness. Rather, Shoreliners need the city to remove legal barriers that discourage Shoreline citizens from caring about their homeless neighbors. This could be Shoreline's collective identity. We could be known not so much for our beautiful Aurora Corridor or sunsets at Richmond Beach, but rather for the warm way our citizens embrace and assist needy people. In my view, that would be glorious.

I want to thank those who put homelessness on the agenda tonight. When the Council reconvenes in January, I will continue speaking about homelessness. I will talk of best practices addressing homelessness from all over the world. I will focus on ideas that do not involve many tax dollars, for such expenditures just drive up the cost of housing in Shoreline generally. I will speak of better attitudes found elsewhere, and of public-private collaborations. At some point, I will make specific proposals.

Tonight, however, I am anxious to hear what you have to say about homelessness.

JANUARY 4, 2016

My name is Brad Lancaster. I live in Shoreline.

I thank the Council for its resolution in support of King County's declaration of emergency regarding homelessness. I want to report the city staff has begun working on these issues. They have acted with me and my spouse, Kim, in good faith. What's more, they have acted intelligently. Intelligence is often in short supply in government bureaucracies. But not in Shoreline.

In the next few weeks, I will be addressing some questions relating to homelessness. Tonight, I want to ask: **Is homelessness the responsibility of Shoreline city government?** Some think it is not. I disagree.

Every community provisions its people. We work together to provide for ourselves, to get what we need. Our Declaration of Independence asserts that governments exist to help people get life, liberty, and happiness. The United States Constitution, in its preamble, states that government exists to promote our general welfare. We debate among ourselves how much provisioning we should do for one another. We rely primarily on our economy to provide most needs. But our economic system is not open to all. Some cannot participate. We recognize this in our school lunch programs and Medicaid and social security and public hospitals and shelters and food banks. The City of Shoreline is one of the groups responsible for homeless citizens. In any of our debates about how much to do for one another, leaving people to face winters outside and alone cannot be one of our decisions.

Some governments act as the handmaidens of rich people. Other governments think they exist only to quash crime and keep trains running. Both wash their hands of the messy business of helping people. Such governments ignore their most fundamental purpose.

The City of Shoreline exists to be a partner to the citizens of Shoreline. This little government should lead us sometimes, follow us sometimes, and puzzle out with us what the good life looks like. Some Shoreliners are homeless. As our partner, the City should take homelessness personally. The City should care, and encourage all Shoreliners to care. The City should put its shoulder, along with ours, to the task of making a place that is warm, clean, and secure for every Shoreliner.

So, is homelessness the responsibility of the City of Shoreline? I hope you will answer, Yes.

JANUARY 11, 2016

My name is Brad Lancaster. I live in Shoreline.

I am talking about sticky questions related to homelessness. Tonight, I ask: **Isn't homelessness so complex that Shoreline can't do anything about it?**

Homelessness is a complex problem. Homeless people suffer from a host of difficulties. Our culture's response to homelessness consists in a weirdly fractured tangle of bureaucracies and entitlements. Increasingly, the United States economy demands highly skilled workers who are very flexible learners. If your reading or computer skills are absent, if you cannot walk, if children make you unable to work parts of days, if your health prevents working eight hours, then you may not be able to find work at all. So, we end up with an underclass of unemployed people with problems that are difficult to address. Some of them become homeless. Surely, the City of Shoreline cannot fix all of this. It is just beyond us. If the United States as a whole changed its priorities, then we might be able to fix homelessness. The whole jumble is a big bird's nest. We grumble about the human condition, and have another beer. Many of us throw up our hands in exasperation.

I encourage a different approach. Shoreline needs modest goals, realistic goals, regarding homeless Shoreliners. We can alleviate important parts of the suffering associated with homelessness in Shoreline. We can make a place for people to live in tents for periods longer than three months. We can let the good-hearted people of Shoreline build tiny houses for homeless people, without burying the volunteers in red tape. We can use surplus city properties, or little used portions of parks, to make a place for homeless Shoreliners. We can encourage neighbors with empty bedrooms to welcome carefully-vetted homeless citizens. We can make access to support services simpler. The City can serve as a partner to citizens and organizations that want to work on the problem of homeless Shoreliners. We can undertake solutions that lie within our grasp. We can do what we can do.

Homelessness **is** a big, complex problem. Not every part of the problem exceeds us. Let's do what we can do.

JANUARY 25, 2016

My name is Brad Lancaster. I live in Shoreline.

I am asking troubling questions about homelessness. Tonight, I ask: **Do homeless people deserve our help?** The historical answer in America has been, No, homeless people should help themselves. But our perspective changes as our culture mutates. Perhaps now we can treat homeless people with respect.

Our nation's story is one of slowly learning to include people. We, frankly, have a ghastly history of exclusion. In the 1600s, we sailed to America to escape European religious persecutions. Once here, we excluded heretics, and burned a few. In the 1760s, we drove nasty Americans loyal to King George into Canada. In 1789, we agreed that Yankee Anglicans could indeed put up with Baptist tobacco farmers, at least to the minimal extent the Constitution required. We let free, white males vote. In the 1800s, we nearly exterminated American native populations. In the 1860s, we killed one and one half million Americans resolving the question whether one man could own another. We abolished slavery, but granted little freedom. In the 1920s, belatedly, women got the franchise. Again, for a time, that meant little. In the 1960s, we belatedly finished the Civil War. We enacted statutes that gave people of color a chance at prosperity. Jim Crowe died (or was badly wounded). In the 1980s, America's women seized their day. In the 1990s, we built some wheelchair ramps. In the 2000s, we recognized that odd sexualities are not all that odd. Always slowly. A little too slowly.

Not surprisingly, the poor's freedoms are off to a shaky start. The Great Depression showed us horrors. FDR intervened. The 1970s saw War on Poverty. Now, belatedly, courts may declare homelessness, even poverty itself, a suspect class. Hating poor people may soon be treated like race or disability or sex discrimination. Where attitudes of exclusion persist, we need such declarations.

So, do homeless people deserve our help? Homeless people need respect. They need homes. Nothing fancy. Just a spot secure, dry, warm, and private. A base from which to re-launch themselves. Can we now say that homeless people deserve our help? Can we lend a hand? We shall see.

FEBRUARY 1, 2016

My name is Brad Lancaster. I live in Shoreline.

I have been talking about homelessness. Homelessness is epidemic in King County. The One Night Count last week found 4,500 homeless persons in King County. That is an increase of 19% over last year's count. The One Night Count conclusion is an underestimate. I have fifteen homeless people in my back yard who did not get counted.

Tonight I want to suggest the most important change that Shoreline can make to improve the life of homeless people in Shoreline.

The first and most important thing to be done is this. **Make a dedicated, year-round place for thirty homeless families with school age children.** Let the citizens of Shoreline who care collaborate to build thirty tiny houses to place on that permanent site. Let them, with the residents, fashion a neat, clean village of families whose children can benefit from uninterrupted attendance at Shoreline's excellent schools. Until those houses are built, erect platforms on which families with children can pitch their tents, up off the wet ground. Provide some power and Honey Buckets. Let the homeless families contribute to those expenses. Do not require families to move from this village so long as they have school age children.

Children are our most valuable resource. The nurture of children is our most critical task. Those children will become Shoreline little more than a decade from now. Children learn to live as do their parents. No Shoreliner wants any child to learn that life is transient, that no one really cares, and that whatever one begins is likely to languish uncompleted.

I spent a few late evenings last week helping a twelve year old and a ten year old, both students at Ridgecrest, with math homework. Neither understood their math problems. I explored the texture of their mathematical knowledge. Each had missed small, but critical, topics in math along the way. These children had moved from the Marshall Islands to Arkansas to Oklahoma to Auburn to Shoreline. At each transition, they lost little pieces, being thrust into classes at different locations on the map of mathematics. So, these children were always befuddled. This week, those children will move yet once more, to Federal Way. They will join yet another math class. They will undoubtedly drop another fragment of math in the transition.

Make a permanent transitional housing location for homeless families with school age children here in Shoreline.

FEBRUARY 8, 2016

My name is Brad Lancaster. I live in Shoreline.

I am identifying ways the Council might change social policy in Shoreline to improve life for homeless people. Before Martin Luther King Day, I asked the Council to authorize a permanent tiny house village for homeless parents with school-age children. I also asked you to fundamentally revise the permitting process for homeless encampments. In that regard, I have begun discussions with a group of students from Seattle University to draft uniform revisions to municipal codes to make them more homeless friendly.

Tonight, I suggest that Shoreline should dedicate two public spaces to homeless encampments. Each should accommodate 100 persons without children. Frankly, it is unlikely that homelessness is going to diminish markedly until the United States restructures itself economically. Manufacturing jobs have fled to cheaper labor markets. The loss of those jobs is rippling downward through the economy, just as the cost of real estate (and rents) rises in urban areas. So, homelessness is going to get worse in Shoreline before it gets better.

The City of Shoreline should shoulder its obligations with regard to Shoreline's homeless persons by dedicating two public spaces to tiny house and tent encampments.

These sites should have the following practices.

First, the encampment sites should welcome placement of tiny houses on trailers constructed by those willing to donate their time and money to building tiny houses. In the interim, the encampment sites should also hold platforms on which campers may pitch tents under nicely arranged tarps (I have a design for that). Over time, we should build common bathrooms, laundry, and kitchen facilities for these public encampments.

Second, only one of the two sites should be in use at any time. Annually, in the spring, the entire camp should move to the alternate location. There is a problem with any encampment. It may, with neglect, become a slum. Living there might stigmatize residents and create marginal apartheid among citizens. The City should require that the tiny house encampments remain clean and well-maintained (by persons who do not work for the City).

Third, this encampment on public ground should self-govern and be treated with respect as another neighborhood of Shoreline.

Several sites have been suggested. Each will require action by the City council and cooperation from other governmental agencies and the public. There may be some fireworks, but homelessness is our problem, not just that of homeless persons. Let's do what we can do.

MARCH 14, 2016

My name is Brad Lancaster. I live in Shoreline.

I am suggesting ways the Council might change social policy in Shoreline to make things better for low-income persons. I have discussed a permanent tiny house village for homeless parents with school-age children. I have asked you to fundamentally revise the permitting process for homeless encampments. I described how the City might use two dedicated homeless encampment sites. I suggested revisions to the City's Accessory Dwelling Unit statute to make those ADUs more accessible as low-rent housing stock.

Tonight I introduce the Open Homes initiative.

This Open Homes idea starts in Europe. In Geel, Belgium, 500 psychiatric patients, all presently under care, live in the homes of the citizens of Geel. The Geel psychiatric hospital has led the way in de-institutionalization of psychiatric care. These many families of Geel provide a home base and social universe for Geel's mentally ill citizens. I speak of Geel to make a point. American attitudes about privacy are not the only attitudes possible. It may well be better for us if we welcome in, rather than shut out, distressed people. It would certainly be better for the distressed people.

The citizens of Shoreline have shown tremendous compassion toward the encampment at my residence. With some encouragement and structure, Shoreliners who are willing might open their homes to one or two homeless people.

An Open Homes initiative might have problems that should be addressed up front. First, families that welcome homeless people to their homes should charge no rent to these guests. A no-rent policy will avoid entanglements with the Washington Residential Landlord-Tenant Act. Second, any homeless person who wishes such housing, and any homeowner who provides such housing, should be deeply screened by the homeless encampment supervisory non-profit. Training for both parties should be provided. Third, a dispute resolution process should be put in place before the program commences. There will be disputes. Fourth, current commission of crimes and active warrants should bar guests from this program. I would, however, recommend allowing people into the program who have served their time and are compliant with their terms of probation.

The Open Homes initiative is an act of conscience and the human heart. It is not legislation. Some Shoreliners may open their homes. That generosity alone might house all of Shoreline's homeless persons. So I ask. Can you open your home?

Thank you for listening.

MARCH 29, 2016

My name is Brad Lancaster. I live in Shoreline.

I have suggested a series of changes to Shoreline law that might make Shoreline more hospitable to homeless persons.

Tonight I want to explain the need for a Shoreline homeless coordinator.

If the city establishes homeless encampments, those camps will need someone to administer them. The membership of camps changes frequently. That is good, because it means people are finding housing. That is bad, because just when a camp administrator gets her feet under herself, she moves out of the camp and into housing. So, the ball gets dropped a lot in the camps. In the weeks since November 15th at my residence, we have had twenty-three persons live in our back yard and house. Only five remain from the original group of sixteen who moved in. To make encampments work, the camps need someone stable and connected.

There are many systemic problems that homeless encampments experience that are not solved by dealing with just one set of campers or just one host. Hosting organizations need to be coordinated so that camps do not need to scramble to find places to be. Campers with specific problems need to be connected to the right services and care. Someone needs to keep a bank account for donations, collect a dollar a day from the campers for their joint expenses, and keep track of who is in the camps. Someone needs to organize camp meetings, create an agenda, and get decisions made with the campers. These are not matters that the campers can handle efficiently themselves. There is no dry paper, no printers, no reliable telephone. Time gets distorted for many campers. And what is administration besides paper, phone calls, and timeliness?

Most of these campers are shell-shocked. Their worlds have fallen apart unexpectedly. Some think their plight is just an aberration, just a bad week. Many have difficulty planning. A few are depressed. Some are pretty thoroughly confused. They need a hand with getting organized, a hand that stays at their ship's tiller longer than a few months.

Shoreline may be able to recruit an existing non-profit to take on this work. Hopelink comes to mind. So does Greater Seattle Cares. If not an existing non-profit, we may need to create one dedicated to administering homeless encampments.

Thank you for listening.

APRIL 4, 2016

My name is Brad Lancaster. I live in Shoreline.

I have suggested a series of changes to Shoreline law that might make Shoreline more hospitable to homeless persons. Two weeks ago, I told you of the Open Homes Initiative, in which Shoreliners welcome homeless persons into their empty rooms and basements.

I have been thinking how very much like Europe's refugee situation is Shoreline's homeless population. Our refugees are not coming from another country. They are home-grown refugees, fleeing collapsed economies and corrupt political schemes. Our local refugees flee the failure of imagination in Detroit, and endemic racism in Appalachia, or unemployment attending South Dakota's anemic fracking fields.

A journalist from Lebanon offers a lesson in absorbing refugees. This bit is from *The Week* magazine, April 1, 2016:

> Lebanon can teach Europe a thing or two about how to treat refugees. . . . [Lebanon's government does not function, its economy is backward, it has no president, and its parliament is gridlocked.] Yet [Lebanon] has absorbed 1.5 million Syrians over the past four years, the highest rate of refugees per capita in the world, with no public outcry or anti-migrant violence. The reason may be because [the Lebanese] do not expect the government to deal with the new arrivals. . . . Here, since government is hapless, civic groups and individuals step up. Refugees find housing in the cities, renting out garages or rooms. Arabic and Islamic charities donate "shadow aid." It's chaotic, but it works. Europeans should try "society-led initiatives." Trust your people to be generous.

Shoreline is not Lebanon, and our problem is not nearly so great as their problem with dislocated Syrians. But perhaps one part of any solution is the Lebanese solution. To achieve a Lebanese degree of hospitality here in Shoreline, we will need to make changes. The zoning code must not tell Shoreliners we are not permitted to care. Our conversations will need to praise those who make a place for dislocated people. And we will need to think about homeless persons differently. They are brothers and sisters, not invading ne'er-do-wells.

So, tonight I ask Shoreline to take a lesson at the feet of Lebanese Muslims.

APRIL 11, 2016

My name is Brad Lancaster. I live in Shoreline.

I have suggested a series of changes to Shoreline law that might make Shoreline more hospitable to homeless persons. Shoreline (and all of America) needs to coordinate the chaotic and duplicative menagerie of systems aimed at helping poor and homeless persons. When seeking public help, the homeless person faces a daunting series of applications. Each application approaches the homeless person as if he had never before contacted public entities. Paperwork obstacles leap up, impenetrable as granite. From the perspective of homeless people, the system, if we can dignify it with the name "system," seems aimed at making sure homeless persons get no assistance.

This is not a new problem. In 1997, almost twenty years ago, the Washington Supreme Court found that DSHS has an affirmative duty to provide for homeless children a "comprehensive and coordinated plan for providing services."[113] Twenty years later, matters have degenerated.

In 1997, the Supreme Court found that the majority of the Washington homeless are families with small children, and homelessness has significant adverse effects upon the growth and development of children. The Court stated, "State agencies have not coordinated their services or their goals concerning homeless families and their children. There is no plan that coordinates the services provided at the state level. At the local level, there is no effort to coordinate with non-profit providers that serve homeless families. It is a very fragmented system."

The Gates Foundation urges that, to bring systemic improvements, the delivery of services needs "one simple way to access the system."[114] This will reduce delay, waste, and redundancy.

Gates billions and the lumbering DSHS behemoth have not remediated this problem. What should Shoreline do for its homeless persons? I suggest that the City could save money by hiring someone to coordinate services to homeless persons. That person could create a system that gathers from homeless persons all the information the various organizations need, and then issues that information in the format each department prefers. The homeless people I know are not great at administration. The system we have invented to help homeless persons requires an administrative genius to navigate. The mismatch is stupid. Failure of coordination causes great suffering. It defeats our good intentions.

Set someone the task of making access to homeless services simple and coordinated.

---

[113] Washington State Coalition for the Homeless v. Department of Social and Health Services, 494 P.2d 1291, 133 Wn.2d 894 (Wash. 1997).

[114] http://www.gatesfoundation.org/What-We-Do/US-Program/Washington-State.

APRIL 18, 2016

My name is Brad Lancaster. I live in Shoreline.

I have suggested a series of changes to Shoreline law that might make Shoreline more hospitable to homeless persons. Tonight, I want to speak about one way to prevent homelessness.

People become homeless a bit at a time. First, something bad happens. One loses a job, gets divorced, gets injured, suffers a crime, or any other of life's insults. Then one's budget capsizes. That budget had been working, just barely, paycheck to paycheck. But the insult is too much. So, one is forced to choose: kids' food, health care, the car, electricity, water, rent. All cannot be sustained. Finally, something gets shut off. The landlord evicts. And you are homeless. You couch surf until you wear your friends and family out. Then you stay in your car, if you have one. Finally, the car won't start any longer, and gets hauled away. And there you are—homeless. At that point, this instance of homelessness rises into our consciousness as a society. We start reconstructing all of those components of life for the homeless person. It is no small task.

Looked at as a system, homelessness interventions work better the farther upstream they occur. One must cut off the crisis that makes a homeless person homeless. Offering $200 of utility assistance might, at one point, have prevented the collapse, and saved $20,000 of emergency room care eighteen months later. Offering $500 in rent assistance when a person breaks his arm might mean his children never are pulled from their elementary school, interrupting their math education.

The Homelessness Task Force of Redmond, Washington, did a major investigation of homelessness in their area. They made useful recommendations. One recommendation is the creation of a flexible funding pool. These grants and loans are made available to people teetering at the brink of homelessness to assist them in keeping their residences. Once people collapse into homelessness, they are likely to do so over and over again. Preventing homelessness is much less expensive, both financially and in degree of suffering, than allowing homelessness. *All Home*, from whom the Council has heard, aims to make homelessness rare. A flexible funding pool on which Shoreline residents might draw could help keep Shoreliners in their homes, even when bad things happen.

APRIL 25, 2016

My name is Brad Lancaster. I live in Shoreline.

I have suggested a series of changes to Shoreline law and policy that might make Shoreline more hospitable to homeless persons. Tonight, I want to speak about a way to get things done and help homeless people too.

Mayor Richard Berry of Albuquerque, New Mexico had a homelessness problem. Their panhandlers were out of control. So, the city took steps. The city did not drive the panhandlers away. They did not jail them. They did not forbid them to loiter on busy corners. Instead, Albuquerque hired them.

This homeless work program addresses the need of homeless persons for a bit of cash to stay afloat. That is, after all, what panhandlers are seeking. So, Albuquerque put up permanent signs at the busy corners preferred by panhandling people. The signs encourage drivers to make a donation to a homeless website, run by United Way, instead of giving directly to panhandlers. The signs also tell the homeless where to go for day work. Donated money goes to wages for homeless persons willing to do day jobs. The city also kicks in funds, and foundations have been making contributions as well. A city van delivers workers to the day's workplace. Workers pull weeds, pick up trash, and do other things the city needs done. Since the inception of Albuquerque's homeless work program, day workers have picked up 50,000 pounds of trash and weeds. When the day of work is complete, the workers are delivered to their pick up point, a church homeless hospitality site. There, volunteers help the homeless link up with social services. And successfully so, it would seem. Eighty-four have found help with substance abuse. Thirty-four got permanent jobs. Eight chronically homeless people have found permanent housing. And 7,200 people have called in on the social services hot line. The first year's budget in Albuquerque was $50,000. This year's budget is $181,000. The city has been asked by neighboring communities how their program works, because they want to replicate it.

I like this program. It turns an annoyance into useful enterprise. It is your classic lemons to lemonade story.

I like lemonade.

MAY 9, 2016

My name is Brad Lancaster. I live in Shoreline.

I have been suggesting a series of changes to Shoreline law and policy that might make Shoreline more hospitable to homeless persons. Tonight, I suggest that the Council could form a volunteer citizen's advisory board to address homelessness in Shoreline. The group could offer reports to the Council and make proposals for needful changes to Shoreline policies. There are several reasons why the Council should take this step:

First, the citizens of Shoreline have shown great compassion and support for homeless people this last long, gray winter. Formalizing that voice within city government could give those concerned citizens a venue for translating their concerns into action.

Second, the homelessness crisis shows no sign of abating. Summers camping in Seattle are generally easier than winter outside. We can expect to see difficult circumstances for families once again as winter settles in. Shoreline should not be the sort of town where children live on the streets.

Third, and perhaps most important, we as Americans have become more and more disconnected from one another over the last fifty years. Our isolation has made us rich, but not made us better. As our social connections have waned, so too our spirits have shriveled. We have become misers, dwelling with our televisions and pets behind locked doors. When in public, we tint our windows, and avert our eyes. We rush about in our little imported cars. Some of us have become moral midgets.

The point of a citizen advisory council on homelessness is to care about others. Such committees swim against America's tide of isolation. They pry open our hearts toward one another, toward our homeless neighbors.

I encourage the Council to establish a volunteer citizen's advisory board on issues relating to homelessness. Show that board some respect. Give them a place to meet here in the City's building. Invite them in to report to the Council every quarter. Take their recommendations, when well-conceived, to heart.

Maybe it will make us better people.

MAY 16, 2016

My name is Brad Lancaster. I live in Shoreline.

I have been suggesting a series of changes to Shoreline law and policy that might make Shoreline more hospitable to homeless persons. Tonight I pivot to begin a series of talks on what other towns are doing to address their homelessness problems. Some towns are trying workable approaches that deserve praise. Others have gotten spanked by the courts and media for harsh or bigoted actions. These tales are the stories of America. We all struggle to know just what to do when families in our midst fall out the bottom of our economy.

Daytona Beach, Florida, has a homelessness problem. The weather is great. The beach is beautiful. The homeless love the benches. The tourists hate the homeless. In 2014, Daytona homeless advocates counted around 175 homeless people within Daytona Beach, and another approximately 700 in Volusia County generally.

Daytona Beach decided to remove its benches. Then they had a beach near which no one could sit, except in the sand. The homeless learned to camp just outside the city limits, so city regulations would not impact them. They would walk downtown every day. Many good-hearted Daytona Beach residents helped feed the homeless population. A researcher studying the Daytona Beach problems with homelessness concluded that such feeding enables homelessness, and makes the unhoused population grow. The researcher recommended engagement, rather than enablement. Address the root causes of homelessness substantively. Providing meaningful care could be financed by the funds saved in public services, of which homeless people are voracious consumers.

So, Daytona Beach decided to create Tiger Bay Village just outside the town. Homes will be provided for people, with onsite services to address the various problems that drive homelessness. The service agencies plan to consolidate, offering other savings. Just so you do not think these folks daft, in Florida in August of 2014, shelter for a homeless person cost $11-28 per day. A night in jail cost $53-94 dollars per day, and each booking cost $764 dollars. A night in the hospital cost $1,278. So, the savings are there to be snagged, if one can only find a way to do so.

We can follow the success and failure of Tiger Bay Village from a safe distance to see how it works out in Daytona Beach.

JUNE 6, 2016

My name is Brad Lancaster. I live in Shoreline.

I attended the State of the City meeting last week. A nice event. During the breakfast, I spoke with a member of this Council and listened to the excellent pianist. That council member said that he has not been too interested in the statutory changes I have proposed concerning homelessness in Shoreline. I was, of course, crestfallen. This councilmember was, however, pleased to learn of Dayton Beach's attempt to move their homeless persons into Tiger Bay Village, just outside the city. That Florida development would contain semi-permanent housing with a host of associated services. As he spoke, I wondered what the thousands of homeless persons in Puget Sound are supposed to do while waiting for Shoreline's equivalent of Tiger Bay Village to be conceived and erected. According to this council member, encampments of homeless folks should be the province of churches and religious charities.

As I thought about that council member's view, I recognized that we differ in what we mean by the word "home." The council member hunkers in a view of "home" that is the American gold standard. One's "home" is where one lives, a place one owns, purchased by one's sweat and diligence. Public spaces differ from home. We all own public places together. Citizens use public spaces, but briefly. After enjoying an afternoon at the park, we go "home" to our private spaces. Citizens are those with homes. Citizens make this limited use of public space. Citizens have jobs and savings so they can afford this pattern of life and thought.

My homeless friends have a different view. Home is where one lives. My homeless friends may stay overnight at a park, or several overnights. These friends do not want to be hiding in the park. They just lack alternatives. Their government evicts them every ninety days or so, if they live in a camp. Most of my homeless friends feel that they are something less than citizens. To me they say: No one makes you move. No one forces you to rely upon the charity of strangers merely to exist. We are not really citizens. My homeless friends are right. Some towns have attempted to criminalize homelessness. Others, more rarified in their deportations, turn up their noses and lavish inattention upon homeless persons.

So, my council member's solution is a good one, if only one has sufficient time. His solution remedies homelessness by housing everyone. Excellent! That, however, sounds better than it is. His view means that the vast majority of homeless persons, thousands of them, will remain annoying vagrants, until that distant point in time (which never arrives) when lions graze with lambs and the homeless are housed.

We simply must do better than that.

JUNE 13, 2016

My name is Brad Lancaster. I live in Shoreline.

Santa Ana, California, became famous for its approach to homelessness. The city passed an anti-camping ordinance. No one could camp on a street, in a park, or in a parking lot. The city council of Santa Ana consciously engaged a war against homeless people. It wanted them gone. The city tore down tents. The city adjusted park sprinklers to douse homeless groups. After litigation ensued, the city entered a stipulation with its homeless opponents that it would end its "war on the homeless." But the City did not stop. Its harassment of its homeless population persisted.

So, eventually, the California Court of Appeals found against the City of Santa Ana. There the court found that Santa Ana's anti-camping ordinance employed a butcher knife where a scalpel was needed. The court said: "[The anti-camping ordinance] is a transparent manifestation of Santa Ana's policy, adopted five years ago, to expel the homeless. The city may preclude the erection of structures in public places and it might ban "camping" in select locations with a properly drafted ordinance, but it may not preclude people who have no place to go from simply living in Santa Ana. And that is what this ordinance is about."

So, you might think that the law of California welcomes homeless people. That is not so. The *Tobe v. Santa Ana* case went on to the California Supreme Court. The high court overturned the court of appeals, and upheld Santa Ana's anti-homelessness statute. I listened to portions of that Supreme Court argument today on C-SPAN. The high court was determined to find some basis for upholding Santa Ana's anti-camping statute. It made much of public urination and drug use. The high court pretended not to know who homeless people are. Generally, the court exhibited all the worst aspects of results-oriented decision-making one ever finds in the judicial system. The court's responses were, frankly, demeaning for homeless persons, and disheartening for this lawyer.

We learn two things from the *Tobe v. Santa Ana* case. First, cities sometimes go great distances to make themselves unwelcoming to homeless persons. When they do so, they simply discriminate. Second, whenever one decides to discriminate against homeless persons, one will find allies, sometimes in high places. Such supporters of ugly measures erode the judicial system itself.

Shoreline should avoid Santa Ana's approach. Do not make war on homeless people, directly or indirectly.

JANUARY 30, 2017

My name is Brad Lancaster. I live in Shoreline.

Fourteen months ago I asked you to remove provisions from the Shoreline Code that discriminate against people without homes. You instructed the City Staff to do just that. Tonight you publicly consider the results of the efforts of City Staff and the Planning Commission. Those two groups could not have failed more egregiously.

First, Ordinance 762 throws up new obstacles to transitional encampments. It requires twenty foot setbacks for camp locations. That makes hosting an encampment unworkable for all but two or three of Shoreline's churches. A twenty foot setback puts any encampments in the middle of parking lots, rather than at their edges. What church will host encampments if it means they have to give up their parking lots to do so? Of the three remaining church sites for transitional encampments, one has already opted out of hosting campers.

The second utterly unworkable theory Staff and the Planning Commission put before you tonight is the concept of "managing agency." No camp in Shoreline has ever been managed by the hosting church or citizens. The camps are self-governing. They have boards of directors. None of the "managing agencies" own or lease land on which to locate encampments. What church would consent to be legally liable for the activities of persons over whom they exercise little control?

The third error in Ordinance 762 is its express intent to prevent citizens in Shoreline from hosting campers in their back yards. Regularly, so far, Shoreline's churches and city government have failed to help people without houses. They have forced pregnant women and sick old men and elementary age children to hide in parks, hoping the police do not roust them. Some citizens are willing to step up when churches and governments fail. Proposed Ordinance 762 would violate the United States and Washington Constitutions. It punishes people for caring. If authorized, Ordinance 762 could embroil the City of Shoreline in protracted litigation as citizens fight to preserve their fundamental right to practice their religious convictions.

Finally, Ordinance 762 still requires elementary school age children to move mid-school year. The Staff took refuge in the idea that the school district is required to bus students who move. The problem remains that no one knows where the camp will go when it moves. Will the school district bus the camp's children from Tukwila? From Tacoma?

The solution is quite simple. Kill Ordinance 762. Don't revise Ordinance 762. Don't spiff it up and pass it. End Ordinance 762. Send City Staff back to the drawing board. Tell them to review once again the instructions you gave them. Instruct the Planning Commission of your purpose to make Shoreline a place that welcomes and cares for people with problems, even if those people lack houses. Tell them both to get it right next time.

Thank you for listening.

FEBRUARY 27, 2017

My name is Brad Lancaster. I live in Shoreline.

We now suffer another version of staff's proposed code revisions concerning transitional encampments in Shoreline. As with the previous proposal, staff throws up new obstacles to homeless people. Fourteen months ago you instructed the city staff to remove, not create, obstacles to homeless people in the Shoreline code.

The revised transitional encampment ordinance proposes new, and unrealistic, minimum square footage requirements for transitional encampments. The provisions will reduce the number of churches with sufficient space to host a transitional encampment from its present four to a questionable three. Of those three potential locations, only two have expressed readiness to host transitional encampments. So, as a result of the staff's and planning commission's work, the number of locations for transitional encampments has declined from the number of all of the churches and back yards in Shoreline to two places only. How do these changes reduce obstacles to transitional encampments?

These revisions still require elementary school age children to move in the middle of their school year. All the evidence indicates that such moves are disastrous for elementary school children, and not much better for older school children. Why would the City put such a requirement in the zoning code? In what sense is this proposal reducing obstacles to homeless people in Shoreline? The School District indicates there are hundreds of children in the district without permanent homes. Why make their lot more difficult? Why further injure their educations?

To solve problems, one must risk something. Obstacles to homeless people have skyrocketed as the staff has done their work. Remove obstacles. Do not create new obstacles. Spend some of your political capital on this issue. Some people complain of homeless encampments from their well-heated homes in their safe neighborhoods with their full refrigerators. Homeless people ask no more than a place to exist, to be cold in their tents, exposed to every predator that lives in Shoreline, with no refrigerator at all. Make Shoreline safe for homeless people. These code revisions will not accomplish that.

You have joined Seattle in recognizing homelessness as an emergency. Are the staff's zoning proposals consistent with your understanding of how our city should cope with an emergency?

My spouse says that this is a cranky talk. She is right. I am cranky about these proposals.

Thank you for listening.

MARCH 20, 2017

My name is Brad Lancaster. I live in Shoreline.

I address proposed zoning amendments for transitional encampments, Ordinance 762. If staff's purpose is to regulate homeless people out of Shoreline, the proposed amendments are a grand success. If staff's purpose is to remove obstacles to vulnerable populations in Shoreline, staff has failed abjectly. So, my question to you tonight is what are you trying to accomplish: helping homeless people or driving them out of Shoreline?

Being a city council person is no easy job. I believe each of you to be a good person in a difficult position. I believe you intend to do well for us. When you get things right, life gets better for Shoreliners. When you get them wrong, matters get worse for us.

As Americans, we have gotten things right, and we have gotten things wrong.

Native Americans. Our ancestors drove the native peoples across the continent, disparaged them, gave them diseases and alcohol, and murdered them. Ultimately, we put native Americans in ghettos. We feared the Indians. We behaved badly. But our political leaders were well-intentioned. They just got it wrong.

Slavery. America bought the human products of the African slave trade. We used those kidnapped peoples as agricultural machines, held them as property, and ultimately killed a million Americans changing those laws. All involved were well-intentioned, but wrong.

Internment Camps. Japanese maniacs destroyed our Pacific fleet. We responded by incarcerating useful American citizens because they looked like the Japanese maniacs. Well-intentioned people made those terribly errant decisions.

Tonight, you consider Ordinance 762. The statute singles out a group of people for intensive government oversight. Poverty is not illegal, though one would never guess that from Ordinance 762. The statute hides invidious discrimination beneath a veneer of bland zoning talk. That statute makes school children move mid-school year. That statute gives inordinate discretion to city staffers. That statute reduces possible homeless encampment sites from many to very few. That statute infringes the constitutional free exercise liberties of citizens of Shoreline, in violation of both the First Amendment, and Article I, Section 11 of the Washington Constitution. Worst, the statute douses human compassion. The statute leaks fear. Discriminatory fear. Loathing and fear of homeless people.

You have good intentions. But are you doing the right thing?

Ordinance 762 does not do the right things. Please vote "No."

Thank you for listening.

On March 20, 2017, Shoreline City Council passed Ordinance 762 by a unanimous vote.

PLEASE DON'T MAKE ME SWIM AGAIN....

64
THE OTHER AMERICA

On the morning after Donald Trump's election, I almost vomited. I sat on the toilet in my crappy little post-war cottage. My mouth gushed saliva. Nausea mugged my balance. For months, during the GOP debates, Trump's lackluster performances met wild adulation. I puzzled. What was I missing? I am a recent Democrat, driven from the GOP by its nutty nationalist lunge. I voted for Richard Nixon and Ronald Reagan, twice each. I would probably do so again. My worst political nightmare was to be forced to vote for Hillary Rodham Clinton. Invited for an imaginary meal, Clinton offers hot porridge of prevarication, rustic sandwich de la snobbery, or artichoke of avarice. Like George W's speechifying, Hillary's homilies chill me. Yet Donald Trump prevailed. He hog-tied me. I filled the little ballot oval for HRC—slowly, deliberately, painfully. God. What was America thinking? Millions voted for Trump. What in the world.....?

Before the rest of this brief cogitation, I want to be clear. Donald Trump is not qualified to be President of the United States. Unhinged narcissism makes of him a humorless joke. Modest (and declining) abilities highlight extravagant immorality. He seethes racial animus. He lives in ignorance of the Constitution he pledged to protect. He revels in serial sexual assaults. As the saw goes, you know he is lying because his lips are moving. This President takes joy in shame. His presidency is illegitimate. He paid more money than some full-time workers make in a decade to muzzle mistresses in the run-up to the election. He needed, asked for, and got election assistance from foreign enemies. He prevented investigators from exposing his crimes. Once was not good enough. Mr. Trump again sought east European help to bolster his flagging election prospects. Donald Trump has demeaned our finest institutions, subverted them to his purposes, and corrupted their players. Mr. Trump has been impeached. But cowering Senators, elected by those who voted for Mr. Trump, gave him a walk. So, he lingers in office. Then Covid-19 stormed our beaches. Tens of thousands have died, who need not have died, for a single reason: Mr. Trump's defects of heart and mind. An election approaches. The circus reconvenes. . . . To grasp my meaning, some perspective may help. The most dangerous thing that has happened in American history is not slavery. Not the Civil War. Not the 1918 influenza pandemic. Not the Great Depression. Not Hitler's Reich or the Emperor's Japan. Not Stalin's Cold War or Three Mile Island or proliferating mass murders by suicidal fanatics, or resurgent racist nationalism. The grave danger lies in Donald Trump. He steals equanimity. He spews disillusion. He eviscerates optimism. Mr. Trump has done what no other could. He makes us doubt America. There. I've said that piece. To be clear.

Back to what the other America, the America I left, was thinking in the last election, is thinking now that they see what messes they have wrought. I vote Republican. Or at least I did until the party wandered off about ten years ago. Around Tea Party time. At festivities with Redsters, to get a rise, I sometimes poke a strident blatherer: Republicans are just Democrats without compassion. It is no joke. I, as do many of my Democratic friends, share Republican values. Hard work. Self-reliance. Fiscal sobriety. Keeping friends and allies safe. Family. Friendship. Truth. Honor. Faith. What has become of those values in Red states? I know Red state people. I grew up in Idaho. There are MAGA hats in my family. More Red than Blue, if you count. For God's sake, my step-daughter-in-law harvested a moose yesterday; she and hers will butcher and eat the beast, every last muscle. Like Arby's, they have the meats. Denizens of fly-over states ooze grit; some deem gristle as the finest cut of a cow. These are not the sort of folks that compromise core values because their convictions prove inconvenient. Moral amnesia affects sociopaths. And con men. And imbeciles. It is tempting to assign Red state moral collapse before the Trumpist tsunami to one of these categories, to call "those people" nuts or crooks or idiots. This is beyond me. I cannot believe that story. Thurgood Marshall spoke truly when he said: "Prejudice, once let loose, is not easily cabined." *City of Cleburn v. Cleburne Living Center*, 473 U.S. 432 (1985) (finding that mentally impaired people are not a protected class in Equal Protection analysis). We cannot, with impunity, dismiss our neighbors so lightly. We are them; they are us. Our togetherness is fractured. Let us cabin our mutual disparagement.

Antonin Scalia, recently deceased from the United States Supreme Court, offered, in dissent, the following thought: "It is hard to admit that one's political opponents are not monsters, especially in a struggle like this one, and the challenge in the end proves more than today's Court can handle. Too bad." *United States v. Windsor*, 133 S. Ct. 2675 (2013) (finding the federal Defense of Marriage Act violates the Fifth Amendment). Despite scolding his brethren for mutual intolerance, the rancorous imp in Nino Scalia took a parting shot, calling the majority opinion "legalistic argle-bargle." Yet, one must recall that Antonin Scalia and Ruth Bader Ginsburg, though polar opposites (he the tradition-mired conservative, she the rabid feminist liberal; he the robust bullock, she the fragile hummingbird), shared friendship. RBG described their odd couple togetherness as "best buddies." Their families spent New Years together. They rode an elephant in India together and attended operas. Ruth loved Nino's "peppery prose," and thanked him for skewering her argle-bargle. His testy Ninograms made her revise, improved her opinions. Ruth and Nino knew that the best way to destroy an enemy is to make him (or her) a friend (Abraham Lincoln, American 19th century).

Perhaps, the other America is just stuck. Most voted for Donald because they (like me) could not stomach Hillary. Perhaps they just dismissed Mr. Trump's incapacities. Perhaps they believed, wrongly, that there are no real qualifications to be President. Perhaps they just voted for "anything else." Now, now that our Incompetent-in-Chief has flown his colors, now that he has thrilled skinheads and racists, now that he has touted pointless walls and terrified children, now that he has rallied despots and enfeebled democracies, now that he has fractured global economic stability, now that he has eroded strategic partnerships, now that he has butchered the English language, now that he has weaponized social media, perhaps now Red America just feels stuck. The only game in town, for them, is Mr. Trump. Red America discarded its dissenters. Me, for example. So, the Other America just holds their collective nose and soldiers on. Hoping. Hoping. But for what?

The Trump delusion will collapse, unless America comes apart at the seams first. I saw two officials, a former sheriff and a southwest politician, pupils blown, sputtering spittle. They declared their intention to kill any bastard who seeks to part them from AR-15s. This berzerk spectacle is what, in specific, it looks like to doubt America. Once we doubt our togetherness, the spiral surges downward. Like a sucking drain. Mr. Trump is a symptom of degenerate politics. Lacking imagination, we embrace self-promoting demagogues.

Rome died. Rome had its Trumps, insinuating eerie metaphorical and psychological parallelisms. Nero Claudius Caesar Augustus Germanicus (37-68 A.D.) ascended to Rome's imperial throne at age sixteen, carried on winds of fortune and maternal ambition. It helped to be adopted by his great-uncle, Emperor Claudius, a good Emperor, a thoughtful Emperor. His childhood tutor was Lucius Annaeus Seneca, a worldly Stoic philosopher and politician of first century Rome. When Nero rose to the seat of power, Seneca and Sextus Africanus Burrus, prefect of the Praetorian guard, advised him. They ran the Empire, with the help of Nero's mother Agrippina, for perhaps the first decade of Nero's reign. Seneca wrote Nero's first speech before the Roman Senate. Nero became a tyrannical and fiscally profligate ruler. High taxes alienated those who paid them. Several attempts were made upon Nero's life. Nero proved indecisive. He relied upon others, among whom was Seneca. In 59 A.D., four years after becoming Emperor, Nero ordered his mother, Agrippina, killed. He sent her to travel and arranged a shipwreck. When Agrippina managed to swim to shore, a Neronian minion murdered her and reported her death as a suicide. Nero divorced his wife, Octavia, alleging she was infertile. Banished, Nero accused her of infidelity with the murderer of mother Agrippina, and had Octavia executed. In 64 A.D., the great fire of Rome swept the city, burning for a week. The inferno razed three and damaged seven others among the fourteen hills of the capital. Nero may have set the fires himself, though the egg of these details is jumbled in history's omelette. Regardless, Nero took advantage of the newly vacated urban land to build the Domus Aurea (Golden House) on Palatine Hill. Its gigantic gardens adorned a thirty-meter bronze statue of the Emperor himself, the Colossus of Nero. The Domus Aurea had 300 rooms, but no sleeping quarters, kitchens, or latrines. It was a narcissist emblem, a sanctuary in which to meditate upon Nero's splendor. Its interior was faced with semi-precious stones and ivory and marble. The exterior was covered, as the name might indicate, in gold leaf. Nero destabilized. He kicked his pregnant successor wife, Poppaea, to death. In 65 A.D., another attempt upon Nero's life led to accusations, probably false, that Seneca, his philosopher-tutor and co-regent, had participated. Nero ordered Seneca to commit suicide. Seneca denied regicidal conspiracy. Nero persisted. Ever the faithful Roman, Seneca drove a sword though his heart. Nero asserted he could sing the Gauls into submission. He murdered people he did not like. Nutty Nero lost the confidence of supporters. The Senate sentenced Nero to die by crucifixion. The young emperor stabbed himself in the throat, after uttering his final self-adulatory words, "What an artist dies with me." In his contempt for Roman traditions and elites, Nero proved his own undoing.

Like Nero, Mr. Trump views his office as a command to self-flatter. Whatever he does, so he claims, is perfect, intelligent, beautiful, necessary, imbued with genius, divinely inspired, or compelled by the corruption of others. The escalator on which Donald announced his imperial intentions, shone, like the Domus Aurea, of shimmering gold. Minions, when merely suspected, disappear. These underlings never last long enough to be anything other than "acting" whatevers. Perhaps one can say that

Donald Trump is kinder to his several spouses than was Nero. Then again, perhaps we should ask Ivana and Marla and Melania their views of spousal Donald. Nero was a symptom of a rotting empire. Is that Donald's role? Is America done?

I hope for more. I expect Red America's Donald delusion to crumble. When it does, that will be a bad day for half of the country. What path for those of us who have held the torch while Redsters toyed with despotism? Shall we oppress? Shall we ignore? Shall we chide? Shall we shun? I say, No. For America to endure, we must forgive. If there is to be an America worth having, we must find some way to heal the infected wound that separates red arteries from blue veins in our body politic. How, I ask? Nothing comes to mind. For I am angry. I suffer spite.

Some of us, Red and Blue, turn to religious traditions for guidance. The Hebraic Writings (*Ketuvim*) advise: "Do not rejoice when your enemy falls, and let not your heart be glad when he stumbles" (*Proverbs* 24:17). The easy path lies in rancor. Pettiness slides from the tongue, like butter from a hot knife. We might "lock him up" as he hoped to "lock her up." If we are satisfied with Lilliputian souls, that will work. But binding the wounds of opponents, with heartfelt care, tests mettle. One must summon forgiveness, and probably a generous dollop of humor. Toranic scholars went farther, assigning priorities: "If two men claim thy help, and one is thy enemy, help him first" (*Talmud*). De-delusioned, Red America will suffer. How can we offer succor? We whose hearts are scorched by disillusion? We who need help ourselves?

I cannot embrace Redsters, at least not now. I search for a path that makes me kinder, more open, gentle with opponents. La Rochefoucauld (French, 17th century) said, "We forgive to the extent that we love" (*Maxims* 330). That's it, I suppose. My love is attenuated. Once there is diagnosis, hope for cure may emerge. Perhaps I will find a way to embrace an affection less conditional. Less political. Less puny.

We shall see.

BLAZING...

65

DECAFFEINATION

Out my office window, while mulling some human tangle, I occasionally watch traffic. Every day thousands of cars pass our intersection bearing Shoreliners about their tasks. We Shoreliners are busy people, serious people. Not many smile, capsuled in their automobile universes. More than a few honk, gun waiting engines, swerve onto sidewalks to steal that tempting right turn. Many speed, screaming breakneck by. Some deem stoplights mere advisory opinions.

I wonder, *What drives my neighbors? Financial pressure? Spousal conflict? Habits of hurry? Panic? Depression from desperate loneliness?* I too rush, for no obvious reason, though not usually behind the wheel. Some noxious imp whispers at my ear, *Do more faster, you goldbricker.* Pestered, I pick up my pace, without actually choosing to hurry. Perhaps my pesky urchin chides my neighbors as well. America cherishes productivity; haste can appear reasonable, even patriotic. Worn, we look for help. Coffee befriends bustle, making hearts beat to quickened feet. We gulp soul accelerators: Jitters or Sexpresso or Perkies or Jumping Bean or Don't Be Latte or Jiffy Java. Life demands that third triple mocha. Grogginess withdraws; some rationality and much calm slink away with it. We are stoked, caffeinated, on top of our game. Still, our hearts murmur inaudibly: *late, tardy, lazy.*

> **MAKE HASTE SLOWLY.**

America did not invent this malady. Before cars and cell phones and airplanes and television, Matthew Arnold (British, 19th century A.D.) complained of "this strange disease of modern life, with its sick hurry, its divided aims, its heads o'ertaxed, its palsied hearts" (*The Scholar-Gipsy*, 1853). Britain hastened to stretch its Empire around the globe, to convey to England the extravagances and baubles of the planet. Bustle bit Brits. Nineteen hundred years earlier, Romans thundered through Mediterranean climes to subjugate the known world. Rush rankled Romans. Gaius Julius Caesar (*Caesar Augustus*, Roman, 1st century B.C.) advised his countrymen: "Make haste slowly." Now, acceleration aggravates Americans. We share a misshapen mindset of long, if sordid, pedigree. Alice Walker (American, 20th century A.D.) said: "I think it pisses God off if you walk by the colour purple in a field somewhere and don't notice it" (*The Colour Purple*).

When sane, I counsel myself: *Slow down. Have a chat with a neighbor. Smile occasionally. Refuse to multi-task. Take a deep breath. Notice that moon. Rescue a self from yourself. Try life decaffeinated.*

Sometimes I even do so. Briefly. Before I hurry off.

GUARD DOG

66
SQUIRREL BUDDHA

My law office nestles on a suburban corner lot. Adjacent arterial streets bear much traffic, and dwindling patience. Commuting bullets scream down the thirty-five mile per hour four-lane arterial. I call the intersection "Chucklehead Speedway," to denominate by its denizens. When impeded from speeding, people honk pointlessly. They alert none to dangers, but sigh satisfaction venting irascibly on neighbors. Washington law permits drivers to use horns to alert others to dangers, but a driver "shall not otherwise use such horn when upon a highway." RCW 46.37.380(1). Some blare at old women with grocery bags who dawdle in crosswalks. A few honk at school buses disgorging rosy-cheeked babes. The worst careen onto the handicap-accessible sidewalk to squeeze past poky law-abiders who wait for the light to turn green. Just yesterday, a prodigal son jerked around traffic, toppling my recycle bin that waited its weekly Recology pickup. He lurched over the adjacent sidewalk, across the crosswalk, turned into oncoming traffic with scarcely a harried glance. This time-hoarder banked two seconds at most. (Now I just sound old. Wait. I am old.) Regularly, these many scoff-laws collide. Beauties applying mascara smash boys trumpeting their sexuality with blaring mufflers. Harried delivery people T-bone school buses. The young and swift mangle the old and hesitant. Bang. Screech. Scrape. Parts spin and bounce. Cell phones deploy. Sirens approach. So far, on my watch, none has died, though more than a few have departed with paramedics. I do not write to berate the beleaguered hurry of Seattleites; that, another day. Rather, I narrate the ambience of an intersection. This crossroad demands fortitude. I, being timid, foreswear its crosswalks. Jaywalking tickets beam sunshine, when juxtaposed with the potential of crimson haze lurking beneath tires of careening soccer moms. Traffic enforcement seems extinct. Speeds and rates of collision wax. The traffic light, cycling its reds, greens, and yellows, murmurs mere advisory opinions to its harried horde. The roadway is, sadly, a hazard.

So, imagine my surprise to be smacked between the eyes with extravagant compassion in this very intersection. It transpired All Hallows' Eve, the sun scraping horizon. Gaggles of ghouls and Disney princesses coursed between houses, collecting loot. Parents hovered protectively. A young squirrel, perhaps sick or injured, wobbled across my office front yard. Crows harassed the little guy, confusing him terribly with hungry swooping. The juvenile gnawer wandered off the sidewalk, directly into hurtling traffic. I tried to reconcile myself to the bloody splat this little rodent was about to become. Then it happened.

Cars from both directions slowed and stopped. Our squirrel fell over then struggled back to its feet, grinding to a halt in mid-intersection. Children across the way got down on hands and knees on the sidewalk, trying to make eye contact, to offer solace and encouragement. The light turned. No car moved in any of the twelve lanes affected. None honked. No engines raced. No one cursed or shook a fist. The traffic signal again turned. None moved. A pickup driver popped open his door. He grabbed a basket from the bed of his vehicle; he jogged to the squirrel. With his camo baseball cap, he shooed the disoriented squirrel into the woven refuge he carried. The squirrel nestled, satisfied to have some help. Our rescuer walked across the wide intersection, then a parking lot, to a line of trees. There he deposited the squirrel in foliage secure from ravens. He walked back to his battered Toyota. The light changed again. None moved. People rolled down their windows. One hollered, "How's the squirrel?" Truck man gave a thumbs up. Applause rippled. Our squirrel savior replaced his hat, plopped into his truck, and drove through the green light. Traffic, slowly, resumed its accustomed frenzy.

Buddhists credit Siddhartha Gautama (the Buddha: Indian subcontinent, 5th century B.C.) with inspiring compassion for all living things. This Enlightened One taught that all should preserve sentient life. One flees what hinders and seeks what enhances enlightenment. Thus, one escapes the karmic wheel of life, death, and re-incarnation. The Dalai Lama (Tibetan, 21st century) argues that the Buddhist insight boils down to showing compassion. One practices compassion. One inspires others to compassion. Albert Schweitzer (German, 20th century), who was no Buddhist, nevertheless voiced Buddhist sentiment: "A man is truly ethical only when he obeys the compulsion to help all life which he is able to assist, and shrinks from injuring anything that lives." And Gandhi (Indian, 20th century) saw widely, as was his penchant: "The greatness of a nation and its moral progress can be judged by the way its animals are treated." Francis of Assisi (Italian, 13th century A.D.) warned that those who care not for creatures will care little for humans when the time comes.

On this Halloween, a baby squirrel in distress taught compassion, channeling Siddhartha. A rodent: the squirrel Buddha of Chucklehead Speedway.

CLEO

67

LOSS

Death knocked for my great grandmother Ley. I was twelve. Louise Ley had bristly whiskers that scraped when she kissed, very white hair, and the pungent odor (not unpleasant) of aged women. The phone rang; she was gone.

My grandparents, in their own time, passed. Howard Rhynard baited my hooks. He taught me tools, fixing things, and mowing lawns. He constructed the *Tyrannosaurus Rex* skeleton that even now haunts my study. ALS stole his body at sixty. Howard departed with dignity despite daunting disabilities. Ada Lancaster left next. She poured great iced tea. Her hugs made night frights vanish. Ada stocked maraschino cherries and beef jerky, to accommodate my foibles. Ada endured chronic stomach ulcers, and smoked. On her death bed, Ada spoke of God to indulge me; she knew, for me, metaphysics matter. Emphysema slowed, then killed, her. Ada's affection was a perpetual torrent. Paul Lancaster took me stream angling in Montana and Alberta; he bequeathed his passion for dogs and YMCAs. He told jokes. Paul abused his liver and driving privileges with tippling. Paul died a decade after ears and eyes failed him. Edith Rhynard passed last, clinging to life despite chronic cardiac insufficiency. She baked supreme cinnamon rolls, and taught me Jesus and Selah summers. Edith died by merciful morphine overdose. The hollows each grandparent left in my heart brim with memories.

My high school sweetheart, Debbie, succumbed to flesh-eating bacteria. She was forty. Debbie endured adolescence with me, and revealed miraculous femininity and empathy. At her death, we were no longer close. I still feel (oddly) that we may bump into one another in the Safeway cereal aisle one day.

Dolph, Tom, Sterling, Velma, Olga, and others. Aging friends: time has stolen each. Some fought wars. One fled war. Some naturalized. They raised families, or chose childlessness. They scraped through the Depression, and watched Americans walk on the moon. They fought World War II and Korea and Vietnam and the Soviet Union. One lost a son at the Pentagon on September 11, 2001. They survived obstacles, lived full life. Some fell where they stood; attrition wasted others. Losing each was painful. Shakespeare (English, 17th century A.D.) understood. His King Claudius said: "When sorrows come, they come not single spies, but in battalions" (*Hamlet*). We pray flat water, but maelstrom death churns our passage. Our boat shudders in dark winds on a troubled sea.

Life gives, but also takes. Depredations bid us reshape ourselves. We knit new faces into our fabric with loose threads where friends are ripped away. Death rends the weave again and again. We darn and patch. For we are this tattered tapestry, loomed of life and death. The dead live in us. We, in our turn, become the dead, living in others. Life's skein unwinds toward a future. Death walks by our side, hand in hand.

I nurse wincing gratitude for the company. Sometimes.

SOFIE

68

THREE MILES
MAY 2020

Yet another coronavirus has arrived. This one is unruly, though not the nastiest among its siblings. Virologists call the bugger SARS-CoV-2, first detected in Wuhan, China, in December 2019 (probably—the Chinese are not admirable reporters). This coronavirus is that one called the "novel coronavirus" on the news, and is frequently confused with its associated disease syndrome, COVID-19, by most of us. Each new coronavirus arrival is novel, and so the name "novel coronavirus" has graced previous relatives of our current unwelcome house guest. This loathsome visitor was never invited, but never leaves, like carpenter ants or cockroaches or a free-riding alcoholic uncle in the basement.

I heard some news-blatherer, waving his hands and sputtering spittle, compare flu season with the coronavirus pandemic. It is true. Every year, Earth also has a flu season, that is, an influenza outbreak. Flu is a weakling, compared to this current coronavirus, SARS-2. Flu's death rate is one-tenth of one percent. The COVID-19 death rate is about five percent. If these numbers are correct (and they may not be accurate), SARS-2 is fifty times more lethal than flu in the United States. Influenza viruses, not coronavirus, cause flu. We, as mere sufferers, without gene sequencing machines in our extra bedrooms, are not well-positioned to know our diseases; their symptoms overlap greatly. Annually, tens of thousands of Americans perish by influenza, predominantly vulnerable populations—young, old, immune-compromised, poor. Flu also regularly reaches pandemic proportions. Famous influenza plagues are the 1918 Spanish flu (>50 million deaths), the 1957 Asian flu (> 1 million deaths), the 1968 Hong Kong flu (> 1 million deaths), and the Swine flu (H1N1) of 2009 (>250,000 deaths). Annually around the globe, about 500,000 humans perish before the incursions of the many mutating strains of influenza. In America, 23,000 to 61,000 lives fall to flu each year, according to the Centers for Disease Control and Prevention in Atlanta. We stand near the beginning of this SARS-2 pandemic. Already more than 100,000 of our neighbors have died, in a mere three months. SARS-2 is not the flu. SARS-2 is a battle axe, when laid next to the paring knife of influenza.

> **MY FRIEND DICK HAS DIED OF COVID-19.**

Perhaps it helps to visit the human family's stressed relationship with the Corona family. Every year, most of us suffer a common cold two or three times. Colds are caused by some 200 viruses, mostly rhinoviruses. But fifteen percent of colds are caused by coronaviruses. What of coronavirus, which is SARS-CoV-2, which causes COVID-19? Here are six other coronaviruses known to infect humans and some lethality rates (which are probably guesstimates):

Date	Coronavirus	Death Rate
1950	OC43	?
1965	229E	15%
2003	SARS-1	11%
2004	NL63	?
2005	HKU1	?
2012	MERS	35%
2019	SARS-2 (COVID-19)	5%

As you can see (though the data are incomplete and doubtable), COVID-19 is a sissy among coronaviruses. It kills a mere five percent of its infected. Unfortunately, the virus has spread widely, so five percent of millions is a big number. Deaths crush tens of thousands, gut-punching hordes of friends and families. We suffer. Where poor social choices and belated interventions retard response, the COVID-19 death rate soars. Italy's fatality rate is eleven percent. Sweden, which has forsaken suppression altogether, has seen its death rate shoot past that of the United States, despite our mostly tepid, often confused, genuinely inane, national response.

Some opine that herd immunity will protect us. A few dim bulbs even throw COVID parties, seeking to spread the infection, to hasten an imagined herd immunity panacea. Herd immunity means that so many people have had a disease in a population that the disease organism has a hard time finding purchase in new victims. The viral "good meat" becomes widely spread and seldom accessible. Bad for the virus. People who talk as though they know (the formula for a herd immunity calculation is quite complex and requires information we have not yet collected) indicate that sixty percent or more of a population needs to be immune (because they have survived the virus and now have effective antibodies to protect them from re-infection). Assuming that sixty percent of America gets COVID-19, that means some 9.9 million Americans might die buying the rest of us herd immunity. Globally, that would be 228 million souls. So, pray for a vaccine. Lacking a vaccine, most of us will eventually contract COVID-19. Some of us will die. So, pray for a vaccine. Good people are working on such a substance with the wit God gave them. Wish them well. Buy them what they need. And, as I say, pray for them (I am not much given to prayer, yet here I am on my knees...)

Until that blessed day, we are stuck with SARS-2. In a few years, most of us will have survived the minuscule menace; others will have perished in droves. After those years, the coronavirus will recede to become wallpaper in that cubby of our mental morass, which I call the mortal threats hospitality suite, where we sequester earthquakes, volcanos, hurricanes, tornados, locusts, famines, the black plague, global warming, malevolent maniacs with automatic weapons, pointless wars, ozone depletion, killer asteroids, hostile alien invasions, and supernovas in our galactic neighborhood. The universe seethes threat. Human imagination fertilizes this fodder, trembling before yet more sinister nightmares.

Until the SARS-2 threat recedes, what to do? Atul Gawande, a doctor and writer of good books, urges America to lean on five pillars: hygiene (wash your damned hands), screening (stay home if you are ill, and maybe even if you are not ill), social distancing (yes, this means you), masks (yes, this means you), and, last, culture. We collectively possess resources to change our various cultures, by creative problem-solving, compassion, and liberal doses of self-restraint. Perhaps we might not merely adapt, and so limp bravely, but, rather, fashion cultures vastly improved, and so stride serenely toward an onrushing, but promising, future. We might become *better*, which is the goal of all thoughtful people.

I drag you through virus facts to say what I have learned so far, and to confess the deficiencies of this "knowledge." I have no medical education. These facts are eminently doubtable. They may evidence nothing more than my confusions. Even the educated are still learning about our new, unwelcome companion, so none can doubt that some of my "facts" are irresolute. Still......

From a deeper recess of what I call "me," I write also for a personal reason. I clutch for fleeting rationality before the adamant grimace of grief. My dear friend, Dick Harwood, died of COVID-19. I read his obituary today in the Seattle Times. I cried again. Dick has been gone weeks now. Not my first lachrymal cloudburst at his memory. I do not write to extol the man, though, as you will see, there was much that deserves praise in Dick. I write of Dick because, among my loved ones, he is the first to succumb to COVID-19. Probably not the last. This disease tears from our affectional warp the woof of persons. Ripped, our social fabric frays. We are weaker for these losses. Time and new affections eventually darn our holes. But we are never again what we were. We are not a new sock, but an old darned sock. Familiar, but plainly war-worn.

Years ago, I planned service projects for my Rotary Club, small undertakings of no great import. But endeavors appropriate for a group of old, white, mostly-men. Twice, I set up for a project, and no one came. I worked alone—except for Dick Harwood. Dick always showed up, unless he had some junior football to coach. On service projects, Dick would work hard, then putter, then sit on the tailgate of his truck to make rude remarks. "More to the left." "Missed one." "Can't you do that faster? I'm getting thirsty." I would banter back. "Good where it is." "Nope." "If it makes your eyes tired watching me work, take a nap, you old fart."

Our exchanges were always frank, sometimes withering. Dick had doubts. Doubt visits any mind that listens to humans talk. Dick could doubt Mother Teresa's chastity. I would call Dick skeptical, but that word drags behind it hints of jaded and angry and self-important. Dick doubted. But he was not bitter, small, or stupid. Dick just had doubts. Especially when folks put down others to promote their own piety. Or when some imagined themselves cruising high above life's frantic fray. Dick could then be downright biting. Dick never doubted his Welsh Corgi. The rest of us were fair game. When Dick and I first got to know one another, I took Dick to lunch at our local old-people-diner. When we finished our mid-day meal, Dick asked, "So, what you want?" I sputtered, "Nothing. Just to know you." Dick doubted my answer. He speculated about hidden motives. Maybe he insinuated. So I asked, "You've been around a while. How often do you meet someone who has a good heart, is intelligent, does important work, and has nothing of the ego-maniacal about him?" "Not often." A wry little smile touched his lips. I offered, "Perhaps, if you met such a person, you might take him or her to lunch." Dick let it drop. We became friends.

Dick studied psychology and American history. His academic studies led to heart work at the Suicide Hotline. There, Dick touched the lives of people gripped by lethal ideation; he talked them back from precipices when he could. He mentored and managed others who did the same. The work took much from Dick. Such work measures a person. It gulps whatever one is willing to give. Dick retired from his labors when his body told him to do so, with kibitzing cancers and frequent fatigue and piercing pains. He spent time with Judy, his beloved spouse, and doted on Zach, their Corgi with spine-gone-bad in a little cart to haul around his canine back half. Zach and Dick suffered simultaneous declines. Both are now gone.

Retired, Dick joined the Witless Protection Program. Saturday mornings, we eight or ten met around a table fabricated from a cross-section of a huge cedar trunk. We shared our week's tribulations, our fascinations, and a huge stack of fine works of philosophical ethics. In these last of his years, Dick would arrive early. I bought him a cinnamon roll or almond croissant. He would chew slowly and complain about his catheter. We would chat. Since our wee-President was elected, we shared frustrations and fulminations about emptiness-at-the-top. Often, Dick led me to obscure facts of American history, analogies fraught with grim resonance to our current plight. Poor choice often precedes senseless suffering; America has chosen poorly. Finally, Dick came to Witless one last Saturday morning, but departed mid-meeting. His energy guttered. Cancers gnawed. I visited Dick at the nursing home. Dick entered hospice, conceding the inevitable. COVID-19 took Dick, so weakened by other illnesses. Like many in skilled nursing facilities, the novel coronavirus truncated life, even if, as in Dick's case, only a bit.

When young, Dick served two years on a Pacific submarine. Being trapped in a tin can full of explosives, traveling under millions of pounds of saltwater, submariners' humor skews toward fatalism. Dick reported the submariner poke: "Don't be afraid. No matter how far out in the ocean your boat goes, you are never more than three miles from solid land." SARS-2 reminds us that we all face threats. Life proceeds in peril's shadow. Everyman, no matter his journey, stands no more than three miles from solid ground.

LUCY

69
HOWARD AND BEV

High school sweethearts from fruit country in Washington's Yakima Valley. Howard bashed his face in football and idolized dogs. Bev cheer-led and, being socially adept, built her diminutive dominion. Both their families were middle class, but his parents at its upper edge, hers the lower. All were lovely people, hard-working, possessed of non-stellar gifts and sensible habits. They (the parents and their offspring) harbored a not uncommon menagerie of foibles: occasional inebriation or foregone education or neurotic dependence or Catholic rebellion or clueless arrogance or mirror-bound primping. Each shortcoming made life harder. But none debilitated.

These families, Rhynards and Lancasters, took shape in the Great Depression, and endured the Second World War. Both events left scars. Not the scars of war per se, but the post-traumatic stress of existential uncertainty and economic deprivation. Ada married Paul to secure Howard's young life; she was Paul's third spouse, he, her second. Paul's first bride was institutionalized with ill-defined psychosis. The second died of cancer. Ada's first was banned by her over-reaching mother and excised from the family like an unholy wart. To wed Paul, Ada departed Catholicism. That went poorly. Howard Rhynard married Edith, so they could secure family blessing to escape Oklahoma together. Howard had a Cherokee grandmother (America Hayes), and wished to shake off racial stigma as an Okie half-breed. Besides, he and Edith both had family in Washington.

When Bev graduated, Howard wed her to his heart, and his affection for dogs to his vocation. Washington State College made him a veterinarian. He joined the army as a first lieutenant, inspecting meat for soldiers and nursing the pets of generals. Three children intruded. Beverly bore me during a stint at Fort McArthur, San Pedro, California. Karen followed shortly at Fort Huachuca, Arizona. Jill landed when my family did, in Coeur d'Alene, Idaho. We kids were much loved, erratically disciplined, and taught to be "normal," which mattered to my mother more than it ought. She was disappointed. We children, each in different ways, fled conformity. We knew, and eventually mom granted, that only dead fish swim with the stream. From my perch in life's cheap seats, I see that my parents stamped habits, good and ill, on their brood. Perhaps every life consists, at least in part, of coping with parental imprint. We each have cause to "lament what man has made of man" (Wordsworth, American, 18th century).

After decades of work and considerable hardships, after the Vietnam War, after Lyndon Johnson's demolition of Barry Goldwater, after the Age of Aquarius, and the ignominy of Richard Nixon, after the fall of the Berlin Wall, my parents retired. To confirm the American cliché, Howard and Bev helped raise a granddaughter, traveled Europe and the United States, and golfed. Their friends began dying like a fractured pipe, first a trickle, then a torrent.

Diseases etched Howard and Bev. Bev, a lifetime smoker, got an inoperable lung cancer diagnosis. She survived after some chemo sleight of hand, but a brain metastasis led to gamma knife excision, which deflected Bev's personality. Always a dynamo, she grew sedentary. Howard picked up slack. He cooked and washed and mowed, but he began losing weight, she gaining. Howard chose triple cardiac bypass surgery when the hospital told him to do so. His Parkinson's disease worsened. Getting out of bed, Bev fractured her ankle. She departed their Dalton residence for rehab, but never returned. Howard left and sold the family home (reluctantly) to make a new nest in a graduated care facility. Together again, after a time, Howard and Bev watched, rather than played, golf. Evenings held Jeopardy and Wheel of Fortune. Alex Trebec and Vanna White and Pat Sajak became unilateral week-night friends. Howard and Bev cycled in and out of cohabitation as health crises escalated.

Bev's heart began failing. Her ankles swelled. Bev knew she would soon need full time care, and become mired in a nursing home. She wanted none of that. Metal allergies left her needing a gold-plated pacemaker. That did not suit my lower-middle class mother. Too puffed. Too hoity-toity. She declined. Bev died with daughter Karen at her side, from cardiac failure.

Howard survived longer than he wished. Parkinsons disease eroded consciousness. Howard regularly hallucinated water on floors and sleeping dogs. He was unable to process Bev's passing. He instead believed that she was living across the hall in the nursing home, so angry with him that she would not speak. All Howard's hallucinations bode ill. With a sweeter disease, he might have died awash in fictive joys. That was not his lot. Howard died with daughter Jill at his side. Jill and Howard had become, in Jill's adulthood, best of friends. Jill cared for

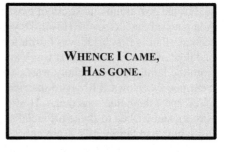

**WHENCE I CAME,
HAS GONE.**

Howard daily during his decline. None knows which of Howard's bodily systems led to the cascade that became his death. He is, despite our ignorance, gone.

Bev and Howard were cremated. Their ashes were scattered in a stranger's field for a fee. This was as they prescribed. Unpretentious. Quiet. Normal. I published the obituaries they wrote in the local paper. No horn tooting. No cloying praise. Like Sergeant Joe Friday on 1950s Dragnet, "Just the facts, ma'am."

Grief has subsided, now these years later. Only occasionally do I wake, a little panicked, that I have not called my parents in so long. I tried to excise from mind distressing images of their decline by substituting photos of their middle life, days of productivity and humor. It did not work. It appears that every life traces an indivisible arc: nothingness, then colliding gametes, then youthful incompetence, then mature vigor, then aged decline, then dollops of dust, and, finally again, simply nothing. We survivors are permitted no emendations. I say grief has subsided. I lied. Tears wet my cheek, just now.

I miss mom and dad. But grief yields to a better posture for one positioned as am I: gratitude. A child of loving parents: life's seminal gift.

Thanks, Bev. Thanks, Howard.

HOME, A CHEW, AND AFTERNOON SUN

IMPERIOUS

70
WOODHAVEN

I write in praise of Woodhaven Veterinary Clinic.

Woodhaven beckoned because red geraniums clung to their chain link fence. I would like to say we sought Woodhaven's expertise because of the manifest professional competency of veterinarians Brudvik, Creason, and Endicott, supported by the caring ministrations of their staff. Of that, we knew nothing at the time. It was the geraniums. Geraniums and Lucy.

Ten years ago, Lucy was a teacup of puppy sass. Woodhaven administered juvenile inoculations and spayed Lucy. Dog-rearing advice ensued. There came, as Lucy matured, paw pustules to excise, raccoon attacks to mend, teeth to clean, assorted bumps and bruises to nurse—all the common nibbles that canine life portends. Then, while still young, Lucy had her first "infection of unknown origin (IUO)." Diagnosis proved elusive. It was pancreatitis. It was a congenital bowel defect or liver injury. It was something she ate. It was an internal puncture wound. We and Woodhaven guessed and watched, hoping to ferret out the root of Lucy's periodic affliction. Antibiotics and love chased away the demon, for a time. The IUO recurred, but was managed. From IUO we learned the mettle of the Woodhaven staff. Life's nameless unknowns expose our characters.

Lucy entered her last year in the fall of 2008. A second challenge emerged. A pituitary tumor overstimulated her adrenal glands. Cushings, they called it. We treated Lucy's Cushings by chemically ablating Lucy's adrenal tissue. Then all hell broke loose. Lucy's hyperactive adrenals had masked her chronic IUO. As her cortisol plummeted, the infection ran amok. Lucy neared death. Woodhaven puzzled and tested, then referred us to a specialist in veterinary internal medicine, who puzzled and tested. Finally, we determined Lucy had an IUO, which told us what we already knew. With substantial hospitalization, Lucy rebounded, commencing Woodhaven's high wire act. What was good for IUO was bad for Cushings, and vice versa. Our veterinarians balanced interventions to optimize Lucy's waning quality of life. We became Woodhaven regulars; efficient, caring staff shuffled us to examination rooms again and again. Our little dog declined, but savored many joys and comforts. On September 25, 2009, Lucy died upon the gentle ministrations of Ann Brudvik.

Drs. Brudvik, Creason, and Endicott showed us depths. Americans sometimes (unfairly) ask their professionals to be omniscient. Egos tempt doctors to accept such fawning flattery. Our Woodhaven doctors showed humility and persistence in the face of veterinary unknowns. The finest professionals harness technical education, experience, and cognitive dexterity to the best impulses of their hearts. Woodhaven staff did so for Lucy.

In the final minute of our year-long struggle, Lucy breathed her last. Death's impenetrable door clicked shut. We call now, but there is no yip. Lucy's food is untouched, her bed cool. We cry.

That sad September afternoon, tears wetted Ann Brudvik's face as well. The finest professionals serve hearts with minds.

Thank you, Woodhaven. You have our gratitude.

GRAY, AND LOVED

71
REQUIEM LUCY

Lucy has passed. Our hearts wither in the sirocco of her absence. Others, canine and human, passed from our lives before Lucy departed—beloved dogs, grandparents, friends. None has so wilted our souls.

Perhaps the blade that now lacerates us was whetted upon the smooth stone of Lucy's long final illness. A year passed after her peril surfaced. As days piled upon one another, Lucy's pain found veterinary names: pituitary tumor, infection of unidentified origin, adrenal hypertrophy, cortico-steroids, subcutaneous fluids, pancreatic inflammation, renal insufficiency, and intractable nausea. Despite Lucy's pain and waning capacities, despite our worry, despite hated Ringer's lactate injections and gagged pills, our last year together was the sweetest of Lucy's ten. Our knit hearts welded as we faced Lucy's insidious black wall together. We cuddled. We nursed symptoms. We sang life's song, reluctantly humming its somber undertones. We grieved, Lucy's sad eyes on ours, tears and laughter jumbled with tail wags and little groans. Lucy licked Brad's toes. We scratched her scruff, stroked her ears in lingering pulls. We massaged her. We cleaned potty errors. Lucy napped and sighed and labored at faltering normalcy. Her squirrel chases shortened and slowed. Her appetite disappeared. We brooded at Lucy's water bowl, counting her laps at its undulating surface.

At the end, Lucy could no longer bother with rodents, so insistent were her pains. Sweetness grew as ministrations intensified: the needles, the coaxing, our hopeless attempts to be rational. As extremity's darkness rushed over us, inextricable bonding illuminated our grim murk. At Woodhaven Veterinary, Lucy lay in Brad's lap, her right hip full of sedative. Lucy raised her head, reached a paw toward Kim. Our trembling hands conveyed Lucy to her other packmate's lap. Lucy's tongue lolled. Dr. Ann Brudvik, our wise guide, entered, found a vein, and ushered Lucy where go we all.

> **REST WELL,
> LITTLE DOG.**

Life with Lucy was not all end. A rich, rewarding, often hilarious nine years preceded. As a puppy, Lucy burst upon the heart of our life. Mirth became an affliction from which we suffered gratefully. Lucy ran and swam and frolicked. She guarded and snarled and alerted. But those are the stories of other, less grieved, days. This is a tale of Lucy's end.

I mowed my lawn a languorous week after poison stopped Lucy's heart. From a flowerbed protruded a half-buried sweaty headband clumped with compost. Lucy cherished that fecund stew of aromas. When tears and heaving subsided, I retrieved the stretchy circlet, soaked it in hot water and soap. Washed, I tossed it, stains and all, in with my other headbands. I will sweat again.

We live on, pained. Lucy does not. Death's impenetrable illogic.

Rest well, little dog.

HAPPY LUCY

APPRECIATIONS AND APOLOGIES

The words of this little tome were inspired by the humans and dogs that people it. Some nuggets became publications in Shoreline's local rag, the Shoreline Enterprise, before that paper succumbed to the wasting disease afflicting the newspaper industry generally. Other pieces were penned for occasions apparent from the texts themselves. A few issued to vent pressures which, if left unattended, might have caused my cranium to explode. Some of the more lengthy entries emerge as fragments of other books I have published (or hope to publish), especially if I think the snippets reveal otherwise obscure cubbies of my existence.

I name few people because I find most people do not want to be named; not that many people will read this offering. Not all the humans who matter deeply to me are represented in this book. Of some formative episodes in my life, I hardly make mention. The Cornerstone house church and my first wife come to mind. So too, my step-son and his lovely family, many cherished friends, and a few degenerates. Others appear with prominence distorted by the fact that of some matters I wrote often, of others I wrote not at all. Some persons who are no longer part of my life feature prominently. Others, central to my well-being, are conspicuously absent. Such are the astigmatic vagaries of texts written over the course of fifty years. I have made no effort to remediate this defect in the book, other than to write this paragraph. The photos are mostly mine, or those of my parents. For each, I have some reason to believe I am authorized to reproduce it.

Depicted dogs haunt corners of my life. Not all are mine. However, I may be all theirs. For those pups have peopled the backgrounds of thousands of photos that, for a twinkling, snatch tidbits of my life from oblivion. The maw of time munches patiently onward, however, soon to leave my existence unremembered, as will the life of every person disappear into its gullet. In a distant end, our planet, our solar system, and our galaxy will likewise succumb to the mashing molars of mortal moments. And all will whimper toward entropic oblivion.

It takes a measure of bluster to write a book about oneself. On reflection, I see that each book I have written ultimately recounts my life, even when the book makes no self-reference. I note ego in the writings of others, but take no offense. So, perhaps hubris is too harsh a judgment. To entertain only negative thoughts of oneself is no sentiment I can advise. Perhaps, only those to whom diffidence is a stranger put pen to paper. To such, effacement seems pointless. The bashful do not dare. Authors do. All risk becoming the butt of jokes, or the target of a Horsey cartoon.

Despite evidence to the contrary (here offered in gobs), I am no dog nut. I chafe at the sharp edges of caninity that rub sore the pack-troop interface. We hominids seek love and cooperation and food; dogs want belonging and leadership and food. Not that different, but not identical either. Mutts lack decorum. Hounds find organization mystifying. Canines love routine, to a degree that irritates people. And dogs like to eat. I like to eat, to a fault. But my appetite pales; compared to a dog, I am a piker. Dogs and people. We are different, yet bred (literally) to be together. Strawberries and cream. Hot dogs and mustard. Canine and human. Each good on its own. But better together.

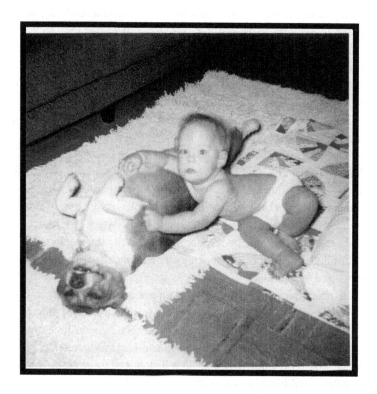

SUZY AND HER PET BOY

PUPPY SOFIE

SAINT GEORGE'S HILL PRESS

On St. George's Hill (southwest of London), in 1648, poor people, under the influence of Gerrard Winstanley, tilled and built shacks on public land to feed themselves, when food prices soared during the English Civil War. They called themselves True Levellers, and sought reduction of the financial chasm between the poor and the wealthy. The king sent a representative, who found the group doing no appreciable harm. A local lord felt otherwise, and commissioned thugs to assault the True Levellers. Some were beaten. Their common meal house was burned. Leaders were tried; the judge refused to let them speak in their defense. The True Levellers, dubbed Diggers by opponents, abandoned their plots for less hostile locations. In the twenty-first century, St. George's Hill is home to an exclusive gated and closely-guarded community, consisting in 450 mansions with tennis club and golf course amenities. St. George's Hill claims to be the premier private residential estate in Europe, close to London and Britain's most desirable private preparatory schools. The median price of a residence on St. George's Hill exceeds £3,000,000. St. George's Hill, then, is the dirt upon which clash desperate diggers and entrenched elites, a metaphor barely metaphorical.

Made in the USA
Middletown, DE
21 February 2021